OFFICE ORGANIZATION and MANAGEMENT

M.E. THUKARAM RAO

ATLANTIC
PUBLISHERS & DISTRIBUTORS (P) LTD

Published by
ATLANTIC
PUBLISHERS & DISTRIBUTORS (P) LTD
7/22, Ansari Road, Darya Ganj, New Delhi-110002
Phones : +91-11-40775252, 40775214, 23273880, 23275880
Fax : +91-11-23285873
Web : www.atlanticbooks.com
E-mail : orders@atlanticbooks.com

Branch Office: Chennai
Phones : +91-44-48531784, 28291383
E-mail : chennai@atlanticbooks.com

Printed & bound in India by Atlantic Print Services

This book is dedicated to the lotus feet of
BHAGAVAN SRI SATHYA SAI BABA
with whose blessings this books is published.

Foreword

It gives me great pleasure to write this foreword to the book on "Office Organisation and Management" by Shri M.E. Thukaram Rao.

Spectacular developments in science and technology and computerisation of transactions have revolutionised communication and information processing. Therefore, this book is a valuable and timely addition to the literature currently available. Due to a variety of reasons, India lost about twenty years in computerisation. We have to catch up so that India could play a dynamic role in the new economic policy of liberalisation and globalisation.

The book is comprehensive and covers some of the latest trends and practices in office systems and procedures. Shri Rao's style is simple, straight forward and lucid.

Shri Rao has been on the faculty of a renowned college; and he has used his vast experience of two decades in presenting the subject in a systematic way.

I congratulate Shri Thukaram Rao for his proficiency in the subject, which is evident from the structure and content. Further, the man behind the book, Sri Thukaram Rao is an excellent teacher. Also, he bears an exemplary character in tune with Indian Values, such as humility and self-effaciveness, simplicity and courtesy, gentleness and friendliness.

I recommend this book to students, particularly in the Pre-University and College levels, and also to common readers, all of whom would find it useful.

N.S. RAMASWAMY

FORMER DIRECTOR, IIM,

BANGALORE

Preface

I take great pleasure in presenting to my readers this book on "Office Organisation and Management". Although many books on this subject are available, this book is written more comprehensively using my long experience and knowledge. This book has twenty one chapters covering all important aspects of the subject.

The book is written in a simple and lucid style so as to enable the readers to understand the subject easily.

At the end of each chapter many standard questions are included which serve as model questions. A select bibliography at the end of the book gives the students an opportunity to refer other works on the subject.

In preparing this book, I have derived constant inspiration from my students and colleagues for which I express my gratitude.

In the course of writing this book, I have referred to many works of various authors. Some useful definitions and contributions have been incorporated in the text by retaining their originality.

The book serves the needs of the students of Pre-University, B.Com., B.B.A., Diploma Course in Office Management and allied courses. It will also be of immense use to the practising managers in the private and public sector industries.

I am thankful to my nephew Shri M.N. Sunil for the valuable help rendered in proof reading the material. I am indebted to my wife Mrs. Rama Bai for her inspiration without which it would not have been possible for me to complete the book.

I shall be glad to receive comments and suggestions, if any, from readers. These will be used to improve the book further.

M.E. THUKARAM RAO

Contents

1

Office and its Functions

INTRODUCTION

The Structure of modern business has become very complex owing to increased number of business transactions. This has led to the establishment of a number of departments such as purchasing, production, sales, accounting, financing, personnel and so on. To facilitate these departments to function efficiently and economically, there arises a need to coordinate the activities of all these departments. This is ensured by establishing a separate department in a business known as office. An office occupies the central position in a modern business. Therefore, it is rightly said that an office is the nerve centre of the whole undertaking.

A well organised office enables the management to plan and implement the operations intelligently and effectively. Appropriate maintenance of records in the office and its timely availability enable management to take quick decisions. Based on reliable and readily available information, communication will speed up the operations of the business. In the present system of production and distribution, the functions of an office are indispensable.

Development of office practice

In olden days, when the size of the business was small, businessmen used to take decision on the basis of knowledge accumulated through experience. As and when business grew in size the need to maintain business secrets was felt. They maintained and protected only those records which were required as per laws of the country. The techniques of maintaining records were simple and adequate for their needs.

With the advent of industrial revolution, which resulted in a series of changes in the production and distribution processes and with the growth of joint stock company form of business organisations, the businessmen felt that the 'traditional' system of recording and preservation of information was no longer adequate. This resulted in the growing awareness of the need for professional management.

The introduction of O and M department of the UK Treasury in 1941 can be considered as the official inauguration of new way of looking at office management. The old methods of functioning of an office are replaced by a planned, scientific method. Instead of allowing the office staff to work according to their whims and fancies, their work was subjected to the universal principles of management.

In the accounting department of the office, the old "counting house" is now replaced by management accounting, cost accounting and statistical techniques. Instead of recording transactions in a bound book, loose leaf records are immensely used. Further, hand written books of accounts are replaced by machine written books.

On the personnel side of office management, employees are scientifically selected and specialised training is imparted as compared to relying on intuition while choosing the right person. Again in the earlier days, for appointing a clerk, his handwriting was given more importance. Today, it is not so as most of the documents are typewritten.

From the point of view of functions performed in the office, most of the work was performed manually in olden days. Today, a great deal of work is performed with the help of modern office equipment. These office equipments not only increase the efficiency of work, but also speed up the work. The improvement in the communication process has revolutionised the office work to a great extent.

Last but not the least, office organisation has gained more importance in modern days owing to increased government legislations relating to office environment, contract of service of employees and payment of salaries to office staff.

Meaning and definition of office

According to the Funk and Wagnall's Standard Dictionary, an office is a place in which business is carried out. In a narrow sense, an office is any room where clerical work is habitually performed as the work of that room. From this point of view, an office implies a place where proper records for the purpose of control and information for effective operations are prepared, handled or serviced.

The term 'Office', however, does not connote the same meaning for all business enterprises. A business unit which provides professional services such as solicitors, accountants, consultants and those who handle documents such as brokers, discounting houses, etc., the office covers the whole business. In a manufacturing concern the office includes the work secretarial, accounting, purchasing departments and also the clerical work done in stores, warehouse and production department.

In modern time, the word office is used in a broader sense to represent the functions performed by the office staff rather than the place where such work is performed. Thus, an office is concerned with the organisation, coordination, standardisation and supervision of paper work, whether it is done by a clerk in a place called office, or by a foreman in the factory or by a salesman on the road. The essential feature of an office is the work itself, but not who does it or where it is done. If it is office work in one place, it is office work everywhere, regardless of where the work is done or who does it. This is because if the office is termed as a certain place only, the paper work done in other parts of the enterprise will remain uncontrolled. But all other records such as sales records, financial records, board of directors records, etc., are the integral part of its operation and hence must be planned, organised and controlled for effective administration.

Definition of office

Robert. C. Appleby in his book *Modern Business Administration* defines office as "a collection of departments carrying out clerical work."

Denyer in his book *Office Administration* defines office as "any room where clerical work is normally carried on whatever name it may be given."

According to L. Hall in his book *Business Administration* "the office describes any place set aside for work of a clerical nature by whatever name it may be called."

P.W. Betts in his book *Office Management* defines office "as a term which is used to provide and maintain an effective information service through an established communication network."

Section 1(2) of the Office, Shops and Railway premises Act 1963 of Great Britain defines an office as "a building or part of a building, the sole or principle use of which is as an office or for office purpose."

The term *office purpose* in the above definition is expressed to include purpose of administration, clerical work, handling money and the use of telephone and telegraph. An extended definition of clerical work is given to cover book keeping, sorting papers, filing, typing, duplicating and computing, etc.

Characteristics of an office

On an analysis of the above definition of office, the following features become evident:

Location: An office is established in a particular locality so as to coordinate the functions of various departments of a business. Several factors affect the selection of an appropriate locality for establishing an office. This is discussed in a subsequent chapter separately.

Accommodation: Spacious accommodation is required for carrying out the functions of office smoothly. Provision of sufficient accommodation requires careful layout of office building.

Departmentation: A modern office performs a number of activities relating to the business. All activities of the office cannot be performed by the same people. The activities are grouped under different types and assigned to people working under different departments. This facilitates specialisation in office.

Work conditions: For increasing the efficiency of the office staff and to meet statutory requirements, it is necessary to provide good working conditions such as lighting, ventilation, air-conditioning, etc.

Clerical staff: Owing to increased volume of office work, we come across several types of clerical staff in an office. The clerical staff in a large sized office may be classified into (*a*) office superintendent who relieves office manager from supervising routine office work, (*b*) clerks of various grades such as first division clerk and second division clerk, (*c*) private secretary to assist office manager and (*d*) typist.

Equipment: To increase the speed of the office work, the office is equipped with modern office appliances and equipment like computers and fax.

Information service: The office is rightly described as a producer of information. The office is responsible for the effective flow of information through appropriate communication channel to all levels of management. In the words of George R. Terry in *Office Management and Control* man's greatest tool today is information... information is required by all members of an enterprise... retaining, analysing and furnishing the appropriate type of information for various purposes to various people and from time to time is one of the important objectives of a modern office.

Organisation: With a view to achieve the above object, an office is to be organised on a systematic basis. Clear cut relations are to be established between superiors and subordinates. The duties and responsibilities of every staff must be clearly laid down.

Requisites of an ideal office

The following are the requisites of an ideal office system:

* To maintain a good flow of work without any bottlenecks.
* To prevent duplication of work and records.
* To ensure movement of staff to the minimum.
* To prevent unnecessary correspondence.
* To divide the work among staff so as to derive the benefit of specialisation.
* To keep paper work to the minimum.
* To apply the principle of management by exception.
* The exceptions to the rules must be kept at minimum.
* To prevent unnecessary checking of records and documents.
* To use modern office appliances to reduce monotony in office.

Importance of office

The modern commercial office is an indispensable department of every business undertaking may it be big or small, trading or manufacturing. The office exists to provide clerical services needed by all the departments of a business unit. In fact, without an efficient and well organised office, business activities can not be carried on systematically and efficiently. Professor Dicksee has aptly said that "the office is to a business what the mainspring is to a watch". The importance of office will become evident from the following:

It helps in identification of business: In undertakings such as banks, insurance companies, etc., office is identified with business. Office enables the investors, customers, public, government, tax authorities, to deal with business undertakings. For enquiries, complaints, etc., people visit only the office but not other departments of the business.

Facilitates preparation of records and reports: The formulation of business policies to a large extent depends upon the reports and records which reflect the success or failure of the business. Management requires information in the form of reports frequently. Some such reports are prepared weekly and some monthly. It is in the office, such records and reports are prepared and furnished to the management. So, office serves as a store room of all records which serves as the basis for the preparation of reports.

Aids management in carrying out its functions: It is through office, managerial functions such as planning, organisaton, coordination and control are performed. In the words of Leffing Well and Robison "a well organised office makes it possible for management to plan its operation intelligently, to put its plan into effect surely, to follow their progress currently, to determine their effectiveness promptly, to appraise the results without delay, and to coordinate all the activities of the business."

It provides employment opportunities: With the increase in the size of business, the office work also increases. To cope up with the increased office work, more number of office staff is required. Thus, existence of office department provides gainful employment opportunities to many people.

Nature of office function

The nature of an office function in a business can be discussed as follows:

1. *Office occupies primary position in a business*: In olden days, the position of office in a business unit was considered to be secondary in importance. The primary position was assigned only to production departments. The traditional view with regard to the nature of office work was that of non-productive. This is so because office work is not directly concerned with production of goods or services. When a clerk records the entries in a book, it does not involve in the production of goods or services directly. Therefore, it was considered that office staff belong to the category of non-producers. But in modern days the office staff are treated on par with producers of goods. Although they do not actually engage in the production of goods directly, they help the production to continue. To identify the product for the office-worker, we must look beyond the particular piece of work done and consider the result that is accomplished. If there is no result, there is no product just as rejected manuscript ceases to be a product when it cannot serve as raw material for finished product (*i.e.*, book) for which it is intended. In this context, the office staff are non-producers. On the other hand, if a useful result is accomplished, *i.e.*, where the work of office staff is used in subsequent stages as raw materials for desired results, then office staff constitute producers. This is justified as economists say any agency that contributes to production is production in the economic sense of the term. However, the following conditions must be fulfilled to consider office work as productive work:

(*a*) The result must be anticipated and believed to be advantageous.

(*b*) It must make possible the performance of one of the primary functions of business.

(*c*) It must do this economically, *i.e.*, at a cost which that function can bear.

2. *It is complimentary to the business*: The modern commercial office is inevitable for the efficient functioning of a business. Today's business, with the existence of a number of departments is ever expanding. There arises a need to coordinate the work of all these departments and this task is performed in the office through a network of office staff. A business unit without an office is incomplete by itself. The establishment of an office makes the business unit a complete undertaking.

3. *Office job is an art*: An art refers to a performance aspect requiring a certain skill and so is an office job. It is a place where several staff and clerks are engaged to perform various jobs such as recording, filing, accounting, communicating, typing and so on. The performance of all these types of jobs requires basic skill which is to be possessed by office staff. Above all, office job also implies the art of getting the work done through the subordinates by the superiors.

4. *Office management is a discipline*: The study of office organisation at one time was considered to be a part of the study of business organisation. But today it is considered to be a separate discipline by itself. It is a branch of knowledge which involves the application of the modern principles of management to office department in order to carry out its function efficiently.

5. *Office management is a profession*: The profession of office management is as old as the history of business. But in recent times the profession of office management has assumed greater importance. This is partly because of the specialisation of office function on one hand and the aspirations by many unemployed youth for the office job on the other hand. Recognising the importance of this profession, many universities and private institutions are offering courses in office management. Some courses are offered as full time courses and others on part time basis. These courses have attracted many young boys and girls, expecting a job opportunity in the office of many business organisation.

Function of an office

The functions of a modern office can be classified into two categories, *viz.*, Primary function and Secondary function. This is shown in the following chart:

Primary functions

The function of an office is mainly concerned with the recording of the business transaction, *i.e.*, making, using and preserving records for future reference. Some of the records and books are to be statutorily maintained as per the requirements of law while other records are maintained to meet the needs of management. The primary functions of an office are:

Function of Office

Primary Function	Secondary Function
Receiving information	Communication
Recording information	Computing
Processing information	Statistical Work
Retrieval of information	Planning and Scheduling
Protecting Assets	Coordination and Direction
Arranging Funds	Supervision and Control
	Function relating to Public relations

Receiving information: Receiving information relating to the business from various sources is the major function of an office. An office receives information either from internal source or from external source. Information received from internal source is from the departmental heads and from other levels of management. The chief forms of such information are reports, letters and telephone messages. Customers, suppliers, government, tax department, investors constitute the external source from whom information is received. Information from external source take the form of letters, orders, invoices, enquiries, telegrams, etc.

Recording information: Having received information from various sources and in different forms, the second primary function of an office is to record them in appropriate books. The first step in recording the information is to sort them out. Then, it involves entering the information in ledgers concerned as, for example, all orders received are recorded in an order book, all communication relating to enquiries in an enquiry book and so on. This helps not only in easy identification, but also enables quick reference. Recording of information is also obligatory for meeting legal requirements.

Processing information: Usually the information received by an office is not in a form which can be used directly by the management for decision making. Therefore, it involves arranging and processing the information systematically by trained staff. Very often it may involve calculation, condensation and simplification which meets the immediate requirements of management. Instances of processing information relates to costing reports, statistical statements, financial statements and other reports of performance in the business.

Retrieval of information: The office provides such information to the management as and when needed from its records. The information to be provided may be of routine nature or special nature and it may be verbal or in writing. Examples of information provided by office are orders, estimates, invoices, progress reports, financial statements and instructions issued on behalf of management.

Protecting assets: This involves safeguarding the assets of the business. By far the most important intangible assets to be protected by an office are the business secrets. The other asset to be safeguarded is cash. Surplus cash which is not required for immediate use is to be deposited in the bank. Necessary steps must be taken to collect outstanding debts and minimise bad debts. All the valuable assets must be insured against probable risk of loss. Contract deeds must likewise be properly protected.

Arranging funds: If the business undertaking happens to be a public limited company, the office has to arrange for funds by the issue of shares, debentures, public deposits, etc. It must arrange for payment of dividend and interest thereon.

Secondary functions

The secondary functions arise in course of business and are incidental to primary function. These functions may be classified as following:

Communication: Communication constitutes the core of the secondary function of the office. The office deals with two types of communication, *viz.*, internal and external. The internal communication takes place between the management and individuals within the business through conferences, interviews, telephone calls, instructions and circulars. The external communication takes place between the business enterprise and outsiders through letters, telephone, telegrams, orders and so forth.

Computation: This function involves ascertainment of cost incurred in manufacturing goods, checking the invoices, computation of wages and salaries payable to employees and assessing the value of by-products, wastes and scraps obtained in the production process.

Statistical work: The statistical work in an office comprises of classifying, analysing, summarising and interpreting the report. It involves the preparation of comprehensive report accompanied by charts and diagrams as a recommendation for prompt action.

Planning and scheduling: The planning function of office is concerned with determining what is to be done, who is to do it and where it is to be done. Scheduling is concerned with the time at which the events planned are to take place, *i.e.*, both planning and scheduling functions are based upon records.

Coordination and direction: One of the functions of office is to coordinate the working of other departments by issuing necessary directions from time to time. This increases the overall efficiency of business enterprise.

Supervision and control: Office is also concerned with supervising the work performed in various departments and maintain pace of work in those departments which lack efficiency. This is ensured through control techniques.

Function relating to public relations

An office is a place to which investors, suppliers, customers, prospective investors and visitors approach to gather information required by them. An office looks after the interest of these people through a competent receptionist. He/she must be a person of pleasing personality, tactful and courteous in order to project a better image of business over the visitors. In this context, an office is often referred to as the eyes, ears and hands of the business.

Types of office

An office can be classified into the three types on the basis of function, location and requirement by law. The following chart depicts the types of office.

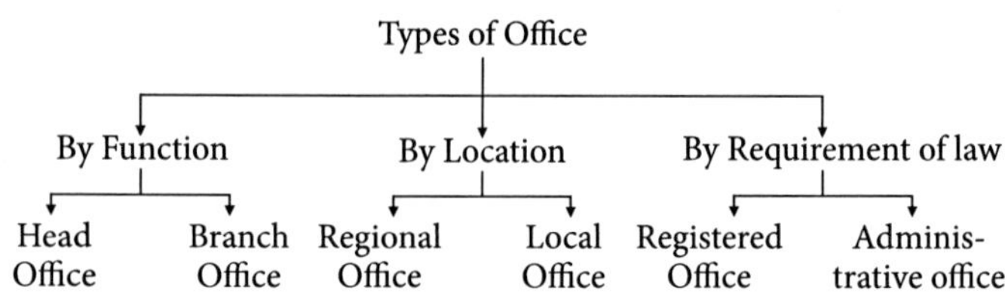

By Function

On the basis of function performed by an office, it can be classified into two types:

Head office and branch office: A big business will have a number of branches spread over different places. The head office is an office which coordinates the work of all such branches established in different localities. The parent establishment is known as head office and its off-shoots are termed as branch offices. The best examples of a business which follows this type of classification are banks in our country which function with a net work of several branches spread all over the country.

By location: On the basis of location, office can be classified into two types: regional office and local office. A regional office is set up at the regional level to look after the business of that region. Indian Railways offer an example for this basis of classification where in it has eight zonal or regional offices. A local office confines its business to the local area where its operations are carried out.

By requirement of law: According to the provisions of Company Act every joint stock company must necessarily have a registered office to enable those interested in a company to communicate with it. A registered office may be established in a place other than actual place of business. An administrative office is situated to carry out the control and supervisory business near the place of business.

Size of office

Very often it is felt that an office is necessary only for a large sized business concern, but not for a small one. The reason is that modern business makes use of different types of office equipment which are needed for a large sized business. But this argument is not correct. Firstly, in modern days, hand operated machines are manufactured and made available to suit the requirements of small business. By using this equipment the efficiency can be maintained in office. Secondly, most of the functions which are to be performed by a large sized business, are also common to small sized business, so the degree of mechanisation and number of equipment can be minimised in a small business but office as such cannot be dispensed with. Thirdly, at one time, office equipments were considered very costly and they were thought to be luxury to a business. But in modern days these equipment have become ordinary and are within the reach of most of the small businesses.

Measurement of the size of office

The size of an office depends upon the nature and organisational set up of a business. The following denominators are used to measure the size of business:

Number of office staff: The number of employees working in an office serves as one of the basis to measure the size of an office. Larger the number of employees, larger is the size of office and *vice versa*. But the presence of a large number of less efficient workers as compared to more efficient ones will not provide the correct basis for measuring the size of the business.

Investment made on office appliances: The capital invested on modern office appliances serves as another basis for measuring the size of office. Usually a large sized office alone can afford to invest huge amount on these office equipments. Hence, this offers a good basis for measuring the size of business.

Payroll: This serves yet another basis for measuring the size of office. But in some businesses, mechanical-office work is simplified to a large extent by using mechanical equipment in place of manual labour in which case the salary bill may be less. However, this will not serve as a correct index to measure the size of an office.

Total administrative expenses: The expenses incurred in maintaining office and administration department offer a basis for measuring the size of the office. But then the question of rented office pose problems as huge amount of administrative expenses are in the form of rent. So unless the ownership of office building is acquired this cannot offer a correct basis for measuring the size of an office.

Recent trends in office practice

The recent trends in office practice can be highlighted under the following:

Recognition of the importance of office management: At one time, office management was almost neglected and huge amount of expenses were incurred as administrative and office expenses. Today, it is considered as one of the most important divisions of business. In many cases, even before the establishment of other departments of business, office is set up first.

Information technology: Information technology may be defined as the art and science of locating, collecting, analysing, recording and transmitting all necessary information to every part of organisation on time and in the most suitable form to satisfy the needs of every executive. The scope of information technology is very wide and includes a number of other disciplines such as economics, mathematics, statistics, operation research, system analysis and cost accounting. The clerks of yesterday who used to perform all these work have been now replaced by persons, specialising in posting, accounting entries, typewriting, filling, calculating, card punching, duplicating and sorting.

Cost-benefit analysis: The cost incurred in the office and administration department is constantly rising in the form of salaries, printing and stationery and investment on office equipment. This has proved to be an additional burden to a business. However, the use of cost benefit analysis technique identifies the crucial areas where huge expenses are incurred and presents a comprehensive picture of the real situation. Attempts are being made to reduce unnecessary expenses by various control measures, *viz.*, budgetary control and personnel control.

The Leadership problem: The present situation in industry and commerce demands an entirely different form of leadership compared to earlier years. The concept of Welfare Sate, the rising level of education, high standard of living and the growth of trade unions have contributed to a great deal of change in the attitude and behaviour on the part of office staff. This demands better innovation which is a key to good leadership.

Mechanisation of office: With the change in technology, office equipment have come to play a significant role. The installation of computer poses the problem of unemployment. With the women employees entering in large numbers into office jobs, men are slowly thinking of jobs relating to other areas of business.

Application of modern principles of management: The scientific principles of management are applied even to office practice to increase efficiency and economy. The principle of specialisation is seen to a marked extent when compared to earlier years.

Other trends

(*a*) The use of loose leaf papers in place of bound book for recording purposes. They are used at all times, in all places, and for all purposes.

(*b*) Office practice and procedure are simplified to achieve the results directly.

(c) Office work is increasingly standardised. The areas of standardisation are: equipment, machinery, selection and operating methods.

(*d*) The size of office is growing continuously owing to extensive use of methods of analysis and pre-planning in business.

QUESTIONS

Objective Type Questions

Answer the following questions in about 4 lines each:

1. Define an office.
2. State any four primary function of an office.
3. Mention any four secondary functions of an office.
4. What do you mean by planning? Why is it included in office work?
5. State four requisites of an ideal office.
6. What is dispatching? Why is it considered to be an office work?
7. What is computing? Why is it considered to be an office work?

8. When is office work 'productive' and When is it 'non-productive'?
9. Define 'information technology'.
10. Distinguish between 'Head Office' and 'Branch Office'.
11. Distinguish between 'Regional Office' and 'Local Office'.
12. Distinguish between 'Registered Office' and 'Administrative Office'.

Analytical Type Questions

Answer the following questions in about a page each:

1. Explain the importance of a modern office to a business enterprise.
2. Examine the nature of office work.
3. "An office is useful only to a large sized business, but not for small business" Do your agree? Discuss.
4. "The office is to a business what a mainspring is to a watch". Discuss.
5. "The office is a coordinating activity". Discuss.
6. Trace some of the developments in office work from ancient days to modern days.
7. "An office constitutes the eyes, ears and hands of business", comments.
8. Explain the recent trends in office practice.

Essay Type Question

Answer in about 3 pages:

1. Explain the various functions of an office.

2

Office Management and its Importance

INTRODUCTION

Office Management is that phase of management which is concerned with the application of the principles of management to the communication problems of business. It is an inseparable branch of Management as it exists not for itself, but to serve the needs of other departments of business. Further, those who are concerned with office management are also concerned with the overall operations of a business. Office management is the planning, organising and controlling of records by the administrators of an organisation. Hence, it forms a part of general administrative management. Office management implements the policy of a business through various departments and hence it is a service and facilitating division of business management.

Definition of office management

(*a*) *Wyle and Brecht in their book Office Organisation and Management* define office management as "the manipulation and control of man, methods, machines and materials to achieve the best possible results of the highest possible quality with the best possible effort and expense in the shortest practicable time and in a manner acceptable to the top management."

This definition aims at optimum utilisation of various inputs with a view to derive maximum results, *i.e.*, output. This definition maintains the achievement of results both economically and efficiently without wasting considerable amount of time. The procedure adopted to achieve the result must be subject to approval of top management.

(*b*) *Leffingwell and Robinson in their Textbook of Office Management* defines office management as "that branch of the art and science of management which is concerned with the efficient performance of office work whenever and wherever that work is to be done".

This definition emphasizes the following features:

(1) Office Management is one of the branches of general management.
(2) It is an art and science.
(3) It is concerned with getting the work done in the office by the superiors from subordinates.
(4) The office function is not restricted to one point of time or place. In the words of Denyer, office management is concerned with the executive control of any room, whether it be a company secretary's accountants', buyers' or even an engineer's office.

(*c*) The Institute of Administrative Management in UK has defined office management as "that branch of management which is concerned with the services of obtaining, recording and analysing information of planning and of communicating by means of which the management of a business safeguards its assets, promotes its affairs and achieve its objectives.

This definition touches upon the primary and secondary functions of an office discussed in the first chapter.

(*d*) E.C. Eyre in his book *Office Administration Made Simple* defines office management "as being concerned with providing a service of communication and records and of safeguarding assets.

This definition lays emphasis on three aspects, *viz.*, (*i*) communications (*ii*) records maintenance and (*iii*) safeguarding assets, *i.e.*, office security.

(*e*) Denyer defines office management as "directing and controlling of an office in order to achieve its specified purpose in the most economical way". This definition attaches importance to the two important functions of management, *viz.*, directing and controlling in executing office functions.

(*f*) P.W. Betts defines office management as "the effective application of all the managerial skills towards achieving the objectives associated with the office function of providing appropriate information and a communication network to all sectors of the organisation". This definition lays emphasis on the following aspects:

Managerial skills: The managerial skills must be effectively applied using office management both as an art and a science.

Administrative knowledge: To perform the job in an office a thorough knowledge of various disciplines is essential.

The communication network: The flow of information to various levels of management depends upon the provision of a formal comprehensive network of communication channel.

Objectives: The objectives must be concise and in perspective with the other main functions.

Office function: The office functions chiefly consists of receiving, recording, arranging and providing information wherever and whenever needed throughout the organisations.

(*g*) G. Mills and O. Standingford quote the following definition of office management. "Office management is the art of guiding the personnel of the office in the use of means appropriate to its environment in order to achieve its specified purpose.

This definition brings forth the following aspects:

Purpose: The office manager must always be aware of the purpose of an office before making decisions. The purpose of an office could be to render service to maximise profit or to attain social responsibilities. Office work is carried out with a view to render service to other departments of a business. Therefore, service is an important purpose of managing office work. There is a close relationship between the efficient office work and increased profit. Social responsibility as a purpose of office lays down the attainment of objectives in accordance with moral and ethical codes of a business.

Environment: Environment here does not refer to physical environment within the office, but the external factors such as traditions, customs and laws of the community, the various statutes enacted by the government of the country and so on. These environmental factors always keep changing and so office must react to change with them.

Means: This refers to making best use of office premises, methods, equipment and techniques by the office manager. When new methods and techniques are introduced, office manager must make use of them with a view to increase efficiency and effectiveness.

Personnel: By far this is the most important element of the definition which includes the office staff who are responsible for performing office work. Since much depends upon the attitude and ability of office staff, the office manager must give utmost importance to this element. The office manager must carefully select the right type of employees, train them, induct them on the job most suited to their talent and guide and control their activities.

Scope of office management

The scope of office management refers to the areas of study included in this subject. The following topics fall under the purview of office management:

Office planning and layout: A careful planning and layout of office is necessary for securing maximum efficiency and economy. This topic deals with three aspects, *viz.*, (*a*) selecting an appropriate location for setting up an office (*b*) making suitable arrangements for providing physical facilities such as lighting, ventilation and air conditioning and (*c*) designing the layout of office so as to utilise the available space to the fullest extent.

Office organisation: Office organisation is concerned with classifying the various office jobs, assigning them to the concerned staff, fixing the responsibilities on the executives, departmentation of office premises for securing specialisation, coordinating the efforts of all personnel so as to avoid confusion in the office.

Office furniture and equipment: Good office furniture and equipment enables smoother and speedy functioning in the office. Systematic arrangement of office furniture enables less movement of staff, effective supervision, and increases the efficiency of office staff. The use of modern office equipment has considerably reduced the stress and the strain on the part of office staff. The installation of computers has made office job more interesting and lucrative.

Office communication and correspondence: Communication refers to the act of conveying information or giving instructions. Communication may be internal or external. The chief modes of communication are oral, written and visual. Office correspondence is mostly concerned with establishing relationship between the office and outsiders. The organisation of correspondence department, drafting correspondence and mailing them are the important activities which fall under this topic.

Records management: By far, the largest proportion of time in the office is spent on recording. Records management is concerned with preparing and preserving new records and destroying the old records once they serve the purpose for which they were meant. The chief areas of study here includes filing system, indexing, micro filming and information retrieval.

Personnel administration: This area of office management is concerned with selection, training, placement, fixation of salaries, control of labour turnover, personnel counselling, personnel safety, implementing benefits to employees, dealing with office trade unions and personnel research.

Office systems and procedures: Office system refers to a network of procedures developed according to an integrated scheme for performing an activity of an office. Office procedure is a sequence of clerical operations, usually involving several staff in one or more departments established to resume uniform handling of a recurring function of an office. To ensure whether systems and procedures are properly adopted, the technique of O & M is applied in modern offices. O & M is the scientific checking of the efficiency of office work.

Office control: Office control ensures whether performance of work in office is as per the schedule. It is also concerned with quality control and cost control aspects of office.

Importance of office management: The importance of office management may be summarised under the following:

(1) It helps the management in providing better physical facilities such as good lighting, ventilation, air-conditioning and furniture. This increases the efficiency of office staff.

(2) It is concerned with recruitment, selection, training and promoting the employees on a scientific basis. The office work progresses with efficient staff as against deterioration with inefficient workers.

(3) It directs and coordinates the activities of all the departments so as to avoid duplication of efforts.

(4) It provides effective leadership in the office and thus improves the morale of office staff.

(5) By scheduling and assigning office work among staff, it ensures quick performance of work.

(6) It exercise control over the various activities of the office and thereby minimises losses and wastages occurring in the office.

Scientific Office Management: Scientific office management is the science of management which is applied to the office practice and procedure. In olden days, much of the office work was performed without applying the scientific principles of management. Consequently, it resulted in considerable waste of time and energy. Scientific management, when applied to office management involves the following steps:

Stating the problem and defining the purpose: The first step involved in the scientific office management is to find out clearly, definitely and specifically the work to be undertaken and its purposes. The office manager has to find out the answers for the questions such as, what is his work? What is its purposes? What results are desired so as to complete the work satisfactorily. Unless the problem is properly defined and its purpose stated, the office manager may spend too much of time to complete it. This is based on the maxim "a problem well stated is half solved".

Analysing the problem: Literally, 'analysis' means the splitting of a thing into its constituent parts of elements. So, analysis of a problem means to find out its elements through organised thoughts. In addition to splitting up of the problem, each element must be given its relative importance, *i.e.*, whether it is a major or minor element, an isolated problem or does it include other subdivisions in it. This process of analysing, facilitates the next step namely search for the facts related to the problem.

Finding the facts of the case: In order to improve the existing method of performing a task it is necessary to collect all the facts concerning it. For example, if the existing method is time consuming to perform a task, it is necessary to find out the cause. Some of the factors which may be responsible for delayed production are difficulty in obtaining tools, equipment, materials, employees and so on. However, it is desirable to study all factors without overlooking any of them. Those factors which are desirable must be retained and the undesirable must be eliminated. The facts can be found out by the following means (1) information from others (2) one's own inference and (3) by actual test.

Finding the right method: This step includes selecting the best method to perform a given task. The selection of the best method depends upon four elements, *viz.*, space, time, energy and materials. A best method is characterised by economy of space, a saving of time, conservation of energy and judicious use of materials. In other words, the best method to be selected is one which eliminates wastages in each of the elements mentioned above.

Finding the right person: Unless a competent person is recruited, the steps of scientific management will go waste. The selection of right person depends upon personal qualities and the aptitude of employees.

Training the right person: Although a right person is selected scientifically, it should not be presumed that he can perform the work efficiently. The person so recruited must be carefully and thoroughly instructed in the standard method of doing the work. This implies training the employee which is an essential principle of scientific management.

Planning: No work can be performed efficiently unless it is properly planned. As a principle of scientific management, the essence of planning is to do the work thoroughly and accurately. Since office work is numerous and diversified, it is impossible to carry it out unless, well-planned.

Getting the work done or cooperating: This step calls for joint efforts of all the members concerned to achieve the objective effectively. Cooperation is said to have been extended when the employees give their 'will' freely, fully and intelligently to accomplish the objective. The cooperation of employees to a large extent depends upon the treatment they get. Good treatment refers to the scientific method of handling both, employees and their work.

Objectives of office management

Zane K. Quible in his book *Introduction to Administrative Office Management* has enumerated the following objectives of office Management:

(1) To Coordinate the activities of the office management function with the activities of other organisational functions.
(2) To maintain reasonable quality and quantity standards so that satisfactory levels of production are possible.
(3) To develop efficient work procedures and processes in order to increase the organisation's profit margin.
(4) To provide a satisfactory physical and mental working environment for the organisation's employees.
(5) To enhance the effective supervision of office personnel.
(6) To make information available when and where needed.
(7) To help in defining duties and responsibilities of employees within the unit and to develop satisfactory lines of communication among these employees and other employees in the organisation.
(8) To schedule work properly so that it is completed on time.
(9) To develop procedures that help in selecting the right person for the right job.
(10) To provide ample opportunities for helping the employees to maintain a high level of work effectiveness.
(11) To make sure that specialised equipment is efficiently and properly utilised.
(12) To provide ample security for materials and information that falls under the jurisdiction of the administrative office manager.

Functions of office management

The functions of general management equally applies to office management. These functions are:

Planning office activity: According to Theo Haimann "Planning is the function that determines in advance what should be done. It consists of selecting the enterprise objectives, policies, programmes, procedures and other means of achieving the objectives." Thus, planning of office activity has the following elements.

(*a*) *Objectives*: The essential objective of an office is to render useful service to all the functional departments of a business so as to enable them to carry out their activities efficiently. However, this service is to be provided promptly and economically.

(*b*) *Policies*: Policies provide broad guidelines as to how objectives of an office are to be achieved. A policy is a guided decision by the office management which guides the office staff to deal with a particular situation in a particular manner. Policies are communicated to the employees through office manuals.

(*c*) *Procedures*: It refers to the process of establishing time sequence for work to be done. Procedure is concerned with fixing a time table for starting a given work, going through its different phases and its completion. The procedures helps to determine (*i*) the specific task to be performed, (*ii*) the time when these tasks will be performed and (*iii*) the person who will perform them.

(*d*) *Programme*: Programme refers to the outline of office work to be done in a proper sequence for the purpose of achieving specific objectives. *Organising office activity*: The function of office management involves (*i*) classifying the office into various sections such as accounts section, finance section, filing section, corresponding section, reception and so on (*ii*) providing required furniture, equipment and stationery so as to carry out the office work more efficiently, smoothly (*iii*) delegating the work among office staff and (*iv*) establishing relationship among superiors and subordinates.

Staffing: This function of office management is concerned with the recruitment, selection, placement and training the office staff at the appropriate time.

Motivating: The process of inspiring office staff is referred to as motivation. The office staff can be inspired by providing congenial environment in office, ensuring job security, recognition of the ability and efficiency of office staff and providing good leadership in the office.

Coordination: The smooth working of an organisation depends upon the coordination of all the departments of a business. Coordination of activities of all the departments can be achieved by effective communication through conferences, meetings and committees.

Direction: Directing a function of office management involves guiding and supervising subordinates. This function is performed by an office superintendent. His job is to orient the office staff towards the policy and philosophy of management, guide towards improved performance and motivate to work effectively to achieve the objectives of the business.

Controlling: This is concerned with the fixation of standards in respect of office functioning, in terms of time or volume of work. The actual work performed is then compared with the standard work. In case the actual deviates from the standard, necessary action is taken to set right the adverse deviation.

The office manager and his job

An office manager is one who is in charge of an office. As regards the role of office manager it is not only responsible, but also flexible. In modern days, the role of office manager has become more challenging owing to rapid advances in technology, modern office equipment, new work processes, and employee unions. Regarding the job of office manager, it varies from business to business. If the size of the office is large, the number of office specialists will also be more. In such an office, owing to increased specialists the job of office manager will be less burdensome.

The primary job of an office manager is organisation and control of the office in relation to various aspects of office management. These aspects of office management relate to:

(1) Make sure that all office activities are directed towards the achievement of the purpose of the office most economically and efficiently.

(2) Personnel or Office Staff—in respect of this aspect the office manager's job is concerned with scientific selection and remuneration of the office staff.

(3) Method of performing the work—wherein the office manager has to decide the mode of doing the work, *i.e.*, manual or mechanical, and

(4) Office Environment—to enable the office staff to carry on their duties successfully. In discharging his job, the office manager must maintain a proper balance among all these aspects as they all equally influence the efficiency of office work.

Position of office manager

At the outset it is to be understood that office manager is not a member of the top management team which formulates the overall policy. The position of an office manager in a modern office is two-fold. Firstly, he serves as a line officer, as he is the last link in the chain of command from top management. In this capacity, his task is to see that the policy of management is properly implemented. It has been rightly said that the position of office manager is 'Man in the middle'. This implies that he has to face both ways, *i.e.*, to represent the workers to the management and at the same time to represent the management to workers. Secondly, the position of office manager is that of staff officer. This position will become evident when the office manager tenders useful advice to various departmental clerks in the business. Under this situation the office manager will have no direct control over the clerks of other departments, but he merely tenders advice to them with regard to organisation and controlling the activities of those departments.

Functions of office manager

The functions of an office manager may be summarised as under:

(1) To interpret and implement the policy formulated by top management.

(2) To plan the organisation structure of the office and define the duties and responsibilities of his staff.

(3) To exercise leadership talents in order to stimulate and inspire the office staff.

(4) To supervise office activities such as correspondence, filing and indexing, handling incoming and outgoing mail, duplicating and reproducing and such other activities.

(5) To set up effective system of control in order to check performance against plans.

Duties of office manager

The duties of an office manger can be outlined under the following:

Duties towards Top Management: To advise top management on all aspects of office matters in formulating policies. To report to top management on such matters as employee grievances, incomplete work and difficulties in executing the work. To work in close coordination with O & M (Organisation and Methods) department.

Duties towards the office work: To ensure that work is carried out as per scheduled time. To ensure that the quality of work is maintained throughout till its completion. To devise best method of doing office work. Where work can be done more efficiently and economically with the help of office equipment, manual labour should not be resorted to. To ensure control over both quantity and quality of work. It is also the duty of office manager to utilise the office equipment to the maximum extent and to arrange for repairs and maintenance in case of need.

Duties towards subordinates: To assist the subordinates in carrying day to day activities. To solve the problems faced by his subordinates. To recommend for promotion and for higher pay. To train the subordinates especially when a new office equipment is installed.

Duties towards associates: To have frequent discussion with his associates so as to have common policies throughout the organisation. To coordinate and cooperate with the activities of his associates in order to maintain a high level of efficiency.

Responsibilities of Office Manager

The responsibilities of an office manager are out lined as under:

Responsibilities relating office building: The responsibilities relating to office building include (*a*) Office building design (*b*) Layout of building (*c*) Lighting of office building (*d*) Colour dynamics (*e*) Heating and Air Conditioning (*f*) Plumbing and electrical (*g*) Noise control (*h*) Expansion of office building (*i*) Maintenance of office building (*j*) Safety and office security.

Responsibilities relating to furniture and equipment: The responsibilities relating to furniture and equipment include (*a*) Selection and procurement (*b*) Maintenance (*c*) Replacement and (*d*) Disposal.

Responsibilities relating to office machines and equipment: The responsibilities relating to office machines and equipment include (*a*) Purchase of modern office equipment (*b*) Computerisation of office.

Responsibilities relating to organisation: The responsibilities relating to organisation include (*a*) Supervision of departments (*b*) Branch office organisation and (*c*) Assigning duties to subordinates.

Responsibilities relating to communications: The responsibilities with regard to communications relates to (*a*) Written communication and (*b*) Oral communications.

Responsibilities relating to records management: The responsibilities relating to record management include (*a*) Filing and indexing of records (*b*) Microfilming (*c*) Protection of records.

Form and Design control: The responsibilities under this area relates to (*a*) Standardisation of size, paper and colour (*b*) Design of forms (*c*) Storage and distribution.

Responsibilities relating to office personnel: The responsibilities relating to office personnel include (*a*) Recruitment (*b*) Training (*c*) Promotions (*d*) Recreational facilities and (*e*) Grievance of employees.

Responsibilities relating to office systems and procedures: The responsibilities relating to office systems and procedures include (*a*) Manuals (*b*) Simplification and standardisation (*c*) Flow of work.

Responsibilities relating to work measurement and work standard: The responsibilities relating to this area include (*a*) Measuring office operations and (*b*) Setting standard.

Qualities of office manager

The essential qualities of a successful office manager are as follows:

1. **Leadership:** A good office manager must possess the quality of leading the office staff rather than driving them. Although leadership ability is inherent it can be developed by training and experience.
2. **Sound judgement:** Sound judgement is required under two circumstances (*a*) Whether the person to whom work is to be delegated, has the ability to do the work and (*b*) In dealing with disciplinary matters with workers.

3. **Impartiality:** The office manager must treat his staff impartially in order to gain their confidence and respect.

4. **Shrewdness:** This quality refers to the ability to deal with a situation and to take appropriate action.

5. **Courage:** This implies backing the shrewdness by courage. He should not contradict his own judgement.

6. **Methodical:** This quality implies orderly performance of office work. He must organise the work of his staff systematically.

7. **Good character:** An office manager must stand firm to his decisions. However, firmness should not be taken to mean stubbornness.

8. **Forward Looking:** An office manager must keep himself upto date in relation to office system, methods and techniques so as to improve the efficiency of the office.

9. **Personal Qualities:** Personal qualities of an office manager is a combination of personal traits such as honesty, sincerity, initiative, self discipline, punctuality, humorous, tact, persuasiveness and an attractive personality.

10. **Professional interest:** In addition to the usual knowledge in the field of office management, an office manager must also have interest in professional fields such as management science, cost accountancy, financial management, secretarial procedure, knowledge relating to law and so on. These professional interests make him to become a wholesome office manager.

However, it is very difficult for an office manager to possess all these qualities simultaneously. While some qualities are inborn, others are acquired by experience and training. Hence, it can be said that an office manager is both born and made.

Administrative office management

The term Administrative office management is often used interchangeably to denote office management. The phrase Administrative office management is popularly used in USA to denote the functions of 'Office Management' which is very commonly used in UK and India. In one sense the scope of Administrative office management can be considered as broader when compared to office management. This is obvious from the fact that the role and position of office manager is not the same today as it was a few decades ago. Over a period of time the responsibilities of office manager has increased and they include selection of office employees (which at one time was the duty of personnel manager), installing systems and procedures (which at one time was the duty of General Manager) purchasing of all materials and equipments required for the office (which at one time was the duty of purchase manager), and playing the role of public relations officer in modern days. So much so, the designation of erstwhile office manager is called today by different names such as commercial manager, office controller, administrative officer and so on.

QUESTIONS

Simple Questions

1. Define Office Management.
2. What do you mean by Scientific Office Management?
3. List out four important functions of Office Management.
4. Mention the two different positions occupied by an office manager in an office.
5. Distinguish between Top level and Middle Level Office Management.
6. List out four important functions of Office Manager.
7. What do you mean by Administrative Office Manager?

Short Answer Questions

1. Outline the importance of Office Management.
2. Explain briefly the steps involved in scientific management as applied to Office Management.

3. State the objectives of Office Management.
4. Briefly explain the functions of Office Manager.
5. Explain the various levels of Office Management.
6. Discuss the position of an Office Manager.
7. Outline the qualities of Office Manager.
8. "An Office Manager is born not made" do you agree. Discuss.

Long Answer Question

1. Define Office Management. Discuss its scope.
2. Explain the Duties and responsibilities of an office manager.

3

Office Organisation

INTRODUCTION

The Term organisation is used in dynamic and static sense. In its dynamic sense, organisation refers to a function of management which is necessary for bringing people together so as to achieve the object of an undertaking. This may well be called as the process of organising. In its static sense of the term, organisation refers to the structure of relationship among positions and jobs which is built up for the realisation of common objectives. In this sense, organisation serves as a means to achieve the end. The scope of organisation includes (1) the human resources who utilise the physical resources of the business to achieve its objectives (2) the respective positions they occupy and the functions they perform (3) the range of authority and responsibility they individually exercise (4) the framework of formal and informal relationship through which they deal and communicate with one another and (5) the mechanism through which they operate and coordinate their activities in the enterprise. It is on the basis of persons, physical resources, positions, authority, contacts, operations, communications and coordination that work is carried on successfully.

Organisation serves two important purposes. Firstly, organisation defines the relationship between the sub-functions so as to coordinate the effort of people in the accomplishment of the overall task effectively and efficiently. The objective places more emphasis on job content, definition, analysis and relationship of organisation structure. Secondly, organisation serves as a pattern of ways in which number of people relate themselves to each other in the planned and systematic accomplishment of a complexity of tasks. This objective tends to emphasize the personal relationship and human element to greater extent. But the common purpose of establishing an organisation is to enable the human resource to work more effectively as a unit. According to Wren "to contribute his best, every employee needs to know what he is expected to do, who his superior is and what his relationship is to other employee, and other parts of the organisation. A sound organisation tends to alleviate certain types of personal problems such as (1) duplication of effort (2) unbalanced work load (3) defining training needs (4) dormant programmes and (5) lack of coordination.

Definition of organisation

P.W. Betts defines organisations as "a plan of the concern's structure indicating all the jobs, their relationship with each other, their function and the duties involved as well as the authority and responsibilities associated with them".

Kimball and Kimball in their book *Industrial Organisation defines* organisation as "the duties of designating the departments and personnel that are to carry on the work defining the functions and specifying the relations that are to exist between departments and individuals."

According to Oliver Sheldon (*The Philosophy of Management*) "Organisation is the process of so combining the work which individuals or group have to perform with the facilities necessary for its execution, that the duties so performed provide the best channels for the efficient, systematic, positive and coordinated application of the available efforts."

The above definition concerns itself with combining and coordinating individual's as well as groups' activities in an enterprise. Organisation integrates the various jobs of the enterprise into an effective system to provide for accomplishing the objective of business.

According to Louis. A Allen (*Management and Organisation*) "Organisation is the process of identifying and grouping the work to be performed, defining and delegating responsibility and authority and establishing relationship for the purpose of enabling people to work most effectively together in accomplishing objectives."

On a careful examination of the above definitions the characteristic feature of an "organisation" can be enumerated as follows:

1. Identifying the work of an office: The various activities of an office can be identified as recording, correspondence, filing, indexing, handling mail, typing, reception and messenger services and so on.

2. Grouping of related activities: Here, the activities are grouped according to similarities and common purposes. This ensures avoiding duplication of efforts and confusion in performing the office work. If we take the activities mentioned above, recording and corresponding can be grouped into one activity, inward and outward mail into second activity, filing and indexing into third activity and so on.

3. Fitting the individuals into function: Once the activities are identified and classified into various groups, the next step is to fit suitable and well qualified staff into these activities.

Each person in the group will be given a specific part of the job for operation and he will be held responsible for the same.

4. Assignment of authority for action: Each member of the group will be given specific responsibility in relation to the authority assigned. In an organisation sense, authority is the right of one person to require another to perform certain duties. This authority may have one or more of the following aspects:

(*a*) It may be formal, *i.e.*, conferred by law or delegated within the organisation.

(*b*) It may be functional, because it is based on special knowledge or skill.

(*c*) It may be personal, *i.e.*, accorded because of seniority, popularity or outstanding qualities of leadership.

Importance of organisation

A well conceived and developed organisation structure will immensely benefit the superiors and subordinates in an organisation. A good organisation structure will not only enable the achievement of objectives more easily and quickly but also the physical operations of the organisation will be greatly enhanced. The importance of organisation is outlined below:

1. Organisation establishes responsibility and prevents 'buck passing'.
2. It provides for easier communication.
3. It eliminates jurisdictional disputes between individuals.
4. It helps in developing executive ability.
5. It aids in equitable distribution of work and personal supervision.
6. It aids in measuring a person's performance as compared to his duties and responsibilities.
7. It permits expansion and contraction without seriously disrupting the structure.
8. It prepares for closer co-operation and higher morale.
9. It points out dead end jobs.

10. It delineates avenues of promotion.
11. It prevents duplication of work.
12. It makes growth possible with adequate control and without literally killing top executives through excess work.
13. It aids in wage and salary administration through forced job analysis and job description.

Process of organising an office

The process of organising an office involves the following steps:

(1) Planning
(2) Recruitment of staff
(3) Procuring equipment
(4) Departmentation
(5) Assignment of jobs
(6) Delegation of authority
(7) Creation of Responsibility
(8) Preparation of an Organisation chart
(9) Preparation of an Organisation manual
(10) Preparation of standard practice instruction.

The above steps are briefly discussed here under:

1. Planning: The planning of an office depends upon the nature, size and volume of activities. Planning of office is essential to avoid wastage of time, money and efforts. While planning, it is also desirable to prepare a budget involving both capital and revenue expenditure. Planning an office is by no means a simple task. It involves a combined judgement to be exercised by Office manager, and Industrial Engineer. The planning of an office involves consideration of other factors such as (*a*) selection of site (*b*) layout of office and (*c*) working conditions on which the efficiency of work largely depends.

2. Recruitment of staff: Recruitment of office staff is based on job specification and job grading. Job specification implies preparation of a list of various jobs that are involved in the office. Corresponding to each job, a list of specific type of staff required to perform such job is also prepared. Job grading enables the recruitment of right type of staff. The American Management Association has listed six types of grade from A to F. A higher grade of work involves a person with high thinking than doing and *vice versa*. In determining the jobs in the office, the following factors must be taken into consideration (*a*) education (*b*) skill and (*c*) experience. Having recruited the staff they must be trained in different areas so as to work independently.

3. Procuring Equipment: The performance of office work involves the use of furniture, machines, appliances and stationery. Proper purchase of these equipments, and continuous supply of stationery ensures smooth functioning of an office. If possible, a separate department may be established for this purpose.

4. Departmentation: The process of grouping allied jobs is functionally called a department. As an example, the account department consists of all jobs such as maintenance of books, preparation of financial statements, calculation of cost of production and so on. Similarly, other departments such as filing department, finance department, correspondence department are set up depending upon the need for such departments. Departmentation of office is based on number of factors and the extent of centralisation and decentralisation desired by the management.

5. Assignment of Jobs: It involves the allocation of jobs to the staff in the office. Proper distribution of jobs avoids confusion and creates a sense of responsibility among the staff. Assignment of jobs creates duty consciousness among all employees.

6. Delegation of authority: Authority refers to the power to take decisions and to order others to get the decision executed. Mere allocation of jobs among the staff do not serve the purpose of organisation. Every assignment of job is to be accompanied by granting power by the superior to the subordinate to perform such job. Authority flows from top to bottom while assigning the job.

7. Creation of responsibility: Creation of responsibility implies holding the persons accountable for performing their duties satisfactorily. Responsibility clearly lays down as to whom a subordinate owes an obligation for fulfilling the job. Responsibility always moves upwards *i.e.*, from subordinate to superiors in the hierarchy of organisation.

8. Preparation of an organisation chart: The organisation chart is a graphic device for portraying the organisation structure. It is used to analyse and assess the existing structure, to identify weaknesses and to plan organisation improvement. It establishes a kind of relationship between superior and subordinates and clearly lays down which subordinate is under whose control.

9. Preparation of organisation manual: The organisation manual defines the nature and extent of the authority and responsibility assigned to each member so that he knows his duties and relationship with other members. The functions of organisation manual are as follows:

(*a*) To set out clearly the general framework of the organisation.
(*b*) To state the various divisions and departments of the organisation.
(*c*) To state different levels of authority, departmental heads etc.
(*d*) To indicate the difference between line authority and staff function.
(*e*) To give titles of different positions and to establish their relationship to the immediate superior and subordinate and the range of responsibility, authority and duties carried under the title.

10. Preparation of standard practice instructions: In order to complete the design of an organisation structure, it is necessary to write up standard practice instructions to cover the established procedures for carrying out the detailed authority within the office. When it is properly organised, it constitutes a written code of practice giving the best method known for performing a given activity. This best method is made into a permanent record and is applied to secure uniformity of performance throughout the office. The standard practice instruction describe how and when a function is to be performed.

Organisation structure

Organisation structure refers to the basic framework within which the executives' decision-making behaviour occurs. The quality and nature of the decisions made are influenced by the nature of the structure. A well defined organisation structure consists of different levels of management with well-defined duties and responsibilities. A typical structure of the organisation is depicted below:

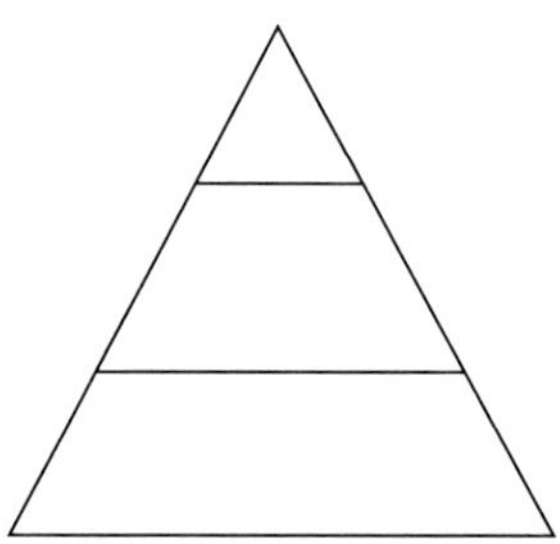

Figure 3.1: Figure showing organisation's structure

From the above figure it is clear that the organisation structure has three levels of management denoting three levels of authority. The authority decreases from top level when it descends down to the lower level of management. The three levels of management which constitute the organisation structure is discussed below:

1. Top level management (Decision support system): The top level management assumes over-all responsibility for all office activities. The executive who heads top level office management is known as chief administrator or administrative manager. He is responsible to the managing director for all activities of the office. His duties are as follows:

(*a*) To control the administration function of the entire organisation at minimum cost.

(*b*) To coordinate all clerical activities with a view to attain the objectives of business.

(*c*) To provide an efficient communication network.

(*d*) To comply with all legal requirements.

2. Middle level management (Management information system): This is seen at various departments of a business. For example, in sales department we have sales manager. The supervisors of a particular section will report to the sales manager about the performance of that section to which he is supervisor. This is illustrated below:

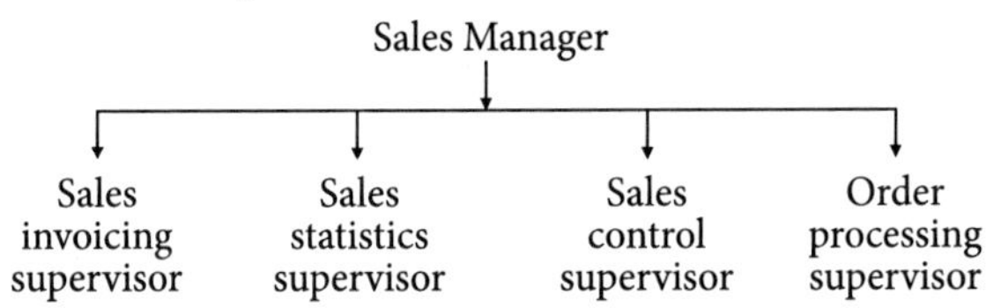

The duties of office manager attached to every department of a business are as follows:

(*a*) To Coordinate the clerical activities of other departments.

(*b*) To ensure optimum utilisation of all office machines and equipment.

(*c*) To keep up-do-date information on all office matters and make recommendations to the administrative manager accordingly.

3. Lower level management (Date processing system): The person who is incharge of lower level management is known as office supervisor. He will supervise the activities performed in the office such as invoice checking, filing the orders, posting entries, scheduling production and maintaining office records.

Principles of organisation

A principle is a general rule that may be expected to apply under similar conditions anywhere. The following are the most important principles of a sound organisation:

1. Principles of objectives: According to this principle of organisation, each and every part of the organisation should be the expression of a purpose either explicit or implicit. Before objectives are achieved, they must be clearly defined, understood and accepted by every individual concerned. Without defining the objectives it becomes difficult to determine appropriate course of action. If the objectives are clearly defined it enables proper utilisation of resources. Objectives may be expressed in numerical terms and it can be either short term or long term objective. Objectives set must be realistic, attainable and consistent with the basic philosophy of the organisation.

2. Principle of authority and responsibility: According to this principle, responsibility for the execution of work must be accompanied by the authority to control and direct the work. Without commensurate authority and responsibility, an individual cannot be held accountable for the successful completion of the task since the individual has very little control over the job.

3. Principle of ultimate authority of supervision: According to this principle, the responsibility of a higher authority for the acts of his subordinates is absolute.

4. Principle of scalar chain: According to this principle, a clear line of formal authority must run from the top to the bottom of an organisation for control. This principle refers to the formal specification of superior to whom a subordinate is to report. Having established a scalar chain it must be strictly adhered to. This facilitates effective communication between superiors and subordinates.

5. Principle of unity of command: This principle states that an employee should be directly responsible to only one supervisor. This avoids both conflicts and confusion in the organisation structure.

6. Principle of span of control: Span of control refers to the number of subordinates a superior is able to supervise effectively. According to this principle, the number of subordinates reporting to a superior should preferably be limited to six at the executive level. The important factors which govern span of control are nature of work, ability of superiors to supervise effectively, nature of responsibilities of superiors and the position of superior in the hierarchy of the organisation structure.

7. Principle of specialisation: According to this principle, the work of every person in the organisation should be confined to the performance of a single function.

8. Principle of definition: The duties, authority, responsibility and relations of everyone in the organisation structure should be clearly and completely prescribed in writing.

9. Principle of homogeneity: According to this principle, an organisation, to be efficient, and to operate without friction, should bring together only duties and activities which are similar and related to one another.

10. Principle of organisation effectiveness: According to this principle, the final test of an organisation is smooth and frictionless operation.

Techniques of organisation

The following techniques are used while designing an organisation structure in an office:

1. Job task: A job task is a document which shows the nature of work and the time involved in performing it. It is filled up every day by the person who undertake to discharge a particular task in the office. It is subsequently consolidated to form a weekly hours of work involved in the office. A typical Daily Job Sheet is shown below:

Job title: Typing Name of Typist:

Section: Accounts Day:

Daily Job Sheet

Job Description	Starting Time	Finishing Time	Time Taken
Replying Enquiries	9 A.M.	10 A.M.	1 Hr.
Processing Order	10 A.M.	11 A.M.	1 Hr.
Preparing Invoice	11 A.M.	12 Noon	1 Hr.
Preparing Reports	1 P.M.	2 P.M.	1 Hr.
Preparing Accounts	2 P.M.	3 P.M.	1 Hr.
Correspondence	3 P.M.	4 P.M.	1 Hr.
Total			6 Hrs

Figure 3.2

2. Activity Analysis: It is an analysis of all the activities conducted in a section belonging to an office. Activity analysis gives a more comprehensive picture of the activities relating to a week. The information for preparing an activity analysis form is drawn from daily job sheet. A specimen of such form is shown below:

Name of the section: Secretaries Office

Week commencing:

Weekly Activity Analysis Sheet

	Activity	Clerk 'A'	Hrs.	Clerk 'B'	Hrs.	Clerk 'C'	Hrs.
1.	Transfers of Shares						
2.	Calls on shares						
3.	Forfeiture and Surrender of Shares						
4.	Dividend and Interest Payment						
5.	Meetings of Directors and Shareholders						

Figure 3.3

3. Organisation chart: It is a chart which shows the grouping of major activities into departments and sections. It shows the main lines of authority and responsibility among these departments and sections. The main purpose of an organisation chart is to enable in Understanding organisational relationships. A typical organisation chart is shown below:

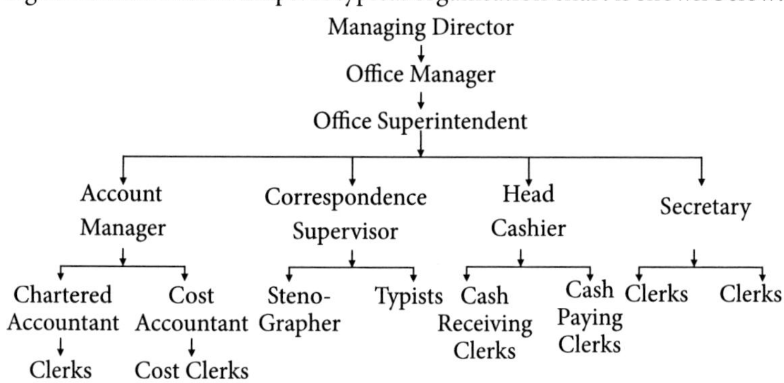

4. Job descriptions: The main features of this technique are to indicate the job title, terms of reference, responsibilities, authority relationship, duties and responsibilities as for example attendance at meetings.

Having gathered all the information through the above four techniques the office manager has to examine the organisation. Based on the particulars so furnished above, he can improve the existing organisation. The following check list helps the office manager in designing an organisation structure.

ORGANISATION CHECK LIST

1. Are the objectives clear ?
2. Does each member know the objectives and the part he should play in attempting to achieve them?

3. Is each employee's capabilities and ability known?
4. Are there clear channels and networks of communication?
5. Are the tasks in each job well balanced. Considering boredom and tasks that are distasteful, enjoyable or demanding?
6. Are suggestions and ideas welcomed?
7. Are reports regular, comprehensive and reasonably correct?
8. Are records upto date and accurate?
9. Are policy, rules and regulations known to everyone?
10. Does each employee know clearly his authority, responsibilities and duties ?
11. Is any member overloaded or underloaded with work?
12. Is the span of control for each supervisor within his capabilities?
13. Is authority delegated as much as possible?
14. Is there sufficient staff flexibility to cope with sickness and absence?

Types of organisation

There are four types of Organisation. They are (1) Line organisation (2) Line and Staff (3) Functional Organisation and (4) Committee Organisation.

I Line organisation

The Line organisation is the simplest and oldest form of organisation. This is also known as the 'military' or 'heirarchical' or 'scalar' or 'traditional' type. The organisation structure here is similar to that in the army organisation and hence the 'military type'.

This type of organisation is based upon exact division of duties, full authority and discipline. The line is the backbone of this type of organisation, that is formed by a series of delegation from the top to the bottom of the organisation structure. This can be illustrated by the following diagram:

Line type of Organisation

Board of Directors
↓
Chief Executive
↓
Office Manager
↓

Correspondence Department	Cash Department	Filling Department	O & M Department	Secretarial Department

From the above figure, it is clear that the board of directors delegate to the chief executive the responsibilities for managing the entire undertaking. The chief executive reserves the overall responsibility and authority for managing the business, but he delegates the day to day routine office work to the office manager, who in turn will delegate various office work to different supervisors working in different sections of the office. The following are the importance features of line organisation:

(*a*) Authority flows from the top to the bottom of the organisation structure step by step, as a result of the downward delegation of the authority.

(*b*) No subordinate will act without the authority delegated to him from his immediate superior.

(*c*) Each subordinate is responsible to his immediate superior for the duties discharged by him.

(*d*) Decisions are made at the top level management which are converted into orders and passed on to the lower level management by successive levels of management.

(*e*) A direct relationship between the superior and the subordinate is established under this type of organisation. While the authority comes down from the superior, the responsibility goes up from the subordinate.

Advantages

1. Direct relationship: The existence of a direct relationship of authority and responsibility, makes every member of the organisation to know his exact position, to whom he is responsible and who his immediate superior is. This renders the performance of work easy and smooth.

2. Fixation of responsibility: The responsibility to discharge a certain duty is fixed to a certain subordinate, so that he is held responsible for any deficiency in work.

3. Simplicity in operation: The fixation of authority and responsibility among the members of the organisation renders the operation of work simple and intelligible.

4. Sense of discipline: The direct relationship of authority and responsibility creates a sense of discipline in the organisation. Each subordinate is compelled to be faithful and loyal to his immediate superior. Discipline is thus the result of the single-man control over the subordinate which aids the improvement in quality and quantity of production.

5. Definite lines of authority: The duties and responsibilities of each and every superior and subordinate are clearly laid down under this organisation. So, the chances of confusion, misunderstanding and conflicts do not arise in this type of organisation.

6. Flexibility in action: The superior in each section has the authority to take effective steps to deal with particular situation without the necessity to consult any other executive in this respect. This freedom or flexibility in action would be helpful in dealing promptly in a situation of emergency.

7. Coordination of effort: There will be effective coordination in the entire organisation, because of the overall control exercised by the administrators in all the departments and because of the control over the activities of each department being exercised by the head of the department concerned. This in turn creates unification in the entire organisation and enables it to achieve its objectives.

8. Direction communication: The direct relationship between the superior and subordinate at different levels results in direct communication which is essential for quick performance of work.

9. Economical: As this type of organisation is simple in nature without involving any other specialists, the cost of setting up of this organisation is very less.

Disadvantages

1. Overburdens the head of department: As the plan of action and control of each department are the responsibility of the head of the department, it is possible that he may be overburdened with work. Most of his time and energy will be required for the supervision of the department, thereby resulting inefficiency. Besides, he will have little time and energy to devote for the improvement of the department.

2. Encourage autocracy: Excessive power and control of each department being vested in the departmental head, may make him autocratic in decision making without taking into the views to his assistants. This may lead to lack of cooperation from them which is essential for effective functioning of each department.

3. Lack of specialisation: Under this type of organisations the departmental manager is expected to look after all the functions such as planning, decision-making, executing and control. This organisation thus suffers from lack of specialised skill of experts. Modern office is so complex that it is extremely difficult for one person to carry on all activities by himself.

4. Lack of scope for the development of the skill and efficiency of the subordinates: The dictatorial rule of the departmental heads may not permit the subordinates to express their opinions in respect of the methods of improvement in work and in turn will curb development of skill, intelligence and efficiency.

5. Difficulty in securing capable executives: The retirement, resignation or death of capable executives may cripple the entire organisation. Such men may not be available for the organisation even in the long run.

6. Difficulty to run large organisation: This type of organisation is not successful where there are complexities in the nature of manufacture and where the industrial unit is large. It may be difficult to obtain competent executives for the several departments of a large organisation, resulting in lack of quality work.

7. Lack of cooperation and coordination among departmental heads: Under this type of organisation, each departmental head concentrates on his own departmental activity without bothering about the remaining departments. The absence of cooperation among departmental heads results in overall inefficiency in the office.

II Line and staff organisation.

This type of organisation consists of the addition to staff specialists to the simple line organisation previously discussed.

Harrington Emerson was the first to introduce this type of organisation. The term *staff* refers to specialists who enable the line officers to work most effectively. They are the supporters providing service and advice to the line officers.

The individuals who constitute *staff* here are experts having no line authority but whose function is largely advisory. Their authority arises from their superior knowledge of a particular function of the enterprise. Although they do not have the power to command the line officer, their advice is generally adhered to because of their status in the organisation. The line officers maintain discipline and stability and the staff officers provide expert information to the line officers. The duties of staff officers are as follows:

(*a*) Conduct research in the areas of technical, operational or managerial problems.

(*b*) Determination and recommendation of the various standards of performance.

(*c*) Keeping of records and statistics on the above activities as a measuring rod of performance.
(*d*) Advice and aid in carrying out plans and programmes.

Types of staff officers

The staff officers are of four types. They are:

1. Personal staff: The personal staff exists primarily at the upper levels of an organisation. The personal staff provides a valuable service by handling much of the administrative burden of his superior by projecting his superior's ideas and wishes to others in the organisation.

2. General staff: While the personal staff is intended to aid his superior in a personal way, the general staff is more concerned with preparing plans. In large business, divisions and departments are often so extensive that it becomes difficult for the departmental heads to concentrate their attention in achieving total organisation goal. The general staff is a medium through which diversified work of large segments of the organisation may be coordinated in the planning process.

3. Specialised Staff: The specialised staff serves in an advisory capacity for line activities based on their specialised knowledge. In helping the planning function, the specialised staff may gather facts, study alternatives and develop plans and programmes for the line officers. In helping control function, they may advise on work standards, gather information on performance and bring to the notice of the management, the deviations between the standards and the actuals.

4. Operating Service Staff: Operating service staff and specialised staff have the common feature of serving the organisation as a whole. The operating service staff facilitates the operation of organisation by directly involving in it.

Features of line and staff organisation

The following are the important features of this type of organisation:

(*a*) In this organisation, we come across two types of officers, *viz.*, line officers and staff officers. The line officers have the authority in getting the work executed whereas the staff officers are the experts who can offer only advice to the line officers.
(*b*) The authority of the staff arises because of their specialisation in particular branch of knowledge.
(*c*) The staff tender advice to the line who are expected to adopt it in practical affairs, although the staff do not have the power to command the line.

The following figure illustrates the line and staff organisation:

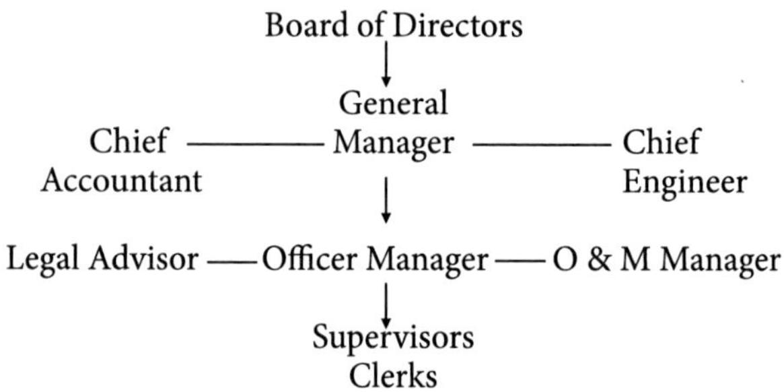

Figure 3.4: Line and staff organisation

From the figure, we can see that at the level of General Manager, two staff officers, *viz.*, Chief Accountant and Chief Engineer advice him. At the level of office manager, we see Legal Advisor and O & M Manager serving as staff officers. The relation of each one of these staff officers is shown only at one level. However, the advice from Legal Advisor may be given not only to office manager, but also to any other line officer. This indicates the cross relationship existing in the line and staff organisation, which provide for more intimate contact between the two, at all levels without breaking down lines of authority.

Advantage

(*a*) It is based upon specialisation within the organisation.

(*b*) It brings expert knowledge which helps the line officers to solve many managerial problems and thus helps in maintaining overall efficiency and success of the entire organisation.

(*c*) The division of duties as the 'doing' functions of the line and the 'thinking' functions of the staff helps in allowing the line to concentrate on its work and achieving proficiency in it with the aid of the staff. Besides, it gives a good amount of flexibility to the organisation, so that it can easily adjust itself to changing circumstances through necessary changes effected in the staff.

(*d*) It makes possible, the principle of undivided responsibility and authority, and at the same time permits staff specialisation.

(e) It provides more opportunity for advancement for the worker, in that a greater variety of responsible jobs are available.

(*f*) The economy and efficiency resulting from the advice of the staff will more than compensate the costs involved in the appointment of the staff.

Disadvantages

(a) There will be lot of confusion as to the functions and positions of the line officers and staff officers in this type of organisation. So this requires a clear indication of duties and responsibilities of line and staff officers by charts and manuals.

(*b*) Since the staff officers lack authority to execute it they may not have the sense of responsibility in tendering the advice.

(c) As the expert information and advice given by staff officers reach workers through the line officer, there is a possibility of misunderstanding and misinterpretation of the advice by the subordinates.

(*d*) Often conflict between the line and staff might arise owing to the inability to appreciate each others' views. Conflicts may also be due to (*i*) the transfer of certain duties from the line executives to the staff resulting in ill-will between the two. (*ii*) resentment on the part of the line officers because they have to take the advice of the staff which may appear to have an over riding authority over the former, (*iii*) the staff may be given undue importance by the management with the result the line officer may feel that they are ignored.(*iv*) the staff may be anxious to get their advice implemented without taking into the practical difficulties involved in it. (*v*) line officers may sometimes resent the activities of staff officers, feeling that the prestige and influence of line officers suffer from the presence of the staff officers.

III Functional Organisation

This form of organisation was devised by F.W. Taylor in 1911 with a view to overcome the limitation of the line type *viz.*, getting sufficient number of trained and capable supervisors to direct production. According to Taylor "functional foremanship consists in so dividing the work of management that each man from the assistant superintendent upto workers shall have as few functions as possible to perform." This system is based on the principle of specialisation, so that men with special abilities are employed to take up specific function. In consequence, workmen at the lowest level will come into contact with the different specialists who are called the functional foremen. Taylor discovered that the typical foreman of his day has loaded with much clerical duty as well as operating responsibility. He found it necessary to remove the planning function from the shop (*i.e.*, production department) where they were performing at low efficiency and hampered production. So Taylor proposed the employment of eight different functional foremen, four of whom would be located in the planning department. They are: (1) Route clerk (2) Instruction card clerk (3) Time and cost clerk (4) Shop disciplinarian. Those dealing with the shop are: (a) Gang boss (b) Speed boss (c) Repair boss and (d) Inspector. When this type of organisation is applied to office it appears as follows:

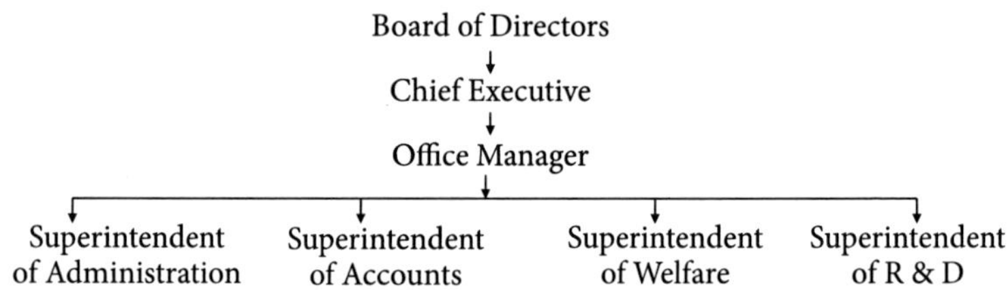

With the line authority the office Manager has not only the right to issue orders but also to take disciplinary action against erring individual over whom line authority exists. Functional authority gives the office manager only the right to issue orders and to make suggestions but not to take disciplinary action against individuals over whom only functional authority exists.

Advantages

1. Specialisation is encouraged: It ensures a greater division of labour and enables the office to take advantage of functional experts' service.

2. Increased efficiency: It makes for higher degree of efficiency as the workers get instructions from experts.

3. Flexibility: It is a very flexible pattern of organisation. Any change in organisation can be made without disturbing the whole organisation.

4. Less burden to the Executives: This aims at increased efficiency on the part of the executives as they are required to discharge a limited number of duties which enables them to concentrate, unlike as in the line organisation where an executive is a jack of all trades and master of none.

Disadvantages

1. Conflict Authority: The authority relationship violates the principles of *Unity of command*. It creates several bosses (Superintendents) instead of one line boss. It creates conflict in the mind of the workers to whom they should obey and whom they should ignore.

2. Discipline is slacked: Due to decentralisation of control and division of loyalty of subordinates the discipline is not maintained.

3. Lack of coordination: The use of several experts in organisation creates the problem of coordination.

4. Lack of fixed responsibility: The inability to locate and fix responsibility may seriously affect the discipline and morale of the workers through actual contradiction of orders.

5. Impracticable and expensive: This pattern of organisation is quite impracticable and also expensive. So small organisation cannot adopt it.

IV Committee organisation

A committee is a form of organisation which supplements the line officers in pooling the ideas of several people on various problems involving different functions in order to bring better plans and policies for operation. The committee only serves in an advisory capacity to the line officers, and the final decision, to be taken rests with the line officers. A committee may be defined as a group of people who collectively make decisions or present view points and whose conduct is governed by a set of rules. The effectiveness of a committee can be increased by following certain basic principles. These principles are as follows:

(*a*) Members of the committee should be selected from those persons possessing an open mind and who are willing to consider all the facts.

(*b*) Members of the committee should possess a wide range of knowledge concerning the operation of the business.

(*c*) The number of members should be generally small. The effectiveness of committees depends on a high degree of interaction among the members.

(*d*) All agenda should be prepared and distributed in sufficient time for study prior to a meeting.

(*e*) Committee meeting should follow the agenda and adhere to a time schedule.

Functions of committees

(*a*) To supply important information to the members or through them to the department concerned.

(*b*) To receive and act on reports from committee members or departments which have been asked for data or information.

(*c*) Assemble facts from many sources and put them together into a combined plan.

(*d*) Test the fitness of the results of operation, arrive at conclusion and formulate report or suggestion.

(*e*) Make intelligent and expert studies of important factors, activities or problems.

(*f*) Develop and recommend procedures of operation.
(*g*) Coordinate or set up time relationship between the operations of different departments.
(*h*) Correlate together the activities of different departments.
(*i*) Formulate and set up standard of various fields.

Advantages of Committees

1. Integrated group knowledge and judgement: One of the uses of this form of organisation is the advantage of group dynamics and pooled knowledge and judgement over individual judgement.

2. Representation of different interest groups: Committees are frequently used to give representation to important interest groups, such as labour unions, Board of Directors and shareholders. At the middle level and the lower level also different interest groups can be represented in the committee, not only to derive benefit of group knowledge and judgement but also to give representation to all such interested groups.

3. Coordination of plans and policies: When many view points are to be unified and when the opinions of individuals differ, committee meets these requirements by bringing together all concerned. The common deliberations which take place in the meeting solve many intricate problems because of the coordination of the efforts of the committee members concerned.

4. Executive team work and personal interaction: Committee organisation results in co-operative attitude and personal association in the development of team work. Instead of individual competition, the committee encourages group accomplishment. Formation of committees brings about integration between all levels of management and thus secures conformity to common goals through sanction of the group.

5. Wider participation and modification: A committee provides an opportunity for a wider participation of subordinates in the decision making process. The mere participation of subordinates give them a sense of belonging and a sense of satisfaction. The resistance to implement a programme is also eliminated by individual participation. Instead the subordinates feel more enthusiastic in executing it.

6. Improved communication: Committees offer a very useful instrument for transmitting and acquiring information face to face. Oral communication is generally a more effective form of communication than written reports and memoranda. Members of the committee learn about mutual problems simultaneously. Opportunity is also provided for on-the-spot clarification of any doubt.

7. Training ground for executives: Committee makes positive contribution to the executive training and development. Subordinates get an opportunity to have an insight into the problem facing others executives and the organisation in general. Senior executives also get a chance to observe subordinates in action and teach them where ever necessary.

Disadvantages

1. High cost of committees: Formation of committees is costly in terms of money and time. The company has to spend money for committee members whenever they attend a committee meeting. It also involves considerable amount of time to collect information and to prepare reports.

2. Delay in decision making: The decisions to be taken by the committee always invariably involves too much of time. This is because, first of all the committee itself is to be constituted. Secondly, the prior notice of the committee meeting is to be served. Thirdly, the deliberation and discussions of all the members have to be pooled and a common consensus to be arrived. Thus, by the time the decision is taken the favourable situation needing a decision might turn out to be adverse.

3. Compromise and indecision: Often conflicts among the committee members lead to a situation of a compromise to be reached instead of taking a best decision. In some cases where a compromise is not arrived at, it leads to even indecision.

4. Minority domination: Often a committee is dominated by a small group of influential members who make up the entire show in the committee. For example, one or two influential members of the committee such as a strong chairman or a high ranking line officer may dominate committee meetings and brow beat it into accepting a decision.

5. Divided responsibility: The committee organisation owes a joint responsibility to the executive of the organisation. Under this type of organisation a single individual cannot be held responsible for taking a wrong decision as he puts the blame on other committee members.

Formal and informal organisation

Organisation can be divided into two parts *viz.*, (1) Formal and (2) Informal.

1. Formal organisation: Formal Organisation is the planned system of goal oriented tasks and authority relationships consciously coordinated in a rational manner. Chester I Barnard referred to organisation as formal, when the activities of two or more persons are consciously coordinated towards a given objective. He stated that the formal organisation comes into being, when persons are (*a*) Willing to communicate with one another and (*b*) Willing to act and share a common purpose. The formal organisation establishes the following types of relationship:

(*a*) *Direct relationship*: This relationship exists between a superior and subordinate at any level in the organisation. This relationship is also known as line relationship. For example, office manager is responsible to General Manager relating to administration of office and Office Superintendent is responsible to Office Manager for various sections of an office.

(b) *Functional relationships*: This relations exists between a specialist and a line executive as for example between a welfare officer and works manager.

(*c*) *Lateral relationships*: This relationship exists between the executives and supervisors operating at the same level *i.e.*, neither is superior, nor the subordinate of the other. Such relationship exists between sales manager, market research officer, advertising manager wherein they must cooperate and coordinate their efforts along the lines indicated by sales manager to whom they are all equally and directly responsible.

2. Informal organisation: Informal Organisation refers to the unstructured network of social relationship and patterns of behaviour among the organisational participants which emerge out of formal activities, personal sentiments and group interaction. To avoid rigidity and restrictiveness of formal relationship, the following two types of informal relationship is recognised:

(*a*) *Adhoc relationship*: To avoid monotony of line of command between departments, this type of relation exists not only on similar level but also at different levels. It hormonises and relieves the line officers from unnecessary contact by shortening communication line.

(*b*) *Line bypass relationship*: Under this type of relationship the contact is established directly bypassing the scalar chain completely. This relation is more useful where a superior wants to evaluate the performance of a lower level subordinate as for example, a general manager, willing to assess the performance of a clerk in the office.

Centralisation and specialisation

Centralisation means the emphasis on control from the centre *i.e.*, head office, over various departments of an office. It implies, issue of detailed instructions from head office as to what work should be done, how it should be done and when. The head office expects regular reports on the progress of work so planned and assigned by it. The various office services that can be centralised are (*a*) Incoming and outgoing mail (*b*) Methods of communication(*c*) Stationery and office supplies (*d*) Office canteen (*e*) Clerical employment and training (*f*) Attendance records and (*g*) First aid.

Advantages of centralisation

1. It means better administrative control.
2. It facilities in handling peak load more easily.
3. Supervision become more effective.
4. It enables better use of machines.
5. It utilises the advice of specialists and experts.
6. It has the advantage of greater flexibility in the use of staff.

Disadvantages of centralisation

1. Too much of rigid control may cause frustration among staff.
2. It involves additional paper work and stationery.
3. It results in delayed work operations.

Specialisation

One of the important factors that is to be considered in organising an office is 'specialisation'. It tends to develop specialists and experts in a particular field of work. For example, when a person is incharge of outgoing mail, he will become expert in affixing the correct stamps even without referring to rates of charge. Similarly, if a typist is given only typing work he can type more number of letters in less time.

Advantages of specialisation

1. It increases the efficiency of workers.
2. It increases the speed of work.
3. It reduces the mistakes while performing work.
4. It maintains uniformity in carrying on the work.
5. It fixes up the responsibility on each and every worker.

Disadvantages of specialisation

1. It builds lop sided knowledge, as workers confine only to a particular type of work and not other work.
2. It results in monotony and boredom among employees.
3. If an employee is absent for any reason, that work will come to a standstill as others are not able to do such job.
4. It fails to adjust the increased work load and thereby makes work schedule very difficult.

Office manual

An office manual is a comprehensive book which offers guidance to the office staff. Whenever a new employee is recruited to the office he would like to know the policy, philosophy, the rules and regulations and procedure of work in that office. In the absence of an office manual, very often the subordinates approach the superiors for getting instructions and advice thereby interrupting the work of superiors which results in wastage of superior's time. Office manual is thus an authoritative book which furnishes all information about the organisation to facilitate the employees to perform the work with full understanding of the business in which they serve.

Contents of office manual

The contents of office manual depend upon the nature of organisation and the volume of work. Generally its contents are as follows:

1. **Organisation structure:** Organisation structure is prepared by means of an organisation chart showing clearly the superior-subordinate relationship. This enables the subordinate to get instructions from and to be accountable to a definite superior.

2. **List of companies' officers or departments:** A complete list of all the officers and departments by name or number together with an outline of their activities are included in the manual. This enables to establish contacts with other departments when the need arises.

3. **Telephone numbers:** The internal as well as extension numbers of the telephones are included in the manual. This facilitates quick communication with internal and external parties with whom the company deals with.

4. **Addresses of Branch offices:** The full address of various branch offices and showrooms together with the telephone numbers are included in the manual.

5. **Office rules:** A detailed set of standard rules and regulations such as office hours, salary, leave and holidays admissible, duties and responsibilities constitute important part of office manual.

6. **Standard procedure:** This is felt in large sized companies where detailed procedures are usually laid down in various sections of the manual. Such sections may include accounting, costing, stock, verification, budgetary control and so on.

7. **Amenities provided:** The various amenities such as staff canteen, sports, recreation and such other facilities are spelt out in the manual.

8. Important decisions: Any new decisions incorporated or revised rules and regulations are to be incorporated at the earliest in the manual. It is important that the manual should be kept up to date and any obsolete sheet is to be removed from all copies of the manual as soon as possible if they have become outdated.

9. Specimen forms: If different forms are used by the company, a specimen of each form used is to be included in an appendix to the manual. Each form must be clearly identified by same number or coding.

10. Signatures: A separate column may be provided in the manual for the signature of the staff to serve as an evidence of having read the manual.

Merits of office manuals

1. Standardisation of methods: It establishes standard methods and procedures to be followed by all the staff of the company.

2. Clear definition of rules and regulations: When rules and regulations laid down in the office manual are clear, it avoids conflicts within the members of the staff.

3. Helps new entrants: It enables new members of the staff to learn the office routine within the shortest possible time.

4. Transfer of staff is facilitated: With the office manual it is possible for the staff of one department when transferred to other departments to adapt more quickly to the new environment and change of work.

5. Improvement in the departmental cooperation: As office manual indicates the source of origin of work, and where it proceeds to, it helps persons in one department to extend cooperation to those in other departments.

6. Assistance for management: It helps managers and supervisors to make decision more promptly by referring to the manual.

7. Easy identification of forms: If the manual includes specimen forms with their respective numbers, even new members of the staff are able to identify the forms used for various purposes.

8. Simplification of procedure: A constant review of the manual helps in improving it by including simple and better methods and procedures.

Demerits of office manuals

Often criticisms are levelled against office manual owing to misuse and neglecting it. These demerits are as follows:

1. Liable to misinterpretation: Very often the description of procedure is misinterpreted when more people are involved. One person interprets in one way, whereas other person will interpret in a different way. So the procedure will be carried out in a slightly different way by each member of the staff.

2. Lacks Precision: Procedure is sometimes described too vaguely which becomes difficult for a few comer to understand clearly. However, this is the result of faulty preparation of the manual, and not the fault of the manual.

3. Requires frequent amendment: Depending upon the changing business environment, the manual is to be frequently amended which is burdensome.

QUESTIONS

Simple Questions

1. Define organisation.
2. Mention the steps involved in organisation process.
3. What do you mean by organisation structure?
4. Mention four techniques involved in organisation of an office.
5. What is 'line' type of organisation?
6. What do you mean by line and staff organisation?
7. What do you mean by functional organisation?
8. Define a committee.
9. What is formal organisation?
10. What is informal organisation?
11. What is office manual.
12. What do you mean by centralisation?
13. What is an organisation chart?
14. What do you mean by specialisation?

Short Answer Questions

1. Explain the importance of organisation.
2. Explain briefly the organisation structure of an office.
3. Briefly explain the various principles of organisation.
4. Briefly explain formal and informal organisational relationship.
5. What is centralisation of office service? State its merits and demerits.
6. What is specialisation? State its merits and demerits.

Essay Type Questions

1. Discuss the steps involved in organising an office.

2. Explain the various techniques involved in organising an office.
3. Explain the advantages and disadvantages of line type of organisation.
4. Explain the advantages and disadvantages of line and staff type of organisation.
5. Explain the advantages and disadvantages of functional organisation.
6. Explain the advantages and disadvantages of committee organisation.
7. What is office manual? Explain its contents? State the merits and demerits of office manual.

4

Delegation of Authority and Departmentation

INTRODUCTION

In Large sized business enterprises, the duties and responsibilities of an executive will be more. In such a situation it may not be possible for him to discharge all his tasks efficiently. He finds it difficult even to supervise his subordinates. So he finds it convenient to get the routine work done through others by sharing authority with them. For example, all work relating to office administration is delegated by the managing director to the office manager. It the size of an office is relatively large, the office manager assigns a part of work to office superintendent who in turn may transfer some of the work to office supervisors. This act of entrusting a portion of authority by a superior to his subordinates is known as delegation. It is a process whereby an individual transfers to other individual, the duty of carrying out some particular action and at the same time taking some particular decision. In this process the superior holds the subordinates accountable for him. While the responsibility of doing the job lies in the hands of subordinates, the responsibility to see that the job is done by the subordinates lies in the hands of superior.

Delegation of authority facilities quick decisions at all levels of management. It reduces the burden of executives as they can delegate routine activities to their subordinates and concentrate only on important functions such as policy formulation and planning and control. Delegation also improves the efficiency of an organisation through the principle of specialisation. It serves as a training ground for the subordinates who can learn the art of decision making. It facilitates administrative convenience as it relieves the executives from the botheration of performing all activities by themselves. In the words of Louis A. Allen "delegation is the dynamics of management. How well one delegates determines how well one manages."

Meaning and definition of delegation

Delegation means the permission granted by a superior to his subordinates to do something. To delegate means to entrust authority by the chief to his deputy in order to enable him to accomplish the job assigned to him. Delegation refers to a process adopted by a manager in dividing the work among his subordinates which enables him to concentrate on the major activities and get the auxiliary jobs done by the subordinates. Delegation of authority assumes the form of direction issued to others to do a particular duty which the person so delegating would have performed. In this process the superior must make sure that the subordinate has sufficient authority and he is informed as to how to utilise such authority. It can be briefly described as a process whereby a manager (*a*) assigns duties to his subordinates (*b*) grants the authority to them to the extent necessary and (*c*) creates a sense of obligation on the part of subordinates for the satisfactory performance of the work. Therefore, delegation means release of lower grade job by a manager to his subordinates so that he has sufficient time to concentrate on higher grade job. Delegation, however, does not mean shrinking responsibility by a superior.

In the words of Robert C. Appleby "Delegation is the process whereby an individual transfer to some other individual the duty of carrying out some particular action and at the same time taking some particular decision."

L. Hall defines delegation as "Delegation is the transference to others of the responsibility for the performance of a specific task and or for the making of decisions in a general or specific area of management activity."

According to Louis A. Allen "Delegation is the dynamics of management, it is the process a manager follows in dividing the work assigned to him so that he performs that part which only he, because of his unique organisational placement can perform effectively and so that he can get others to help him with what remains."

There are three reasons for delegating the authority by the managers. They are (*a*) lack of time on the part of superiors (*b*) changes and complexities in the various Acts enacted by the Government of a country thereby requiring the services of specialists and (*c*) providing a basis for training the managers required in the near future. However, it is to be understood that a superior will not delegate all his authority. If he does so it amounts to passing the whole of his position to his subordinates. While delegating the authority, the superior takes a calculated risk on the abilities of his subordinate. This problem can be overcome by exercising supervision over his subordinates. Delegation of authority is an art by itself and for its success the following points are worth noting:

(1) The superior must make sure that his subordinate has understood what is involved in the delegation process and accept it wholeheartedly.
(2) The superior must outline the task to be performed, fix up control limits and allow the subordinate to do the task by himself on his own initiative.
(3) The superior must supervise the activities of the subordinate frequently and at the same time take into account the ideas contributed by the subordinate.
(4) The superior must trust the subordinates and authority must flow parallel to duty delegated.

The degree of delegation depends upon the following factors:

(*a*) *Policy and philosophy of the management*: If the management decides to decentralise its activities, the degree of delegation will be high. On the other hand, if the management wants to centralise its activities, the degree of delegation will be low.

(*b*) *Size of the firm*: Large sized business will have a complex organisation structure. To facilitate quick decision making, decentralisation can be preferred which means greater delegation of duties and responsibilities. Reverse is the case if the size of the business is small.

(*c*) *Availability of capable managers*: If competent managers available are less, the degree of delegation is high. Where more number of efficient managers are available, the decision making process is centralised and so the degree of delegation is low.

(*d*) *Need for uniform policy*: If uniformity is to be maintained, naturally the degree of delegation is high and *vice versa*.

(*e*) *Cost of decision*: If the problem which is to be decided involves incurring of heavy investment it will be taken up by top level management. For example, a decision to purchase computers involves heavy expenses which is decided by the top management. In such situations, the degree of delegation is less. On the other hand, the problems which involve less amount of expenses can be decided by lower level management. For example, purchase of stationery in the office may be delegated to office superintendent. This implies a high degree of delegation.

(*f*) *Availability of control techniques*: If good control techniques are available in a business, the management can delegate more duties and responsibilities and consequently the degree of delegation will be high. In the absence of availability of control techniques, the management will not be keen to delegate the authority and hence degree of delegation will be low.

Elements of delegation

The process of delegation involves three important elements. They are:

(1) Delegation of duties and responsibilities (2) Delegation of Authority and (3) Accountability. These elements of delegation are explained below:

1. Delegation of duties and responsibilities: The first step in the process of delegation is the assignment or delegation of duties and responsibilities to the subordinates by the superior. Assignment of duty refers to the nature and type of work to be performed by the subordinate as is allotted by the superior. This may relate to discharging certain functions, taking certain decisions, etc. Responsibility means description of role, a subordinate has to play in achieving the objectives of business. The fixation of duties in a way serves as a standard or target which helps to measure the extent of performance of subordinates. Duties in terms of functions and responsibilities in terms of results to be achieved, constitute the basis of delegating process.

2. Authority: Authority refers to the powers and rights conferred on the subordinates by the superior. Authority is necessary to enable the subordinate to carry out the task assigned to him. Whenever any responsibility is fixed, it must be accompanied by the right to act, power to control and to take other administrative steps to complete the task. In office management, authority implies the right and power to purchase stationary, meeting expenses on printing, postage and telegram and other miscellaneous expenses. The authority to be exercised can be classified into three kind, *viz.*, (*i*) Authority of knowledge (*ii*) Authority of position and (*iii*) Legal authority.

(*i*) *Authority of knowledge*: Authority of knowledge refers to the power to get the work done by using specialised knowledge. The authority of knowledge is exercised by virtue of one's own professional and academic knowledge. This may take the form of advice, guidance and suggestions to be offered while commanding the orders. The best example for this type of authority is the management consultants who offer consultancy service by virtue of their special knowledge.

(*ii*) *Authority of position*: In some case, the superiors and subordinates expect some authority on account of their position or status in the company. For example, an office manager expects a better equipped office building because of the status and prestige which he enjoys.

(*iii*) *Legal authority*: This type of authority is derived by the superior owing to the operation of law of the country. For example Companies Act of 1956 vests some authority on the directors of the company.

In terms of the extent of authority to be delegated, a manager will not delegate his entire authority. He will retain the important matters for himself and delegate such matters which his subordinates can perform as good as himself or even better. This implies that the supervisor will not overburden himself by performing all the work. By delegating the authority, it is possible to accomplish much more work by utilising the skill and abilities of superiors.

3. Accountability: Accountability refers to the obligation which is to be fulfilled by a subordinate for having delegated the task. In other words, the subordinate is answerable for completing the assigned task. It is the process of reporting on the performance of duties delegated. In the words of Louis A. Allen "It is the obligation to carry out responsibility and exercise authority in terms of performance standards established."

Importance of delegation

The importance of delegation may be summarised under the following points:

1. **It is a fundamental to the organisation:** The entire process of organisation is based on delegation and without it an organisation structure is not complete.

2. **It lessens the burden of executives:** It relieves the executives by delegating the routine work to subordinates and thereby enables them to concentrate on important matters.

3. **Distribution of work load:** The work is more evenly and fairly distributed among the staff in such a way that no one is called upon to do more work which is beyond his reach. This eliminates the bottlenecks and helps in doing the work more quickly and efficiently.

4. **Development of Managerial ability:** With the delegation of authority, a sense of responsibility is created among the subordinates.

This encourages the subordinates to take part in management, thus, it develops the managerial ability in them.

5. Subordinates are trained to higher-level work: Delegation of authority, in a way trains the subordinates so as to enable them to attain status involving high responsibility.

Process of delegation

The process of delegation can be outlined as under:

1. To list out all the activities that are to be performed in an organisation.
2. The list of activities must be rearranged in descending order of importance.
3. It is necessary to estimate the time involved for performing every activity on an approximate basis.
4. To decide what part of the activities can be performed within available time and staff.
5. Assess the capabilities of the staff by taking into consideration further development of such staff.
6. To match the activity with the capabilities of staff and accordingly allocate the task in which a staff is an expert.
7. Inspect the performance of the subordinates frequently.
8. In case of difficulty, it is desirable to rearrange the activities and reallocate the work among the staff.

Advantages of delegation

The following are the important advantages of delegations:

1. It serves as a basis for effective functioning: By establishing relationship among various personnel, it helps in coordinating their efforts which in turn helps in accomplishing the objectives of an organisation.

2. Reduction of work load to superiors: By delegating the routine jobs to subordinates, it relieves the superiors to reduce their work load and thereby concentrate on important issues of management.

3. Specialised services: Delegation of authority provides the benefits of specialisation or division of labour to an organisation by means of splitting the total work and distributing among all the staff depending on their abilities and skills.

4. Training ground for staff: Junior staff will gain by the process of delegation as it serves as a training ground for them. This improves job satisfaction and morale of the employees.

5. Helps in expansion of business: With the availability of trained and competent staff, it permits the expansion and diversification of existing business unit.

Limitations of delegation

Though delegation is the very basis of organisation, it must be applied within the following limits for its success:

1. Nature of work: The delegation of authority does not apply to highly specialised work and duties of a confidential nature.

2. Permission to delegate: In some cases a superior cannot delegate his authority unless permission to do so is obtained from the person to whom he himself is responsible.

3. Span of control: When a superior desires to delegate his authority to a number more than under his control (which according to U.A. Graicunas if five or at the most six) it become more difficult.

4. Ability of the subordinates: The degree of delegation depends upon the abilities of subordinates which are determined by physical and mental capacity to do the work, extent of training undergone and availability of time.

5. Facility for inspection: The amount of the opportunity for inspection serve as a limiting factor to delegation. Whenever a superior delegates authority, he must check and supervise whether the subordinate is proceeding on the right line of instructions issued. Hence, it has been rightly said that "the corollary of delegation is inspections."

6. Training*:* The nature and extent of training facilities available often serves as a determining factor in the delegation process. Very often training is a necessary prerequisite for the success of effective delegation.

7. Proper communication: For an effective delegation, it is very essential that a proper communication process exists through which proper announcement can be made (to the fact that a certain person has been delegated) to all personnel affected.

8. Size and form of organisation: The extent of delegation is determined by the size of the organisation. Again the form of organisation also affects the degree of delegation. For example, in line type of organisation the extent of delegation is more when compared to line type and staff.

Principles of delegation

For the effective delegation of authority, it is necessary to observe certain fundamental principles which serve as guidelines to management. Unless these principles are consciously and carefully recognised, there is a possibility of managerial process being seriously impeded. These principles are as follows:

1. Delegation to be consistent with result expected: According to this principle, the authority must be delegated only to the extent necessary for accomplishment of results expected. As a prerequisite to this, it is necessary to determine first, the job, which a superior expects of a subordinate. Based on the job to be performed, the extent of delegation is determined. Thus, the possible danger of delegating too much or too little is overcome under this principle.

2. The principle of absoluteness of responsibility: According to this principles, the responsibility of a subordinate to his superior is absolute. A superior cannot escape the responsibility for the activities of his subordinate through the process of delegation. In other words, every superior will be responsible for the act of those under his command. At the same time, the subordinate is fully responsible to his superior for the performance of assigned task.

3. Principle of parity of authority and responsibility: According to this principle, the responsibility always accompanies the authority whenever a task is delegated. Therefore, logically it follows that the authority of a particular manager should correspond to his responsibility. For example, an office manager cannot be held responsible for production failure as he has not been given any authority for undertaking production process. Thus, it follows that both authority and responsibility relate to the same assignment and hence coextensive.

4. Principle of unity of command: According to this principle, each subordinate should report to only one superior. This is so because if a subordinate is made answerable to more than one superior it only leads to conflict in both authority and responsibility. From the point of view of superior also any divided responsibility will undermine his position.

5. Clarity of delegation: Delegation of authority must be very clear in terms of its contents, functional relations, scope and assignment. This implies that the delegate must know the extent of authority delegated, what is expected of him and how his obligation fits into the general plan. Any ambiguity in delegation leads to poor performance and often less impact on delegation. In addition to clarity of idea, it is also necessary to clarify the position of every person in the organisation structure so that in time of need, a subordinate can take assistance from other superiors.

Problems of delegation

The reluctance to delegate is not a new problem. Infact, it is perhaps as old as the history of human civilization. Studies in India and a number of other countries suggest that executives are generally reluctant to delegate because of the following reasons:

1. Desire to Dominate and control: Executives who are in their positions because of ownership, have a psychological desire for power and control over people. They have passion for power and enjoy constant interaction with subordinates.

2. Lack of faith in the ability of subordinates: This appears to be a primary reason as to why many executives find it difficult to delegate, as they feels that their subordinates are not capable of doing the jobs which they should delegate. The real reasons, however, could be that they subconsciously believe that no body else can do the job as best as they can.

3. Fear of subordinates: An executive may be afraid that one of his subordinates, given the chance, may outshine him and attract more attention and recognition than himself. By delegating too much, be may work himself out of his job.

4. Lack of ability to direct on the part of the executive: An executive may find it difficult to identify and communicate essential features of his long range plans.

5. Lack of control: Absence of selective and sensitive controls that give a warning of possible difficulties may often be lacking for proper delegation.

6. Aversion to take risk: Sometimes executives handicapped by a temperamental aversion to take a chance feel that something may go wrong in spite of giving clear instructions and availability of selective control techniques.

While the above reasons make executives not to delegate authority, the under mentioned reasons go to constitute reasons for non-acceptance of delegation:

(*a*) Fear of criticism.

(*b*) Lack of self-confidence on the part of subordinates.

(*c*) Negative motivation, *i.e.*, threat of punishment.

(*d*) When the subordinate believes that he lacks needed information and resources to do a good job he hesitates to accept any new assignment.

(*e*) The subordinate may already have more work to do.

Steps to make delegation effective

The consideration of the following steps will make delegation more effective:

1. Clear definition of plans and policies: In order to facilitate the subordinate to do the job assigned to him, he must be furnished with the guidelines and the plans that affect his area of decision making.

2. Assignment of definite job and authority: This refers to delegation of authority in the light of results expected. In order words, it simply means that granting of authority to enable accomplishment of plan.

3. Selection of right person for right job: The selection of right person to an organisation is the staffing function of management. But while delegating authority, care must be taken to see that the right job is delegated to the right person.

4. Communication: For effective delegation there must exist a free flow of information between the superior and subordinate. The information relates not only to decision making powers but to interpret properly, the authority delegated to him.

5 Proper control: For effective delegation, it must be accompanied by control techniques to make sure that authority is being utilised properly to accomplish goals.

6. By offering rewards: By offering monetary rewards and recognition of status in terms of position and promotion, delegation can be made more effective.

Centralisation and decentralisation of authority

Centralisation of authority: Centralisation of authority refers to the concentration of power of decision making in a few hands, *i.e.*, at the top level management. In other words, centralisation means concentration of authority in the hands of a few people. According to Louis. A. Allen "centralisation is the systematic and consistent reservation of authority at central points in the organisation." In the words of C. Appleby, "if authority is not delegated it is centralised" ... centralisation refers to the withholding of delegated authority. Sometimes centralisation is also used to denote departmental activities as for example, typing pool in the centralisation of office services. The existence of pure centralisation of authority is a rare phenomenon. This is so because it only adds to the burden of executives and destroys the initiative and enthusiasm of middle and lower level managerial staff. Therefore, the principle of decentralisation of authority is resorted to in many organisations.

Decentralisation of authority: Decentralisation of authority refers to dispersal of authority and power of decision making to lower levels of organisation. It denotes a situation where ultimate authority and ultimate responsibility for results is localised as far down the organisation as efficiency permits. According to Louis. A. Allen decentralisation of authority refers to the systematic effort to delegate to the lowest level all authorities except that which only be exercised at central points. Decentralisation is closely related to delegation of authority and is concerned with what should be transferred down together with the policies that are needed to guide the actions. The degree of decentralisation depends upon the following factors:

(*a*) The more the problems confront decision making, more is the scope of decentralisation.

(*b*) The more the number of functions involved in an organisation, more is the extent of decentralisation.

(*c*) The importance of decision making determines the extent of decentralisation. A more specific problem such as purchase of office equipment can be left to the choice of office manager to decide rather than the general manager to decide.

(*d*) The extent of control and evaluation of the performance also decides the degree of decentralisation. If the extent of checking is very less because of the efficiency of subordinates, the degree of decentralisation will be more.

The circumstances that bring decentralised of authority are as follows:

(*a*) When the size of business grows involving problems in directing, the authority may be decentralised to lower level management.

(*b*) Where the products or market segment demand decentralisation for providing an emphasis on a product line or market area.

(*c*) When more branches of an establishment are opened.

(*d*) When technological development necessitates delegation of authority and responsibility.

(*e*) When the management philosophy determines the decentralisation process.

(*f*) When the need for an uniformity in the policy is felt.

Advantages of centralisation of authority

The following are the important advantages of centralisation of authority:

1. Reduction in the burden of executives: In a large sized company, the top executives can concentrate on important and urgent matters by pushing down the authority of normal and routine matters to subordinates. Thus, the top executive relieves himself of the unnecessary burden by shifting the authority to his subordinates.

2. Increases initiative of subordinates: When the authority is dispersed over subordinates, it provides an opportunity for the subordinates to exhibit their talents and skills. This also create a sense of responsibility and foster a team spirit among the superiors and subordinates.

3. Leads to development of managerial personnel: When junior managers are provided with freedom to exercise the authority with their own judgement, they learn over a period of time the process of managing the organisation. This decentralisation of authority serves as a training ground for them to acquire leadership qualities. This serves as the foundation for the growth of future managers.

4. It facilitates better coordination: Under decentralised authority, coordination of efforts will become easy because of participation and better understanding between superior and subordinates.

5. Improves work performance: When a new line of product is added and when expansion and development programmes are resorted to, it may not be possible for the top level management to cope up with increased volume of work. By diversifying the authority among subordinates an executive can effectively carry out his own activities fully concentrating on important issues.

6. Promotes internal and external economies: The internal economies that are reaped by decentralised authority include speedier communications, better utilisation of lower and middle level management, improved training opportunities. All these internal economies will lead to the growth of an enterprise. External economies will be in the form of reduction in the cost of production per unit caused by factors outside the business.

7. Effective control: Control can be effectively exercised under decentralised authority as it is easy to set up standards at various levels of management. Measurement of actual performance with standards and taking corrective measures to eliminate defective performance also become easy under decentralisation authority.

Disadvantages

1. High operating expenses: Decentralisation of authority involves establishment of number of divisions and units. Consequently, the initial operating expenses are high. So, small scale units cannot afford to spend more amount if decentralisation principle is followed.

2. It leads to duplication of efforts: Sometimes decentralisation results in duplication of efforts and responsibilities which proves to be dangerous for efficient management. Often it is characterised by conflicts among employees. Hence, decentralised authority must be properly handled.

3. Impracticability: Decentralised authority is justified only when a large number of departments exist in the company. Where the organisation does not permit division into a number of departments, it cannot be practised.

4. Availability of competent personnel: Decentralisation of authority presupposes the availability of competent staff who can handle the problems carefully. In the absence of the availability of such staff, decentralisation of authority will be inoperative.

5. Where uniformity is desired: Decentralisation of authority will not be effective where uniformity in policies, ideas and decisions are to be taken. Under decentralised authority, each subordinate will deal the matter in his own way depending upon circumstances and need, and it may not be uniform in all cases.

Differences between decentralisation and delegation

The following differences exist between decentralisation and delegation:

(*a*) Delegation is a process while decentralisation is the end result of planned delegation.

(*b*) Delegation is between one superior and subordinate while decentralisation is company wise delegation.

(*c*) Delegation is a must for management and it creates an organisation while decentralisation is optional and appears when organisation grows.

Departmentation

The process of grouping various activities of an organisation into homogeneous group is known as departmentation. In modern business world, owing to increase in size of business, technological changes, changing laws and changing consumers' tastes and preferences, the structure of business has become more complex. It becomes somewhat difficult for the top level management to cope with all these problems. So, the various functions are divided according to their nature and placed under the charge of a competent person. Only then it is possible to carry out all the functions of an organisation successfully. Departmentation can be created on the basis of function, area, customer and so on. A department can again be sub-divided into various sections. For example, accounts department can be divided into number of sections such as book keeping department, costing department and internal audit department. Often, instead of setting up a department, a 'cell' may be set up for the sake of convenience. A 'cell' refers to a small group to which a specialised duty is assigned. For example, we have research cell and inspection cell in some of the big organisations. The following factors determine the number of departments in a business:

1. Nature of business: In a manufacturing business the number of departments will be more when compared to trading business and other non-profit organisations.

2. Size of business: A large sized business requires and can afford to have more number of departments than a small sized one.

3. Specialisation: If the degree of specialisation is sought more, the number of departments created are also more.

4. Availability of capable managers: The number of departments to be set up depends upon the availability of capable and efficient management. More number of departments are created if more efficient Managers are available and *vice versa*.

5. Need for identifying the responsibility: If responsibility is to be fixed for every persons in terms of achieving the performance, the number of departments will be more in number.

Advantages of departmentation

(*a*) The advantages of specialisation, *viz*., greater efficiency, economy of operation and saving in time can be derived.

(*b*) The effectiveness of each and every activity can be ascertained and those departments which are considered to be inefficient can be improved upon.

(*c*) It facilities full utilisation of human resources.

(*d*) It helps top level management not to bother about routine activities as they are all looked after by departmental managers. So they can concentrate wholly on the important issues of the organisation.

(*e*) It increases the initiative and enthusiasm of departmental managers.

(*f*) It facilities recruitment of staff based on the functions to be performed in various departments.

Disadvantages of departmentation

The disadvantages of departmentation arises when departmentation is not properly effected. They are:

(*a*) Difficulty in coordinating the activities especially when too many departments are created.

(*b*) It involves heavy expenses when too many departments are established.

(*c*) With large number of departments it becomes difficult to achieve the common objectives.

(*d*) The success of departmentation depends upon availability of efficient departmental managers.

Various departments of a modern commercial office

The following are some of the important departments that are found in a large sized office:

(1) Financial department
(2) Accounts department
(3) Filing or recording department
(4) Correspondence department
(5) Public relations department
(6) Stores department
(7) Legal department
(8) Staff recreation department
(9) O & M department
(10) Inspection department
(11) Administration department
(12) Secretary's department

1. Financial department: The financial department is headed by a competent authority known as chief cashier. He is responsible for receiving and paying cash on behalf of the company. The chief sources of revenue are sales, rent, interest, subscription, etc. Payments to be made relates to purchases of raw materials, salaries, wages repayments of loans, rent, interest, etc. Whenever any cash is received 'receipts' are issued and when cash is paid vouchers are maintained. Financial department will function in close coordination with accounts department. Where the size of the organisation is large there can be separate sections created in the financial department such as petty cash section, banking section to receive and issue cheques, and so on.

2. Accounts department: The accounts department is headed by chief accountant. The accounts department is concerned with the preparation of final accounts of the business. In accounts department various ledgers are maintained to record transactions of various nature. The accounts department is also concerned with conducting internal audit in large sized business. It undertakes to prepare various reports so as to enable the management to exercise control. The accounts department will work in close coordination with costing department and helps in reconciling the profit as shown by the financial books and costing books. The accounts department functions with the aid of certain equipment such as calculators, computers, billing machines, cheque writing machines, etc.

3. Filing department: The filing department is concerned with systematic and scientific maintenance and preservation of all important documents relating to the business. The person who is concerned with maintenance of records is known as records-in-charge. He is solely responsible for supplying necessary files for reference by various persons as and when required.

4. Correspondence department: This is the most important department of an office as it performs the primary function of office, *viz.*, communications. The correspondence department is concerned with handling the incoming and the outgoing mail. This department is equipped with staff such as stenographers, typists and correspondence clerk. To facilitate the function of correspondence certain equipments such as typewriter, dictophone, telephone, etc., are made use of.

5. Public relations office: The public relations office is in-charge of a competent person who is known as Public Relations Officer (PRO). His duty is to establish contacts with public and create a better image of the company in the minds of people. He attends to the complaints and grievances of the public and solve their problems by taking prompt action. Along with public relations officer a receptionist can also be appointed to serve as a guide to public and to handle internal-communication system.

6. Stores department: A stores department is concerned with storage of all type of materials required by the company. The persons who is incharge of store room in known as store keeper. He is responsible for classifying and codifying all the materials for easy identification. The store department will receive all the materials and store them until they are drawn by various departments.

7. Legal department: The legal department is incharge of a law officer. He deals with all legal matters pertaining to the company.

8. Staff recreation department: The staff recreation department is looked after by labour welfare officer. The welfare department looks after the welfare of employees by providing amenities such as food at subsidised rates, recreational facilities such as sports and games, film shows, and other forms of entertainments, library facilities, medical facilities and so on.

9. O & M department: O & M Department is concerned with conducting research studies in order to suggest improvements in procedure and method of performing office work. The main purpose of O & M department is to simplify the routine functions of office so as to maintain efficiency in the office.

10. Inspection department: A very big company will usually have number of branches and within each branch more number of departments. In such a case, a separate department is established known as inspection department. The inspectors will visit different branches and departments and inspect the mode of working by various departments. Having inspected various departments they prepare a report and submit it to the head office for exercising control over inefficient departments. The Head Office will suggest various remedial measures to improve upon the performances of relatively weaker departments.

11. Administration department: A large company will have a separate department which is divided into two separate divisions known as administration department and management department. The administration department comprises of Board of Directors of the company. Their main duty is to formulate the policies and objectives of the company. The second division is known as management department and is incharge of the General Manager or Managing Director. The General Manager is mainly concerned with implementing the policies of the company. He also coordinates the efforts of all departmental managers such as purchase manager, personnel manager, production manager and so on. Controlling the activities of all other departments also constitutes one of the important functions of General Manager.

12. Secretary's department: This department is headed by a person known as secretary. He does all confidential work relating to the company. His duties include the supervision of application and allotment of shares, preparation and issue of share certificates and share warrants, making calls on shares, forfeiting the shares for the non payment of calls, arranging transfer and transmission of shares, payment of Dividend and Interest to shareholders and debenture holders, arranging all type of company meeting, submitting copies of resolutions to Registrar of joint stock companies and maintaining all statutory and statistical books of company. The secretary also deals with other agencies "such as government; tax department, suppliers, bankers and so on.

Relationship of the office with other departments of the enterprise

A business organisation functions with number of departments such as purchasing, sales, finance, research and development, personnel and so on. The office as one of the departments will undertake to coordinate the functions of all these departments. The coordination is achieved by process of internal communications. Better coordination is achieved by means of the following:

(*a*) Proper organisation of an enterprise by considering the principles of organisation.

(*b*) Appointing competent secretary to perform all activities of the office.

(*c*) Constitution of a committee wherever necessary by a good representation from each and every department.

(*d*) Organisation of seminars, lectures, group discussion, etc., frequently so as to take approximate measure to solve problems.

(*e*) Maintenance of a good internal communication system.

(*f*) Providing training facilities and promotional opportunities for better participation of subordinates.

(*g*) Appraising of the activities of each department to ensure that the performance of every department confirms the planned programme.

(*h*) Prompts reporting of achievement by various department to undertake control measures.

QUESTIONS

Objective Type Questions

1. Define delegation.
2. Mention three reasons for delegating of authority.
3. Mention of elements of delegation.
4. Mention the four principles of delegation.
5. What do you mean by centralisation of authority?
6. What do you mean by decentralisation of authority?
7. Distinguish between centralisation and decentralisation of authority.
8. Distinguish between delegation and decentralisation.
9. What do you mean by departmentation?
10. Mention any eight departments of a modern commercial office.

Analytical Type Questions

1. Briefly explain the factors which determine the degree of delegation.
2. Explain the different elements of delegation.

3. Outline the importance of delegation.
4. Outline the process of delegation.
5. State the advantages and limitations of delegation of authority.
6. Briefly explain the principles of delegation.
7. State the problems faced in delegation of authority. How can they be overcome?

Essay Type Questions

1. Explain with merits and demerits of centralisation and decentralisation of authority.
2. State the merits and demerits of departmentation. Explain the various departments of a modern commercial office.

5

Office Systems and Routines

INTRODUCTION

The Term 'system' is derived from the concept 'systematic' which refers to an organised and orderly approach to solve any problem as against the haphazard approach. In the context of studying office management, a 'system' may be regarded as a planned approach to activities necessary to attain desired objectives. A business enterprise has a number of activities to perform such as sales, production, purchase, distribution and so on. In order to perform all these functions efficiently, they require a systematic approach. Office system, to a large extent, helps in simplifying the procedure involved in the performance of such activities. For example, a system of trading on credit basis with credit customers involves considering such steps as checking references, ascertaining the credit worthiness, interviewing the customer and finally deciding the extent of credit to be sanctioned. The purpose of credit sales is to make sure that the debts are promptly paid while increasing the volume of sales. Similarly, when purchasing activity is concerned, it involves selection of appropriate supplier, proper storage and control and prompt payment of bills to derive cash discount. The objective of purchases is to make purchases at the most economical price and to ensure prompt supply of materials.

Definition and characteristics of office system

Definition of system

Neuschel in his book *Streamlining business procedure* defines system as "a network of related procedures developed according to an integrated scheme performing a major activity of the business."

P.W. Betts in his book *Office Management* defines office system as a cluster of procedures closely relating to each other and each consisting of a number of operations which collectively provide adequate information in various suitable forms for staff to work efficiently and for managers to control and direct effectively. According to C.L. Littlefield and others, *system* is defined as a group of inter-related and interdependent parts operating in sequence according to a predetermined plan, in order to achieve a goal or series of goals.

The above definition has the following characteristics:

(*a*) Office system consists of various parts of segments which are inter-related, operating in a sequence but not in isolation.

(*b*) Office system is mainly concerned with achieving the objectives of an organisation.

(*c*) They set out a definite procedure for performing the activities.

Requisites of an ideal system

The following are the important requisites of a good system:

1. Effectiveness: Office system is considered effective when it accomplishes the purpose for which it is established.

2. Efficiency: An efficient system must achieve the object at a reduced cost to consider it efficient.

3. Dependability: An ideal system is one which produces consistent results and which does not fail in terms of operation.

4. Flexibility: A system, to be called ideal, must be capable of adapting itself to the changing environmental conditions and it should not disrupt the operations.

5. Simplicity: A good system should not be complex in terms of its design. Simplicity of system facilitates understanding on the part of users of system.

6. Acceptability: In order to constitute a good system it must be accepted by every-one, irrespective of how well it is designed and technically perfect.

Importance of office system

The importance of office system in the field of office management can be enumerated under the following points:

(*a*) A good system is conducive to smooth running of an office and as such helps in reducing delays and bottlenecks in work.

(*b*) As office systems are based on different methods of performing work, they ensure speed.

(*c*) Office system can be designed in such a way where it can serve as a basis for internal checking. This helps in preventing fraud and to exercise better control over the work.

(*d*) Very often a well designed office system reduces labour cost and overheads. By mechanising the various processes of work, it is possible to save large amount of expenses which otherwise would have been incurred.

(e) An office system involves the use of *form design* and *form control.* This in turn increases the efficiency of office work.

(*f*) A good office system ensures better coordination of all the departmental activities.

(*g*) Training can be offered to junior managers with the help of office system.

(*h*) An office system reduces to a large extent, the common mistakes and errors which are inevitable in an office.

(*i*) It facilitates induction of new *clerks* in office.

Principles of office systems

Office systems are based on certain principles which are as follows:

(*a*) They should be simple in order to relieve supervision.

(*b*) It is based on the principles of specialisation.

(*c*) Avoidance of unnecessary writing, movement or efforts.

(*d*) Avoidance of bottlenecks and instead seek the best flow of work.

(*e*) Avoidance of duplication of work, particularly with forms.

(*f*) There should be as few exceptions to the rule as possible.

(*g*) Avoidance of unnecessary checking.

(*h*) Systems should be flexible and adaptable to changed condition.

(i) Proper distribution of work among the staff.

(*j*) Continuous exercise of control over the performance of the work.

(*k*) Utilisation of office equipment to maximum use.

(*l*) Use of best sequence in performing the operations.

Techniques for establishing an office system

(*a*) To study and analyse in detail, the work being done using suitable charts.

(*b*) To determine which part of the work is essential, bearing in mind the purpose of the office.

(*c*) To eliminate unnecessary operations. The questions to be asked are: *Are they used? What for? How often?* and *by Whom?*

(*d*) To consider all alternative methods for remaining operations.

(*e*) To select the best method for each operation with regard to control, cost and staffing.

(*f*) To determine fair work standards for each operation for purposes of control and staffing.

(*g*) To calculate the personnel required and seek the right sequence of operations to give the smoothest flow of work.

(*h*) To design the office layout, with regard to flow of work.

(*i*) To train the personnel and install the procedure.

Steps involved in designing an office system

The following steps are involved in designing an office system:

1. Overall assessment: Under this step, it involves gathering of as much information as possible such as the background of the company, operating conditions, the financial situation and the philosophy of the concern. This familiarisation leads to a comprehensive picture and evaluation of the information requirements.

2. Activity Analysis: To ensure continuity of activities, it is necessary to study the entire set of functions and divide them into sequential groups. Thus, the various functions of a company can be divided into purchase, sales, accounting, finance and so on. To facilitate inter dependence of activities, they may be grouped together wherever necessary.

3. The system model: This stage is also known as prototype stage and includes establishing a suitable model by analysing all the functions.

4. The operational model: Under this stage, the protytype is developed into operational form. This stage includes sequence of processing, *viz*., input, output and feedback, the preparation of reports and means of control. Thus, a complete plan is assembled which is often called operational plan.

5. Documentation of the system: This stage involves preparation of a complete document which includes the description of the system and the operational plan as mentioned above. After obtaining the approval of everyone concerned, it is submitted to management.

6. Introducing the system: The final step is to implement the scheme and to ensure that the proposed control system actually satisfies the requirements.

Advantages and limitations of office system

The following advantages can be derived by an office systems:

1. Elimination of duplicate operations: By adopting identical procedure for performing similar type of work, uniformity in office routine can be maintained. Thus, the possible duplication of operations is eliminated in an office.

2. Avoidance of delays: The usual occurance of errors and delays can be overcome by following a definite system in office. Similarly, idle time could also be eliminated by adopting a proper system and smootheness in functioning of the office can be ensured.

3. Economy in operations: Owing to elimination of unnecessary operations and avoidance of duplication of efforts leads to economy in the operation of office.

4. Training ground for employees: A well designed system always serve as a training ground for the office staff and this in turn improves their efficiency.

5. Fixation of responsibility: When a proper system is followed, responsibility can be fixed at the time of assigning the work. A sense of responsibility is created when a proper method of work is to be followed by him.

6. Facilitates coordination: When a uniform system or routine is followed by every staff in the office, it facilitates coordination of efforts. This is so because performance of work by an individual depends upon the work done by another person.

7. Facilities control: It is possible to exercise better control under circumstances where a common system is followed. Comparison between actual performance with standard performance and feed back process becomes easy when a standard system is laid down to perform a given task.

8. Improves speed of performance: With a well established system and routine, the chances of confusion and need for consultation by subordinates with superiors can be minimised. This increases the speed of operation of work.

9. Use of form design and form control: When an approved system and routine is followed, it is always accompanied by the use of standard from control and form design. This eliminates inefficiency in performing office activities.

10. Reduces the burden of top management: A good system always helps top management to concentrate on important matters, thereby entrusting routine matters to the subordinates.

Limitations of office system

Office system is beset with the following limitations:

1. Difficulty in establishing system: It is very difficult to establish an approved system in practice. Devising a suitable system is based on many factors which may not always be favourable to the setting up of a system.

2. Difficult to adhere to system at all times: When a system is rigidly imposed, it may not result in attaining designed objectives within a specified time. Certain work always requires flexibility in terms of operation and when a system is rigidly imposed it may hamper procedure of performing such work.

3. System cannot be useful at all time: A system can work out well only under a certain set of circumstances. But in the present dynamic world, where everything is changing fast it may not be possible for strict adherance to the system.

4. Investment in system: Implementation of a standard system involves incurrance of additional expenditure. For example, if a standard system is to be followed in mechanising the accounts, it involves investments on computers. But it may bot be within the reach of small and medium sized concerns to invest heavy amount of such systems.

System integration

When the various systems in an office are interwoven so as to get one master system, it is known as system integration. When systems are not integrated, it works in a haphazard fashion, which produces ineffectiveness, duplicates the efforts and results in unnecessary paper work. The present trend in management of all organisation is to develop a master system plan which provides a basis for coordination, operating efficiency and total optimisation of the enterprise objectives. The systems integration can be brought about by adopting the following two steps.

1. The Master system plan: The development, of a master system plan involves consideration of the different levels of systems which are likely to be found in any enterprise. They are:

(*a*) *Sub system:* The various sub systems in an enterprise are purchase, production, personnel, finance, accounts and so on.

(*b*) *Procedures*: For carrying out every sub system, an appropriate procedure is followed. For example, purchase sub system is made up of a series of operations such as preparing requisitions, ordering and so on.

(*c*) *Methods*: Methods refer to means of performing individual operations. For example by using a standard form and a typewriter, a clerk prepares a material requisition note.

(*d*) *The total systems*: This includes consideration of all the systems to achieve the overall objectives of an enterprise.

(*e*) *Combination of major sub systems*: This refers to clubbing of one sub system with another such as production control with inventory control and sales with bills receivables and so on.

2. The flow of information: The process of system integration is also based upon the flow of information among different sub-systems. Integration of any system involves consideration of input and output data of each sub-systems. For example, input data on resources used can be obtained from production sub-system, material inventory data from inventory sub-system and so on. The output data takes the form of reports. The purpose of this step is to provide information needed by people to guide each work steps.

Office routines of procedures

The term routine or procedure connotes a planned sequence of operations for handling recurring activities uniformly and consistently. It refers to a series of related steps which constitutes a planned method of doing any work according to a system. For Example, in purchases system, the various procedural steps involved are selecting the best supplier, placing of purchase order, receipt and inspection of materials and settlement of accounts. Efficient purchasing involve strict observation of all these steps. Thus,a routine or a procedure implies a specific work sequence. It is a series of operations directed towards achieving a particular objective. A procedure or routine stands in between a system and a operation. Procedure brings down the system to the level of actual work operations.

Definition of routine or procedure

Neuschal defines routine or procedure as "a sequence of clerical operations, usually involving several people in one or more departments established to ensure uniform handling of a recurring transactions of a business."

J.C. Denyer is his book *Office Administration* defines office procedure as "the sequence of steps (or operations) in which they are performed and is concerned with what is done, how it is done, when it is done, where it is done and who does it?"

Leffingwell and Robinson in their book *The Book of Office Management* define office routine as "a series of steps in the performance of work, each step in the series being performed in the same order and in the same way every time."

An analysis of the above definitions bring forth the following elements of a routine or procedure:

(*a*) Procedure denotes a sequence of predetermined operations.
(*b*) It is determined to achieve a uniform method of performing a work.
(*c*) Procedure lays down the name of the person who has to do a work in relation to time, place and nature of work.
(*d*) It specifies the steps necessary to perform a work.
(*e*) It involves creation of authority and relationship when the work is assigned to a subordinate.

Differences between systems and routines

	Systems	Routines
1.	A System is a plan of work.	Routines are steps to perform a particular work or particular task. The routine operation required to perform a work is so planned that a particular work is performed by the same sequence and in the same manner.
2.	The term system is applied to the performance of major functions of the business such as purchase system, production system, etc.	The term routine is used to denote small division constituting the system, For example, under the major function of office organisation, we have filing and indexing for which different procedures can be followed.
3.	Systems means designing and linking together the method of work with procedure.	The procedure refers to the sequence of operations only.
4.	A system is concerned with broad relationship which is expressed in one or more flow charts accompanied by a group of procedure that make it up.	A procedure is the working level of system. It actually guides employees to proceed each time when a particular recurring type of work is to be performed.

Type of procedures or routines

On the basis of purpose served by routines, they may be classified into two types. The first type of routine may be termed as 'primary routine' and it is intended to expedite the dispatch of day's work. Some examples of this kind are order and billing routines, purchasing routines and so on. The second type of routine may be termed as 'secondary routine' and are intended to facilitate the work of the people handling the primary routines by means of rendering the services. Some examples of this type of routines are mail and messager services, telephone service, filing service, stenographic service and so on.

Aims of a procedure

It is not always possible for an accepted procedure to attain its aim. It is the duty of office manager to continuously strive to improve the procedure under his control to find better ways of operating. The following list of aims applies to most of the procedures established in office:

(*a*) To ensure the smooth flow of information in correct sequence.
(*b*) To avoid any possibilities of fraud.
(*c*) To provide appropriate control points.
(*d*) To allow for insertion of missing information according to the requirements of the system.
(*e*) To adjust any inaccurate information.
(*f*) To insert any additional information as considered necessary.
(*g*) To confirm to legal requirements.
(*h*) To provide appropriate information to supervisors and managers on time.
(*i*) To integrate with other procedures and systems.
(*j*) To be economically viable.
(*k*) To satisfy quickly any queries from staff, customers, suppliers and others.
(*l*) To design in such a way that the staff develops interest in the work and performances are maintained at their highest levels.
(*m*) To present all information on time and in its most suitable form for the purpose.
(*n*) To indicate the accuracy of the infonnation from its source, such as factual, second hand and opinion.

Principles underlying the establishment of routines

The following principles govern the process of establishing routines:

(*a*) Every step must have a justifiable purpose.
(*b*) Each step must advance the work.

(*c*) The order of each step should be such that records required to be taken off will not delay the service.
(*d*) Equality of the time required for each step should be striven for.
(*e*) Guard against duplication of work.
(*f*) Avoid unnecessary writing.
(*g*) Needless effort should not be expended.
(*h*) Make as few exceptions as possible to the general routine.
(*i*) Avoid unnecessary checking.

Step involved in establishing an office routine or procedure

Very few office managers have experience and knowledge in establishing routines or procedures in an office. Even in the case of newly, organised offices, office routines are frequently copied from other business units dealing with same products. This process of adopting the routines of an existing business results in wastage as it may not fully fit into the system of newly organised office. Therefore, this routine requires reconstruction. The steps involved in such a situation are as follows:

1. To undertake a preliminary investigation of routines: Under this step detailed analysis is made in relation to (*a*) the main objective of the office, (*b*) the staff and their contribution to the work, (*c*) the method used for performing the work and (*d*) how best the work is being done. This analysis helps whether the purpose is justified and whether the routine should be continued, altered or abandoned. The two important ways of improving office performance are by eliminating unnecessary routines and eliminating unnecessary steps in routines.

2. To make a detailed analysis of each step: This step involves a careful analysis of each step in the routine to see if there are any defects in the routine of each step. The following points helps in conducting such an analysis:

(*a*) *Name and purpose of the step*: The true purpose of every step is to be known for, unless the purpose is known, the rest of the analysis is useless.

(*b*) *Justification on the purpose*: The justification of purpose can be known by asking such questions as: is it necessary? If so why? If not, why not? After taking a decision it involves explaining the reasons in detail.

(*c*) *Accomplishment of purpose*: This involves determining whether the purpose is accomplished or not. If the purpose is not accomplished the reasons for the same is to be known.

(*d*) *Performance*: Step in the right place is to be known.

(e) *Duplication of work*: This analysis involves in determining whether the step under consideration duplicates with the work done elsewhere.

(*f*) *Time required to perform this step:* It involves determination of the time required to perform the step.

Thus, the above information helps in restructuring the routine.

3. Preparation of work charts: The purpose of a chart is to portray the flow of work in a simple way so that it can be grasped easily. The study of the chart then reveal where the subject needs improvement. The following are the different kinds of chart prepared in this connection:

(*a*) *Procedure analysis chart*: This chart outlines the different operations along with an analysis of the type of operation. It gives the sequence, time taken for each operation and distance travelled by documents.

(*b*)*Procedure flow chart*: This chart shows how office form and its different copies move from one department to another department.

(*c*) *Work distribution chart*: This chart shows how office form and its different copies move from one department to another department.

(*d*) *Production study chart*: This chart shows the extent of manual and machine labour employed.

(*e*) *Operation chart*: This chart shows the distance and time of movement of the detailed work of an individual.

4. Making the final analysis: This step is useful for the purpose of discovering defects in the earlier steps. The final analysis considers the (*a*) necessity of a particular step, (*b*) critical review of the method used and (*c*) the amount of time required, in making this study. Each operation should be written up completely, showing the present method, highlighting the defects involved and offering suggestions for improvement.

After considering the above steps, a new routine can now be designed. This involves the following steps:

(*a*) *Elimination of supefflluous steps*: By eliminating all superfluous steps, new methods are to be devised.

(*b*) *Determination of order of various steps*: By following a common step, it may be possible to perform two or more steps simultaneously.

(*c*) *Provision of even flow of work through the routine*: This step is very essential as a large part of the waste in office work is due to uneven flow of work.

(*d*) *Underlying correct mode of working*: Instead of following different method for performing a work it is better to adopt the appropriate method of doing the work.

(*e*) *Use of best tools and equipment*: This involves provision and prescription for the method of using tools and equipment.

(*f*) *Training the clerks*: Proper training is essential for enabling the clerks to discharge their duties satisfactorily.

(*g*) *Determination of speed*: It implies inculcating the habit of a speedy work.

(*h*) *Determination of accuracy*: Inaccurate performance of work is owing to lack of interest in the work. So interest should be cultivated to emphasize the accuracy of work.

(*i*) Re-charting the procedure and redrafting the forms.

(*j*) Installing new procedure with new forms and new methods.

(*k*) To take follow up action to see how the procedure is working and wherever necessary, it is to be modified.

Application of procedures in performing some important functions in office

In order to illustrate how routines or procedures improve the efficiency of office, the following functions are considered. Along with each function, the observation of important procedural steps are mentioned which serve as the application of procedure in office organisation.

1. Purchase procedure: The aim of purchase procedure is to ensure that the most important arrangement is made between the concern and the supplier to deliver specified items at the right price, in the right quantity and quality and at the right time. In order to achieve this aim of purchase procedure, the following routine is followed:

(*a*) Receiving of purchase requisition slips by purchase manager from store keeper and others for those materials which are to be procured.

(*b*) Inviting tenders from all competent suppliers in order to choose the best supplier.

(*c*) Placing of purchase order with the best supplier.

(*d*) Taking follow-up action in case of delay in delivering materials.

(*e*) Receiving of materials supplied by the supplier.

(*f*) Inspection of materials so received.

(*g*) Returning of materials which are defective and damaged accompanied by Debit note.

(*h*) Arranging for the payment of bills.

2. Wage payment procedure: Payment of wages form part of accounting system. In a large sized concern, the following procedure is observed for the distribution of wages and salaries:

(*a*) Obtaining the information regarding the hours of work done from the time keeping officer, if the basis of wage payment is one time rate system. Similarly, under piece rate system of wage payment, particulars about the number of units manufactured are obtained.

(*b*) From the above information, the monthly wages of each and every employee is calculated.

(*c*) The pay roll is then prepared so as to include the basic pay, over-time wages and bonus if there is any. From the gross wages and salaries the usual deductions such as P.F., E.S.I., house rent and such other deductions are recovered.

(*d*) For payment of net amount of wages and salaries, cash is drawn from the bank.

(*e*) In a small concern, the cash is enclosed in pay envelops along with pay slips and in large concerns salary is paid by cheque.

3. Sales procedure: Sales constitutes one of the important functions as it is this function which is responsible for earning revenue to the business. The following procedure is observed while executing sales orders:

(*a*) Receiving customers orders either by the sales manager or by the production manager directly.

(*b*) To issue an acknowledgment indicating the customer that the order is receiving due attention for execution.

(*c*) If there is no stock of such goods, necessary instructions are given to production manager to arrange for the production of required quantities of goods according to the specification of customer's order.

(*d*) If the finished goods are available in the warehouse, then necessary arrangements are made for packing the goods in required quantities.

(*e*) The accounts department is notified to prepare the invoice for the customer.

(*f*) The goods are then delivered to customer along with a delivery note and an invoice.

(*g*) Collection of bills from customers and closing the account of that customer.

4. Procedure relating to handling cash: The control of cash is one of the essential aspects of modern commercial office. By following a definite procedure, it is possible to prevent frauds and misappropriation of funds in an organisation. The following procedure is observed while handling cash in an office:

(*a*) Obtaining the signature of payee whenever cash is paid.

(*b*) Maintenance of cash book upto-date for receipt and payment of cash.

(*c*) Cash should be banked as soon as possible.

(*d*) Preparation of vouchers whenever cash is paid.

(*e*) Proper recording of money received through mail.

(*f*) The issue of receipts should be done only by those with appropriate authority.

(*g*) Payment of money and signing of cheques are to be under the control of one person.

(*h*) Petty cash system must be operated with a receipt for any item of expense incurred.

(*i*) The cash book should be balanced regularly and reconciled with bank pass book.

(j) Any cash discrepancies should be immediately reported to the chief cashier.

Procedural manual

When the office procedure is in the written form, either in the form of a booklet or loose-leaf, it is termed as 'Procedural manual'. It includes (*a*) written instructions relating to the person, place and time of doing the work, (*b*) the system or method of dealing with the work, (*c*) the forms and the way of using them and (*d*) instructions as to how to use the manual.

Advantages of procedural manual

1. Clarification of instructions: When procedures are clearly written, it enables everyone to understand clearly what one is expected to do, how and when.

2. Saving in time: Once the instructions are written down, it serves as authoritative document. Employees spend less time in understanding the routine aspect of processing. It gives them a sense of confidence and they are more certain about their duties.

3. Preserve the experience of firm: The standard procedure once prepared remains for a long period of time. Even if there is too much of labour turnover, the firm will retain the ideas and knowledge of people who are no longer with the organisation.

4. Helps in training thg employees: The written instructions serve as the basis for on-the-job training for the employees.

5. Promotes morale: The procedural manual reduces uncertainty because the employee knows what his job is and is expected of him. This understanding builds confidence and enhances morale.

6. Facilitates delegation of authority: The superior is assured that the subordinate will perform the work in the same manner in which he would have performed. Thus, procedures manual make delegation more effective.

7. Facilitates management by exception: Management is relieved of performing repetitive functions and decision-making by the process of delegation. Thus, an executive is able to focus his effort on more critical matters.

8. Establishes a basis of control: As procedure manual provides a standard procedure, it serves as a good basis to measure the performance of individuals and departments. Thus, it establishes a basis for control.

Disadvantages of procedural manual

1. It is expensive: The process of analysis, writing in brief, periodic reviews and necessary revisions are time-consuming process and costly. The management has to, therefore, weigh these costs in relation to benefits accruing from manual and the potential losses resulting from their absence.

2. It is rigid: It takes away the initiative of staff because they are to be strictly followed.

3. It is difficult to understand: Very often it may be misunderstood and misinterpreted by those who are not familiar with manual. In such a situation as a device of communication, its effectiveness is diminished.

4. It is unreliable: In today's changing organisation, procedures may change substantially and to this extent it loses its status of authoritative document.

Office methods

Any discussion of office systems and procedures will be incomplete without mention being made on office methods. Neuschel defines office methods as a manual or mechanical means by which clerical operations are performed. The method to be adopted for every operation differs from organisation to organisation. For example, training of staff can be undertaken by following such methods as lectures, film shows, seminars, group discussions and so on. Similarly for recording the attendance time of employees, the different methods available are: Signing in attendance register, disc methods, time recorder method and such mechanical devices. The method followed in correspondance may relate to dictation of letter to shorthand typist, or to a dictating machine, using standard letter forms, entrusting the letters to the private secretary and so on.

Flow of work

Flow of work is concerned with the way work moves along from one operation to another. More specifically, it implies the movement of work load, the rate of speed at which it moves and the smoothness of its movement. The efficiency of office to a large extent depends upon the quick flow of work. A steady flow of work goes to improve the efficiency of work and an uneven flow of work goes to retard its progress. This is so because an uninterrupted flow of work makes the clerk to wait for the work. Thus, flow of work determines the speed of work and the idle time of workers. The capacity to do the work or volume of work in certain cases can definitely be completed even with less staff provided there is even flow of work without obstruction. Most of the work is delayed owing to lack of flow of work steadily because of some obstruction. From the above discussion it is clear that the flow of work is the problem of management but not of clerks. So, it must be the endeavour of management to control the uneven flow of work by anticipating them in advance and by taking appropriate measures. In the words of Leffingwell and Robinson "in controlling output, the first and most important consideration is to handle work so that it shall flow steadily without any interruption; that is, velocities at all points should be equal and uninterrupted."

Factors which affect smooth flow of work

The smooth flow of work is impeded by the factors mentioned here under:

1. Daily or seasonal fluctuations in the volume of work: The volume of work may not be the same all through the year and in some cases even on the same day. For example, during the peak seasons such as festival and marriages the orders for gifts and such other articles will be more. Consequently, the volume of work in the office will be more. Similarly, if the delivery of mail is undertaken twice a day, the number of letters received by the first mail is more and consequently the correspondence will also be more compared to the delivery of mail for the second time. It is better under such circumstances to prepare statistics which helps in knowing the fluctuations of work and adjust and work accordingly.

2. Interruption to work: Every interruption of work adversely affects the flow of work causing considerable delay. The important causes of delay are: (*i*) Non-availability of information when required (*ii*) Change in work owing to change in the method of performing the work (*iii*) Change of work because of defective planning and (*iv*) Other causes such as interference of visitors, telephone calls, absence of employees, laziness on the part of employees, brief visits by staff outside the office.

3. Different timing involved for performing different types of work: The performance of different work requires different span of time, say, varying from 2 minutes to four minutes. If the first clerk takes four minutes to perform the operation and the second clerk only two minutes to perform the same job, the latter will sit idle waiting for the work. Thus, the flow of work is interrupted whenever a person takes longer time to complete his operation.

4. Lack of standard: The lack of uniform distribution of work will hamper the flow of work. If a person is overloaded with too much of work compared to others, he may not complete all the job within the allowed time. This slows down the flow of work.

5. Defective layout of office: Layout of office refers to systematic arrangement of office equipment and furniture. A good layout provides for better use of available space. The related work and staff must be placed close by to one another. Otherwise the work to be performed moves in a round about way thereby delaying the process of work.

6. Lack of Planning: Planning is concerned with what is to be done, how it is to be done, who is to do it and where? When office work is not planned properly it will only lead to haphazard means of performance rather than systematic method. An unplanned work only involves waste of time, money and material thereby causing delay in the flow of work.

7. Lack of scheduling: Scheduling is concerned with the time within which the flow of work is to be ensured. Very often this is neglected in most of the offices which is responsible for delay in flow of work.

Use of charts as a means to improve flow of work

In order to overcome the difficulties of flow of work, it is necessary to analyse the flow of work carefully. The actual flow of work may be depicted on flow charts. This helps management to know whether the present system of flow of work is satisfactory or whether it is to be improved. In preparing the charts, it is desirable to follow the method of 'Straight line flow'. According to this method the progress of work should follow a course of a straight line. That is to say, the work should always move in a forward direction but not in the backward direction. This method increases the speed of work, without losing the documents and enabling the staff to be in their place and not to go in search of papers and files. Two important charts used in this connection are: (*a*) office layout charts and (*b*) flow process chart. An office layout chart depicts the analysis of the flow of work throughout the office. A line is drawn which indicates the movement of work along the line. For comparison purpose, the layout chart can be drawn before or after the movement or flow of work. This gives scope to know the extent of delay, waste of effort and time. Flow process chart which is otherwise known as work simplification chart is used to depict the office routine graphically. The American National Standard Industrial Engineering terminology defines a flow process chart as "a graphic symbolic representation of the work performed or to be performed on a product as it passes through some or all of the stages of a process. Typically, the information included in the chart is quantity, distance moved, type of work done and equipment used. Work-time may also be included."

It is common practice to make use of the following symbols while preparing a flow process chart:

Symbol	**Name**	**Activities represented**
O	Operation	Modification of object at a work place depending upon need
⇨	Transportation	Change in location of object from one place to another
☐	Inspection	Examination of object to check the quality
D	Delay	Retention of object in a location awaiting next activity
Δ	Storage	Retention of object in location in which it is protected against unauthorised removal

The flow process chart is useful as it helps in improving the flow of work by considering the following questions:

(*a*) Can an operation be eliminated?
(*b*) Can an operation be combined with another operation?
(*c*) Can the sequence of performance be changed?
(*d*) Can the operation or inspection be simplified?
(*e*) Can a movement be eliminated?
(*f*) Can a delay in storage be eliminated?

Organisation and Method (O & M)

In large companies, the office manager may not have time to review specific clerical procedure in detail. Under such circumstances an advisory service department is established with a full-time staff who are concerned with analysis of office practice. Such establishment is termed as O & M. It first originated in UK in civil service procedures in the 1940s as *organisation and methods*. This term is now widespread by establishing a division named as *system and procedure or clerical work study*. While the term O & M is properly used in UK, it is denoted by *work simplification* in USA.

Meaning of O & M

O & M is a section of specialised staff which investigates systems in an office and tries to redesign and replace them with a more efficient or economical system. In simple words, it refers to the scientific checking on the efficiency of office work. Its scope includes office organisation, office system, methods, machines, office forms and work measurement.

Definition

L. Hall in book *Business Administration* defines O & M as "O & M is the name given to any conscious attempt, scientifically applied to improve organisation, simplify and improve methods and generally create and maintain an efficient administrative machine."

J.C. Denyer in his book *Office Management* gives two definitions on O & M. Firstly, O & M or work simplification is defined as "the organised use of common sense to find easier and better ways of doing work." Secondly, he defines it as "a scientific checking on the way work is done, to ensure that utmost efficiency is obtained".

Need for O & M

It is the rule of the day where the organisation tends to grow continuously. In an office, paper work multiplies infinitely owing to growth in the organisation. It may not be possible for the office manager to supervise personally all types of office work. In addition to increase in the volume of work, the techniques, organisational structure, method of performing work, standards of performance keep changing. In the light of these changes, a continuous review becomes necessary on the part of office manager. O & M serves as a tool in the hands of manager to conduct such a review of work operations. The need for O & M has arisen owing to the following three reasons:

(*a*) To cooperate with the challenge of change and to improve upon the efficiency, O & M is used as a tool with which changes are explored.

(*b*) The industrial revolution has brought about radical changes in the methods of production and management. O & M studies are felt necessary to bring these methods upto date.

(*c*) Lastly, the vast increase in the size of organisation and its complexities necessitate a professional staff to advice on managerial problems. O & M staff constitute this professional body of people.

Objectives of O & M

The following are the important objectives of O & M:

(*a*) To reduce the cost of office work to the minimum.

(*b*) To establish the most efficient procedure for performing paper work.

(*c*) To relieve the executives from performing routine work.

(*d*) To provide the right information to the management to exercise control over operations.

Functions or duties of O & M officer

(*a*) To assist top management in various ways in order to improve administration and methods of work, both in office and factory.

(*b*) To review office oganisation and systems for suggesting work simplification measures.

(c) To advise on devising form design and form control.

(*d*) To assist in starting new departments and branches and planning their layout.

(*e*) To offer advice on the introduction of new machines to meet special requirements.

(*f*) To organise and supervise training of short-term courses.

(*g*) To publish O & M bulletins so as to improve efficiency by providing a medium for the exchange of ideas on office methods.

(*h*) To conduct investigation to solve departmental problems.

Setting up O & M Department

Whenever an O & M department is to be set up, it involves the following considerations:

(*a*) To appoint an O & M officer to head the department, who shall be responsible to the general manager.

(*b*) To recruit required number of O & M assistants. The important sources of recruitment are costing department, accounting department, secretary's office and production, control department.

(*c*) To establish the status of the department in the organisation structure.' The O & M service is that of advisory service and has no authority of its own. It is desirable to build up the O & M gradually instead of establishing it suddenly.

(*d*) Before O & M department is created necessary information must be given to all departments regarding the purpose and status of this new department.

Procedure involved in O & M or methods of operation or techniques of O & M

The following steps are involved m conducting an O & M study:

1. Determining the objects. This step involves preparation of a statement of purpose which helps the O & M officer to conduct his investigation. The statement of purpose contains (*a*) the general or specific objectives of the investigations, (*b*) the nature and extent of the information required to achieve the objectives and (c) sources of information, both internal and external.

2. Planning the assignment: This step is based upon the scope of assignment, the size of the organisation, extent of concentration and dispersion of various departments.

3. Collecting the facts: The facts can be collected by using techniques like personal observations, studying existing records, by conducting interviews, by written questionnaire and by holding discussions with employees and departmental heads.

4. Analysis of facts: Analysis of facts is a prerequisite to the work improvement. The O & M officer will examine the various office procedure. This step involves the following two sub steps.

(*a*) To study and analyse the existing procedure and to ascertain in respect of each procedure.

(*i*) The purpose of each operation.

(*ii*) The method of doing it.

(*iii*) The amount of skill required.

(*iv*) The person who does the operation.

(*v*) The department where the work is performed.

(*vi*) The time involved in performing the operation.

(*vii*) The use of different forms in relations to the procedure.

(*viii*) Number of documents handled, in peak and normal conditions.

(*ix*) Special requirements (arising out of legal or customers) influencing the procedure.

(*x*) Cost of operations.

(*xi*) Extent of mechanisation.

(*xii*) Degree of supervision.

(*b*) To study and analyse the source of information used in respect of each procedure with particular reference to the following:

(*i*) Whether information is prepared manually or mechanically.

(*ii*) Degree of accuracy and reliability of information necessary.

(*iii*) Delay in preparation and receipt of information.

5. Designing a new or modified procedure: Having analysed all the above factors, now it involves designing a new or modified procedure purely as a basis for comparision. Several alternatives can be developed and measured against the basic one to know the best alternative.

6. Submitting to the Management. The O & M officer will submit the procedure to the management at whose request he undertook the investigation. The O & M officer must convince those concerned, by:

(*a*) presenting to the board of directors the economics and increased efficiency arising from such a procedure.

(*b*) impressing upon the departmental managers about the advantages accruing from such procedure.

(*c*) convince the lower level managers that there is no need to fear about the redundancy. In this process he obtains consent from the management for the installation of the procedure.

7. Preparation of procedure statement: Under this step, a procedure statement is prepared according to the nature and extent of the investigation. The investigator having obtained the consent to his recommended procedure now describes and establishes it by recording the following:

(*a*) Defining clearly the purpose and scope of the procedure.

(*b*) Full description of the procedure explaining the principles involved.

(*c*) Preparation of 'key terms' with explanatory notes concerning their applications.

(*d*) Definition of any new terms introduced in the procedure if they are liable to misinterpretation.

(*e*) Effective date on which the new procedure will become operative.

Subsequently after taking a trial the relevant items of the above procedure statement will be included in the office manual as a standard procedure.

8. Installation: Under this step, the O & M officer will (*a*) prepare an installation plan (*b*) assist in the actual installation (*c*) inspect the working of the new procedure and (*d*) review the procedure periodically and modify if necessary.

Advantages of O & M

1. Simplification: The O & M study helps in simplifying the procedures and forms. This helps in the speeding up the procedures and easy understanding of the fonns.

2. Better control: Through O & M studies, the management will be able to exercise better control over all the aspects of business.

3. Improvement in communication: It improves the communication process owing to better designed forms and from changes of the organisation structure.

4. Prevention or Reduction of errors: By using machines which employ built-in-checks and from the simplification of forms, it is possible to reduce the errors in the procedure.

5. Use of new techniques: The adoption of new techniques through O & M studies enables management to meet new developments and cope with the expansion of business.

6. Reduction of cost: The increased efficiency derived from O & M techniques go to reduce the cost of production.

7. Increased prestige: With the increased efficiency of the business, it improves the image of the business. The improved external communication and the use of simpler, better designed and more legible documents improves the public relations.

8. Staff improvement: More attention will be given while selecting, training and promoting employees so as to suit the environment in which they work.

9. Work measurement: O & M technique permits work measurement and assessment of performance of employees which keep the staff at a high level of efficiency.

10. Improved security measures: O & M department often helps in improving the security of the cash, stock of materials and information secrecy of the business.

Applications of O & M

The O & M techniques are applied to the following fields of office organisation:

1. Comunications: O & M is applied in studying the existing means of communications with the object of improving the means of communication. The important considerations in replacing the existing mode of communication with an improved means are the potential benefits to be derived and the cost involved in such replacement.

2. Dividend payment: To improve the method of paying dividend and to maintain proper records for unclaimed dividends, this technique is being applied.

3. Forms control: In order to dispense with outmoded types of forms and to redesign new forms which involves improvement and reduced cost, the O & M technique is applied.

4. Office layout: Whenever the layout of office is to be revised for meeting the legal requirements and for the efficient performance of work, this technique is applied.

5. Personnel records: To improve recording and storing of personnel records, O & M techniques are made use of.

6. Material control: O & M techniques are applied to a greater extent to exercise control over material all through the stages of receipts, storage and issue.

7. Transfer of shares: O & M studies are applied to examine the existing procedure of transfers of share and to offer suggestions with a view to accelerating the process of transfer of shares.

8.Wages payment: O & M studies are applied in improving the system of wage payment.

QUESTIONS

Objective Type Questions

1. Define a system.
2. What do you mean by systems integration?
3. Define a routine.
4. Distinguish between a system and a routine.
5. Mention different types of office routines.
6. What is a procedural manual?
7. What do you mean by 'office method'?
8. What do you mean by flow of work?
9. Mention the charts used to improve work flow.
10. Define O & M.
11. State four objectives of O & M.

Analytical Type Questions

1. Briefly explain requisities of an ideal system.

2. Outline the importance of office system.
3. Outline the principles of office system.
4. Explain the steps involved in designing an office system.
5. Explain the steps involved in systems integration.
6. Outline the various aims of office procedure.
7. Outline the principles underlying the establishment of office routines.
8. State the advantages and disadvantages of procedural manual.
9. Briefly discuss the factors which affect the smooth flow of work.
10. Explain the need for the importance of O & M.
11. List out of the functions of an O & M officer.
12. Explain the advantages of an O & M.

Essay Type Questions

1. What do you mean by office system? Discuss the advantages and limitations of office system?
2. Explain the steps involved in designing an office procedure.
3. Discuss the procedure as applied in (*i*) Purchases (*ii*) Wage payment (*iii*) Handling cash in an office.
4. Explain the procedure involved in O & M studies.

6

Forms Design and Control

INTRODUCTION

Office Forms are one of the important tools used in an office for its efficient functioning. A form is a piece of paper used for communication purposes. In the words of Frank. M. Knox "*nothing happens in an office except to or by means of pieces of paper*" Very often communication process involves use of certain matters which can be avoided by means of printing them on forms. The other part of the information which is to be furnished can be written in the blank space provided in the forms. Thus, considerable amount of time can be saved while preparing various type of reports. Besides saving time, such forms also present the information in a more understandable way to the reader. With a view to achieve these two objectives in all offices more attention and care is taken in designing and controlling the office forms. Unless proper design of form is used, it only leads to confusion, waste of time, effort, money and paper. The study of 'Form design' is concerned with simplification of forms and that of 'Form control' is concerned with the proper use and the supply of such forms.

Definition and aims of forms

J.C. Denyer in his book *Office Management* defines an office form as "a printed piece of paper or card, and on which entries are usually made against marked headings."

Ricks and Gow in their book "*Information Resource Management*" defines forms as "carefully designed documents used to gather and transmit information necessary for operational functions and for historical records."

According to P.W. Betts "A form may be described as sheet of paper with printed information indicating the date required in the blank spaces provided."

The main aim of office forms are:

(*a*) To provide concise and sufficient information, according to procedural requirements.

(*b*) To minimise repetitive writing of information by printing the essential data on the form.

(*c*) To provide a number of copies of similar information for injection at various points in the procedure.

(*d*) To indicate clearly their filing location, reference and identification.

(*e*) To record systematically so that the data appear in the same place each time for operational effectiveness.

Type of office forms

The following are some of the important types of forms used in an office:

1. Continuous forms: It is a set of forms that are attached to one another. In order to separate one form from another, perforations are used. Continuous forms are especially suited for automatic printing equipment such as computer printers. It saves considerable amount of time because continuous forms are automatically fed through the equipment. This process eliminates the task of individually inserting each form in the equipment.

2. Unit-Set forms: As the name indicates; it is an individual form or a separate form and is not attached to another set as in the case of continuous forms. This type of forms may be either single or multiple-copy forms. Where multiple copies are desired, a sheet of carbon paper is inserted within each form.

3. MICR forms (Magnetic Ink Character Recognition): It is a type of form frequently used by banks on which MICR number appear. Such forms are used by banks to expedite the sorting and processing of numerical data found on banking documents. The equipment reads the numbers printed with a magnetic ink and then transmits the data to the computer.

4. OCR forms (Optical Character recognition): The OCR forms arc both alphabetical and numerical data as compared to MICR forms which use only numerical data. When the data is read on the OCR form, the data is transmitted to the computer where it is processed.

5. Mark-sense forms: It is a type of form that involves the use of a special pencil for entering data in appropriate areas on the form. The location of mark which is in coded form, can be read by a special data processing equipment.

Form design and its importance

Form design is concerned with (*i*) the size of form, (*ii*) the content, (*iii*) the colour, (*iv*) the number of copies of each form and (*v*) the thickness and quality of paper used. The efficiency of office function, to a large extent, depends upon the use of properly designed form. A poorly designed form cannot be completed easily especially by those who are not familiar with such forms. Further, a poorly designed form may be responsible for recording inaccurate data. Therefore, in some of the large sized office; the services of experts are utilised for a good design of form. The following points highlight the importance of form design in a modern commercial office.

1. Forms serve as tools of office work: Forms constitute one of the important tools of office management as they assist in performing some of the important functions such as receiving, recording, arranging and giving information in the office. If Office forms are badly designed they impede these functions seriously.

2. It improves the morale of staff: A badly designed form will have a psychological effect on the staff using such forms. This will reduce the efficiency of office work.

3. It avoids clerical mistakes: Sometimes clerical mistakes occur as a result of badly designed forms. The decisions based on such wrong information will lead to serious consequences on the management.

4. It reduces cost of maintenance: A well designed form results in saving in the cost involved in preparing, recording and filing the forms.

5. It improves the prestige of the organisation: A well designed form results in building up the goodwill and public image of the concern.

6. It helps in effective implementation of the office system. Office forms are closely related to office system. A well designed form enables the successful implementation of office system.

Objectives of form design

There are two objectives served by form design:

1. Facilitate collection and use of data: A well designed form enables the form originator *i.e.*, individual or department requesting information to rapidly extract the needed data from the form. It also enables the form user as to what information is being requested and to complete the form accordingly.

2. Achieve printing economies: A good form design facilitates in low printing cost by (*i*) use of standard size of paper. The standard size of paper also facilitates easy filing and locating the forms,(*ii*)ordering only required number of forms as this will decide the cost of printing.

Steps involved in designing a form

The step involved in designing a form are as follows:

Preliminary consideration

1. Define the purpose of the form: Defining the purpose of the form is necessary to determine the type of information to be included in the form, the number of copies needed, the nature of instructions for completing the form and the necessity of certain control procedures for the form. The general purpose of a form is to reduce clerical work than what would be possible if a blank sheet of paper is used. If the blank sheet of paper serves the purpose, there is no need for going into a well designed form. The designer should ask certain questions for himself such as why is a form necessary? In case of need, should it be a new form or is it possible to modify an existing form to suit the present purpose?

2. The nature of the equipment through which the forms is processed: The equipment through which the forms are processed determine the minimum or maximum size of the form. For example, a form which is to be used on a typewriter should be designed in such as way that the typist does not waste time in setting the machine. Similarly, while getting the forms printed, necessary instructions must be given to the printer to allow sufficient space for the use of typewriter in filling up the relevant particulars. Sometimes certain equipments determine whether automatic feeding of the form is possible. While certain other equipments determine the type of paper to be used on which forms are printed.

3. The relationship between the form being developed and any other previously developed forms: If the newly developed form has any relationship with an earlier form, care must be taken to maintain consistency between the two. When the information is to be transferred from one form to another, the sequence of items should be identical.

4. The period for which forms must be preserved: If the forms are to be preserved for a longer duration to meet statutory requirements, the quality of paper must be superior. This is so because the paper on which the form is printed must be of sufficient durability to withstand time element.

Layout of the form

The layout of the form depends upon the following factors:

1. Identification of form: In order to facilitate easy identification of a form, it is necessary to give a number or a name at the bottom of the sheet. It is easier to remember the name rather than the number of the form. Therefore, in most forms we come across the use of names instead of numbers. It is better to use standard names of the forms to avoid confusion. The name of the form should be brief and self explanatory. Where numbers are preferred, the forms are to be consecutively numbered. Sometimes the decimal system of numbering is preferred. Under this system, two separate set of numbers are used. The first number indicates the department where forms originate and the second set of number correspond to the number of form. For example, the use of the number 1: 10 would indicate form number 10 in department 1.

2. Alignment of items: There must be proper alignment of items so as to avoid delay in setting up the equipment, say, a typewriter. The following example illustrates the incorrect and correct way of aligning items on a form:

Incorrect Alignment	Correct Alignment
Name:	Name:
Occupation:	Occupation:
Address:	Address:
City:	City:

In the above example, the correct alignment of items facilitates the accommodation of all the items in one tab set of the machine. This also saves a considerable physical effort over a period of time

3. Simple design of the form: The contents a form must be in simple language so as to avoid misunderstanding on the part of those completing the forms and those for whom the forms are ultimately intended. Three broad guidelines serve this purpose *viz.*, (*i*) placement of information at the correct point. For example, identification matter such as name, address, etc., should be placed at the top of form, (*ii*) the second part of the form is to be provided for recording data on the form and (*iii*) instructions, if any such as delivery instructions should be placed at the bottom of the form.

4. General appearance: The forms to be used must be attractive and pleasing. This can be ensured by using colours, well balanced arrangement of the contents, providing columns and rows wherever necessary and such other factors.

5. Size of form: The size of paper depends upon the contents of the form. The size of a form should not be large so as to involve additional cost on it. The size of the paper is affected by the number of columns and rows. In any case, the size of paper must be compact so as to include all matters within it.

6. Use of standard typeface: As far as possible, the typeface to be used must be of one variety only. Where it is necessary to distinguish one type of data with other types, it is necessary to use bold and italic types.

7. Sequence: The sequence in the presentation of matters should be strictly followed on the forms. The arrangement can be made either vertically or horizontally. Wherever related items are involved, they must be grouped and presented as it enables in maintaining proper order of the contents.

8. Filing: Those documents which are to be filed must be provided with an adequate filing margin which is about 20 millimetre width.

9. Use of best paper: The quality of paper used for printing office forms helps in two ways, *viz.*, in preserving the forms for a longer period of time and in easy handling of forms. The paper to be used in printing office form possesses three qualities, *viz.*, weight, grade and grain. The weight of paper on which forms are printed is important as it determines the durability of the form. The grade of paper refers to quality of paper. A good quality paper retains the impression for a long time. The grain of paper refers to the fibres contained in the paper. When the forms are to be fed into machines, the direction of fibres determines how well the paper can be fed through various types of equipment.

10. Window envelope: Where the forms are to be enclosed in window envelopes, the address must be typed on a suitable place with adequate size.

11. Provision of perforation, punching and scoring: When any portion of the forms are to be detached it requires perforations which can be in the form of small holes or indicated by a series of small dashes. Punching of forms becomes necessary for filing purposes which can be done through the printer by issuing necessary instructions. Scoring refers to the use of line on a form which serves as a basis for folding the forms. This can also be arranged for at the time of printing the forms.

12. Distinguishing lines: Where the number of lines are many on the forms as in the case of invoice, it is desirable to distinguish one set of lines with others preferably by drawing a thick line or drawing double lines. This avoids confusion among different lines.

Review of form by using a forms design of check list

After preparing the layout of form as discussed above, it should not be released for printing. The third step involved is to review the form by using a *form design* check list. This ensures that the draft forms design satisfies all the requirements of a good office form. The check list to be used as given by Ricks and Gow is reproduced below.

CHECK LIST FOR REVIEWING THE FORM

1. Arrangement

(*a*) Consider the source of information, its use and does it satisfy the readers?

(*b*) Are all items arranged in the right sequence?

(*c*) Are the forms amenable for proper filing?

2. Spacing

(*a*) Has proper amount of space been provided between each piece of requested information?

(*b*) Is the horizontal spacing adjusted to provide a minimum number of typewriter tab stops?

(*c*) Is all extra space used properly for emphasis, separation and balance instead of looking leftover?

3. Captions

(*a*) Will all captions be understood by everyone who might use the form?

(*b*) Will abbreviation be readily understood?

(*c*) Are group headings used to identify major areas?

4. Instructions and distribution

(*a*) Can someone, unfamiliar with the form complete it without referring to any other source for help?

(*b*) Are the distribution instructions shown in the form in the most effective way for its usage pattern?

(*c*) Is the form designed to fit a window envelope whenever appropriate?

5. Margins

(*a*) Does the form have adequate margins for the required lock-up space on the press?

(*b*) Are the margins adequate for any binding purposes or for other handling characteristics such as filing, stapling and so on?

6. Construction

(*a*) Is the size appropriate for both the printer and all users?
(*b*) Is the paper right for the form's use and retention needs?
(*c*) Is the colour of ink appropriate?
(*d*) Are all appropriate perforations, scores provided?

7. Identification

(*a*) Is the title meaningful?
(*b*) Is the form properly identified with a number of reference.

Preparing a draft form design

Before a form design is finalised, a draft copy of the form design is prepared. This is done on the basis of the factors discussed above. A paper of standard size is used for this purpose. The ruling can be of rough sketch. The particulars are typewritten at appropriate place of the form. The required space in between two sets of particulars are provided for. Necessary changes can be incorporated to give better appearance of the form. This process will save considerable amount of space, time, money and efforts. Where it is desirable the use of professional services can be derived. The form specialist identifies the purpose of a form and accordingly designs it. After the form is designed and is approved by the organisation, the specialist will arrange for the preparation of final copy of the form. The form specialist also offers suggestions for the improvement of forms. Before the final copy is sent to the press, the quantity to be ordered is to be decided upon. Larger the number ordered at a time, lesser is the amount involved. However, the heavy investment involved in bulk ordering as well as the time taken by the printer to deliver the forms should be considered. No standard is available regarding the quantity of forms to be ordered. However, the following points can be considered in deciding upon the quantity of forms to be ordered.

(*a*) Quantity used, (*b*) Quantity required for the future use, (*c*) Amount of capital involved, (*d*) Savings derived if bulk order is placed and (*e*) Possibility of change in the form.

Finally, the order is placed with the printer for the supply of required number of forms.

Principles in form design

Robert C. Appleby in his book *Modern Business Administration* has enunciated the following principles of form design:

(*a*) The number of operations necessary in the use of the form should be reduced.
(*b*) The form must be easy to read and to use.
(*c*) The number of copies and the number of forms should be reduced. This can be done by designing forms to serve more than one purpose.
(*d*) The layout of the form must be such that it is related to other documents with which it will be used.
(*e*) Appearance must be attractive with entries easily made and instructions easily read. Colour should be used with care.
(*f*) The form must be large enough to contain all information required; any limits because of its use with machines must be noted, in addition to mailing and filing facilities.
(*g*) Titles should be concise, the form reference number and destination should be clearly visible.
(*h*) The quality of the paper should be considered.
(*i*) Spaces for entries should be adequate and in the most natural order for use.

Definition and aims of forms control

L. Hall in his book *Business Administration* defines form control as "an important aspect of O & M through which control is exercised over the use and misuse of forms."

According to Ricks and Gow "A form control programme is a record management function designed to achieve the efficient collection and distribution of information through the use of forms."

Zane K Quible in his book *Introduction to Administrative Office Management* defines forms control programme as "a programme whose function includes determining whether or not a new form is needed; eliminating, consolidating or simplifying existing forms, assisting in the design and development of new forms and facilitating the development of efficient work procedures."

According to the above definitions the form control is concerned with:

(*a*) Guarding against the development of unwanted forms.
(*b*) Eliminating existing forms that are not needed.
(*c*) Assisting in the development and in designing efficient forms.
(*d*) Consolidating and simplifying existing forms when found necessary.

(*e*) Providing a continuous review of existing forms.

(*f*) Facilitating the development of efficient work procedures.

In the absence of forms control programme, there is a tendency on the part of managers and supervisors to introduce forms in a wasteful and haphazard way. The other side effects are: lack of systematic ordering of forms which results in storage problems, careless use of forms, little incentive to revise the forms and wastage if the form is obsolescent. To overcome these problems, a form control programme is necessary in the organisation.

Aims of forms control

The aims of form control may be summarised as follows:

1. Necessity: The first and foremost objective of form control programme is to examine the necessity of forms used and to determine whether any kind of form can be scrapped as obsolete. The guiding point in this connection is to question whether the form is really necessary.

2. Design: The second objective of form control programme is to evaluate forms in relation to their design. Depending upon the circumstances and need, forms may be redesigned so as to serve the purpose at the lowest cost.

3. Preparation of forms: The third aim of form control programme is to arrange for the preparation of good forms taking into account the quality and size of paper.

4. Standardisation of forms: The fourth object of forms control is to standardise the form in relation to:

(*i*) *Content*: Where a variety of forms are used for the same purpose but slightly differing in contents, such forms should be reduced to one standard form. The examples of such forms are *materials received note, materials returned note and materials transfer note* which are used in connection with drawing material from and returns to stores.

(*ii*) *Size*: The size of forms is to be standardized for reducing paper cost and savings in storage space.

(*iii*) *Description*: The particulars of description of the forms can also be standardised, as for example, name, address and code in order to facilitate identification.

5. Purchase or ordering of forms: The procedure of ordering the forms must be centralised under the supervision of one competent officer such as Forms Control Officer. Any other officers who are in need of office forms must place the requisitions for the new forms with the forms control officer.

6. Issue of forms: To avoid excess issue of forms and causing wastage thereby, control is to be exercised while distributing the forms.

Setting up forms control system

Forms control consists of the setting up at the head office a separate department to exercise control over the forms. This involves the following steps:

1. Establishment of department or section: To facilitate better control a separate section known as form control section is established. The forms control officer in this case will be responsible to O & M Manager. Where a separate O & M department is already established the form control section is operated by that department.

2. Appointment of forms control officer: To look after the process of control over forms it is desirable to nominate a person who has the knowledge of office procedures and office equipment.

3. Appointment of staff: The required number of staff to assist the forms control officer in administering the new system is the third step. Wherever existing staff are available in the office their services can be transferred to forms control department.

4. Terms of reference: The duties, responsibilities and powers of form control officer are clearly laid down.

5. Conference: Before forms control programme is operated, it is better to have some discussion among the departmental heads so as to explain them the need for such control. If there are any suggestions offered, it can be taken note of by the form control officer.

6. Report to the Board: The forms control officer will now prepare a report for submitting it to the Board of Directors. The report will contain:

(*i*) An outline of the broad principles of forms control.

(*ii*) The potential advantages of introducing the systems.

(*iii*) A recommendation to permit the initiation of the system.

7. Communication: After getting the approval from the board, the form control officer will communicate to all the heads of the department regarding the initiation of forms control system. He can also emphasize the procedure to be followed henceforth for requisitioning new forms and replenishing the supplies of the existing forms.

8. Office manual: The details of the new forms control system are to be included in the office manual.

Steps involved in efficient form control programme

The following steps are involved in designing a forms control programme:

1. Forms cataloging: It helps the staff of forms control section to determine the nature, type and purpose of the forms that are utilised throughout the organisation. This step consists of submission, by each department, copies of each of its forms to the form control officer. This process will reveal:

(*i*) The primary purpose of each form.
(*ii*) The forms utilised by each department.
(*iii*) The frequency of use of each form.
(*iv*) The number of multiple copies of each form.
(*v*) The routing of forms.
(*vi*) The disposition of forms.
(*vii*) The relationship between one form and another form.

2. Forms classification: Classification of forms facilitates the analysis of forms assembled during the cataloging process. Forms can be classified on the basis of functions and by number. Classification by function means organising forms according to their purpose. For example, all purchase forms are classified into one group and all forms relating to sales into another group and so on. This enables the form control officer to analyse similarities and differences among the various forms.

On the basis of numbers, forms are classified according to identification number assigned to each form. This basis is not widely used, but it enables to know the total number of forms already available and helps in numbering new forms.

3. Eliminating forms: On an indication that certain forms are no longer needed, their elimination is considered. This is true because the purpose for which they were meant is no longer felt. Perhaps the purpose of a form is now being served by another form. Yet another reason for discarding a form, is that it may not be consistent with the systems and procedures of office.

4. Consolidating forms: Once the unwanted forms are eliminated, the remaining forms may reveal that certain forms contain same details. A single form may be designed to replace two or more existing forms. This will result in reduced cost of operation in the office.

5. Design guidelines: Design guidelines are established for developing the new forms or revising the existing forms. These guidelines help in maintaining consistency with other forms. Design guidelines can be illustrated by considering the following:

(*i*) When some information appears on different forms, that information may be made to appear in the same location on each form, as for example, name and address of the company.

(*ii*) Information that are transferred from one form to another should appear in same order in both the forms.

6. Development of forms: This refers to the preparation of either a new form or revising an existing form by taking into consideration the principles of form design discussed earlier.

7. Continuous supply of forms: Under this step, efforts are made to get continuous supply of forms without interruption.

Advantages of forms control

The advantages of forms control are summarised under the following headings:

1. Savings in costs: Costs involved in forms handling is reduced through (*i*) eliminating time spent in unnecessary recording, handling and filing of forms, (*ii*) printing costs, (*iii*) paper cost and (*iv*) space, both relating to filing and storage space.

2. Simplification of work: The process of filling the form and its use can be simplified to a large extent through form control programme. This also facilitates better understanding by the staff.

3. Reduction of errors: By issuing proper instructions, errors are avoided on forms.

4. Improvement in communication: A programme of forms control facilitates both internal and external communication smoothly and quickly.

5. Ensures continuous supply: The delay involved in getting the forms printed can be avoided by using such devices within the office from which forms for internal use can be obtained. Even forms meant for external use can also be had by planning in advance about quality and quantity of forms.

QUESTIONS

Objective Type Questions

1. Define office form.
2. State any four aims of office forms.
3. What is a continuous form?
4. What is a unit set form?

5. What do you mean by MICR form? What purpose does it serve?
6. What are OCR forms?
7. What do you mean by Mark-sense form?
8. What is form design?
9. Mention three objectives of form design.
10. Define forms control.

Analytical Type Questions

1. Briefly explain the various type of office forms.
2. Outline the importance of form design.
3. State the principles of forms design.
4. Briefly explain the objectives of form design.
5. Explain briefly the steps involved in setting up form control system.
6. Explain briefly the steps involved in efficient form control programme.
7. What are advantages of forms control?

Essay Type Question

1. Explain the steps involved in designing a form.

7

Office Accommodation and Layout

INTRODUCTION

The Term *Office Accommodation* refers to the space that is available or to be procured to do office work. One of the important problems that confront the management of every business organisation is the selection of an appropriate place for the establishment of an office. This is so because the success of a business depends upon the efficient functioning of an office. This in turn depends upon the location, layout, and physical environment of an office. As large part of the office work relates to mental work, the efficiency of office staff depends upon the availability of good office accommodation and better working conditions. Infact, the provision of good office accommodation is the primary consideration of office management. Recognising this fact, in Western countries, the services of professional experts are engaged. But in out country, this aspect has not received much attention though in recent times utmost importance is given by large sized business units.

Importance of office accommodation

The importance of a good office accommodation is reflected by the following points:

(*a*) It offers protection to office staff and office equipment from bad weather.

(*b*) It provides healthy and pleasant working conditions by the installation of lighting, ventilation and air-conditioning facilities.

(*c*) It facilitates performance of office work effectively and continuously by eliminating work stoppages and interruptions.

(*d*) It enables in maintaining the business secrets.

(*e*) A well planned office accommodation saves area of land through multi-story and mezzanine floor space.

(*f*) It increases the morale of the employees and thus reduces labour turnover.

(*g*) It creates favourable impression on visitors and general public.

(*h*) It increases flexibility in the use of office for future growth and varying needs of the business.

(*i*) It has self-advertising value.

Factors to be considered while providing office accommodation

The following factors are to be considered while providing office accommodation:

(1) Location of office building
(2) Securing office building
(3) Size of office accommodation
(4) Shape of office accommodation
(5) Provision of physical facilities
(6) Layout of office building
(7) Staff services
(8) Cost of office accommodation

1. Location of office building: The selection of an appropriate location enables the office to operate smoothly, efficiently and with minimum cost. Wrong location leads to wastage in efforts and talents of office manager with consequent uncertainity in result. The location of an office has a great effect on the success or failure of the operation of a business unit. If the selection of the site is not proper, then the investment on such office will go waste. The cost of transferring it from one location to another would prove a very costly affair. Therefore, while selecting a site, the management of an undertaking must consider financial, operational and employee factors. The selections of a site is influenced by two important decisions *viz.*, (*a*) choice between urban and suburban locality and (*b*) centralisation and decentralisation principle.

(*a*) *Choice between urban and suburban locality*: Before an actual site is selected for an office, the management must decide between an urban area and a suburban area for establishing an office. This again depends upon the size of the organisation and the nature of function performed by it. A large sized office can be established in towns as it can afford to spend increased cost in acquiring and maintaining an office. Similarly, banking and insurance business, can also be established near towns and cities because of increased business which it can secure. The relative advantage and disadvantages of establishing offices near towns and cities are as follows:

(1) It facilitates establishing close and quick contact with suppliers.
(2) Provides transport facilitates to the office staff.
(3) It enjoys the advantages of banking and communication services.
(4) It provides easy access to public.
(5) It offers housing, recreational, medical and educational facilitates to the office staff.
(6) It creates better advertising value to the company.

However, location of office near towns and cities suffers from following disadvantages:

(1) The price of land will be very high.
(2) Towns and cities are always overcrowded.
(3) Lack of scope for the expansion of office in cities and towns.

(*b*) *Centralisation and decentralisation principle*: Centralisation of office accommodation refers to the establishment of offices of all commercial organisations in one central place which is commonly termed as *commercial complex* or office complex. Such a commercial complex is largely found in the heart of the towns. However, with the growth of commerce and industries and consequent large demand for office accommodation, it is no longer possible to accommodate all the offices in the same area. Further, it restricts future expansion potential of an office. In order to avoid such difficulties there is a tendency towards decentralisation.

After making a choice between the above two alternatives, the actual selection of a site is to be decided upon. The selection of actual site depends upon the availability of the following factors:

(*a*) *Value of land*: The cost of land determines the location of offices premises. The cost of land will be very high in urban areas when compared to suburban areas. Therefore, the trend in office is to establish it near suburban areas.

(*b*) *Cost of construction*: The cost of construction affects the selection of a locality for an office. It is high in urban areas than in rural areas.

(*c*) *Expansion potential*: The additional space available for future expansion of an office is an important consideration in office location.

(*d*) *Climatic condition*: The health and efficiency of office staff depends to a large extent on the climatic condition of the locality. Hence, this factor must be given top priority in locating an office.

(*e*) *Availability of parking facility*: Ample space is necessary for paking the vehicles of office staff as well as visitors. The facility is available is suburban areas when compared to towns and cities.

(*f*) *Availability of banking facilities*: For arranging financial requirements of the business and for prompt deposits of cash from daily collections it is necessary to establish office in a locality where banking facilities are readily available.

(*g*) *Availability of postal and communication services*: As office is the place where communication is exchanged, it is necessary to select such a site where postal and communication facilities are readily available.

(*h*) *Availability of transport*: The availability of various modes of transport enables office staff to reach the office in time. Such facilities are found mostly in urban areas than in suburban areas.

(*i*) *Availability of housing:* To enable office staff to attend to office work promptly and punctually, the area to be selected must be such that it provides housing facilities to them.

(*j*) *Availability of shopping and recreational facilities*: To provide entertainment for the staff of the office and to make all their purchases at one common place, it is desirable to select an area which has shopping centres and recreational facilities.

(*k*) *Adequate police and fire protection*: To avoid disturbances arising out of political, sociological and economical reasons, it is better to select such an area where police protection is readily available. So, also to protect office records and office furniture from the occurance of fire, it is necessary to select an area which is accessible by fire brigades.

(*l*) *Tax rates:* The local taxes levied by municipality and local authority determine the location of an office. Urban localities always involve payment of heavy taxes as compared to rural areas.

(*m*) *Availability of quality labour*: The success of office work, to a large extent, depends upon the availability of efficient staff. Hence, this factor plays an important role in the site selection for an office.

(*n*) *Nature of streets*: It is better to avoid neglected areas and instead select popular streets of a locality for establishing an office. Similarly street which distracts with more noise and which pollute the environment must also be avoided.

2. Securing office building: The second step involved in providing office accommodation after selecting a site is to procure required area for setting up an office. The area to be procured must be sufficient not only to meet the present needs but also for the future expansion of office.

One important decision to be made while procuring area for office accommodation is between leasehold or freehold or ownership land. The freehold land depends upon the availability of capital and availability of land for sale. The purchase of land for owning an office offers the following advantages:

(*a*) It facilitates construction of office building according to the needs and objectives of the business.
(*b*) Owned office adds to the prestige of the business.
(*c*) It facilitates renting out the unused portion of the office building and there by earns interest on it.
(*d*) The office can be remodelled whenever necessary.

However, owned building has certain disadvantages.

(*a*) They require heavy investment to procure the land.
(*b*) It involves cost of maintenance of office building.
(c) Payment of property tax to the local government.

The overcome the disadvantages of freehold or owned land and for deriving the following advantages, often building is acquired on lease basis:

(*a*) The repairs and maintenance cost are borne by landlord.
(*b*) It does not require initial investment for acquiring the land and building.
(*c*) It facilitates shifting of building from one place to another place by acquiring leased land from others.

The few disadvantages of lease hold land are:

(*a*) It involves payment of high rent.
(*b*) It cannot be designed to meet the requirements of the business.
(*c*) It is not available on a permanent basis.
(*d*) Does not add to the prestige of the business.

Yes, another decision that requires consideration is whether to buy an existing building or to build a new office building. This decision is based on the following features:

(*i*) Size of the existing building and the future needs.
(*ii*) Amount of capital required for building the new one as against the rent payable for the existing building.
(*iii*) Rooms available in the existing building and the proposed requirements.
(*iv*) Physical facilities available in the existing building.

While securing office accommodation on lease basis, it is worthwhile to consider the following points:

(*a*) To incorporate all terms and conditions of lease in the lease agreement. The provisions so incorporated must be very clear so as to avoid misinterpretation.

(*b*) To specify the exact date, the lease is to begin. Sometimes the building construction may be delayed in which case the landlord may be asked to provide temporary accommodation.

(*c*) The amount of rent payable and its variation is to be clearly specified in the lease agreement.

(*d*) Any alterations that are to be made to the office buildings by the landlord or by the lessee is to be specified.

(*e*) To specify the period of renewal.

(*f*) To make sure as to who should pay insurance premium for the office building.

(*g*) To get the document checked by the lawyer before it is signed.

3. Size of office accommodation: The third factor that is to be considered while providing office accommodation is the size of building. The size of the accommodation depends upon two factors. Firstly, the nature of activities involving a variety of functions demands big sized building. Secondly, large volume of transactions necessitate a large sized office to cope up with increased number of transactions. Though the size of office building may be small in the initial stages, it may have to be expanded to meet the future requirements of the business. The size of an office building can be expanded either by adding new departments or expanding the existing departments of the office. It is always prudent on the part of management to acquire sufficient area so as to expand the size of the office should the need arise. Where it is not useful at the time of acquisition, it can be sublet on hire basis to others.

4. Shape of office accommodation: The shape of office accommodation is an important factor for the following reasons:

Firstly, the shape of area determines the shape of office building and in constructing single storey or multi storey building. Secondly, the shape of office building determines the layout of the office. Thirdly, the full utilisation of office accommodation depends upon the shape of office building. Usually rectangular shape is preferred to other shapes as it facilitates easy and quick movement of office staff. Further, it also enhances quick flow of work in office.

5. Provision of physical facilities: The efficiency of an office staff mostly depends upon the provision of adequate physical facilities such as ventilation, lighting, heating and air-conditioning. These factors are discussed in detail in the next chapter.

6. Layout of office: Layout of office refers to a systematic arrangement of office furniture and office equipment so as to utilise the space to the maximum extent. This factor consists of setting up of various departments or sections at appropriate places and within each departments, allocation of sufficient space for furniture and equipment.

7. Staff services: While providing office accommodation, it is desirable to provide separate rooms for canteens, wash rooms, cloak rooms, rest rooms, toilets, and for such other facilities. Office accommodation must also provide space for visitors which can be termed as reception and conference hall especially for participating in meetings, seminars and conferences. Where the office building is multi storey building, provision for lifts may also be provided for.

8. Cost of office accommodation: This is by far the most important factor which influence the office accommodation. The cost of providing accommodation for office activities depend upon the locality such as urban or rural, size of the business, volume of business transacted, the design required and so on. However, the efficiency and convenience with which office activities can be carried out should not be under estimated while designing office accommodation.

Shifting the office to the new location

The need for shifting office accommodation to a different locality arises in order to earn more profit, to increase the size of the business, to offer better services to office staff and visitors and to minimise the risks involved in the existing building.

The steps involved in shifting an office building to another locality consists of three stages, *viz*., (*A*) Preliminary State, (*B*) Intermediate Stage and (*C*) Final Stage.

(A) Preliminary state

This stage includes the following steps:

(*a*) *Appointment of a committee*: Before the office building is actually shifted to a different locations a committee consisting of members from different departments is constituted to consider the desirability of shifting the office to a different locality.

(*b*) *Arrangement for shifting the office*: If the locality where the office is to be shifted is at a far of place, it involves transporting the office furniture, equipments and records. Necessary arrangements are to be made by entering into contract with transport undertakings for shifting the office property to the new locality.

(*c*) *Informing the office staff about the shifting of office:* Sometimes, office staff may not be willing to work in a locality where office is to be shifted, where large number of staff decide not to continue their services. In such a locality, the company must make all arrangement to recruit new staff for the office.

(*d*) *Arrange for additional Insurance*: If the new building is to be insured for a higher amount, necessary steps must be taken in this regard.

(B) Intermediate stage

This stage involves the following steps:

(*a*) *Fix up responsibilities on individuals*: Before the office property is shifted, responsibilities can be fixed on individuals to safeguard the assets and company secrets during the transit.

(*b*) *Issue necessary instructions for moving the Assets*: As and when the properties of office are packed and ready for movement, necessary instructions are to be issued for their movement.

(*c*) *Preparation of layout*: To fit into the new building, the head of each section of the office may be asked to prepare a rough sketch of the layout of the office so as to facilitate proper placement of furniture and equipment in the new building.

(*d*) *Arrangement of specialised workers*: If the nature of equipment used is such that it requires any disconnection or reconnection, specialised workers such as electrician and plumbers may be engaged on a temporary basis.

(*e*) *Arrangement of printing new letterheads*: Owing to change in the locality of an office all old letterheads may have to be replaced by new ones.

(*f*) *Notify customers, suppliers and other about the change in the office:* The change in the address of the office is to be informed to customers, suppliers, insurance company, government and post office.

(*g*) *Recruitment of additional staff:* In order to fill up the vacancies caused by resignation of employees and to meet the additional work load, the required number of staff is to be recruited.

(C) Final stage

This stage involves the following steps:

(*a*) *Arrangement of facilities in the new location*: Important facilities such as telephone, water, electricity, etc., is to be arranged for.

(*b*) *Sell out the old furniture not suited for the new building*: All old furniture not suited for the new building are to be sold out and arrangements are to be made for buying new furniture.

(c) *Arranging for post-moving inspection of the premises*: This step enables in detecting defectiveness in the functioning of any department or even equipment, in progress of work in various departments, and such other activities.

Recent trends in office location

1. Decentralisation movement: Traditionally office establishments were mostly located in big towns and cities. The present trend in the location of office building is to move away from cities towards suburban areas. This is so because various advantages such as proximity to market, transport facilities, availability of employees, and such other factors are available even in suburban areas today. Suburban areas provide ample space for future expansion, they are less congested and availability of land at a cheaper rate.

2. Establishment of office amidst commercial establishment: The second trend to be observed in office location is starting of offices, main or branch office—amidst commercial establishments or commercial shopping centre. This is increasingly observed in all countries without exception. This trend is followed to enable everybody concerned with office to take advantage of the presence of all the establishments surrounding the office premises.

3. The office park: As compared to the above trend, the office park resembles an *industrial estate*. In some countries, the real estate owners, construct a series of buildings to be let only for offices. Such an office park resembles a college campus with all the amenities and facilities. Office park offer such advantages as lower rents, availability of more parking space, availability of space for future expansion, reduction in traffic and so on. Further, the real estate owners themselves undertake the responsibility of maintenance and repairs of office parks.

4. The office condominium complex: This refers to the office structures which are constructed by real estate owners, association for selling them to business enterprises. However, the institutions or organisations are expected to become the members of such association. By purchasing an office condominium, the occupants have many of the advantages of building ownership.

Layout of office

The term *Office layout* is used in a broad sense to include location of departments in an office as well as systematic arrangement of furniture and equipment within each and every department. Office layout is a plan or the act of planning to obtain an optimum arrangement of office facilities, including personnel, equipment, storage space and all other supporting services along with the design of the best structure to contain these facilities.

Definition of office layout

According to J.C. Denyer office layout refers to the determination of space requirements and the detailed use of this space in order to provide the best practical arrangement of furniture and equipment necessary for the execution of the work of the office.

In the words of Mills and Standingford "the layout of an office is the arrangement of furniture, machines, etc., within the space available."

Littlefield Rachel and Caruth defines office layout as "the arrangement of equipment within available floor space. Space management may be thought of as providing space which will yield maximum productivity and effectiveness at minimum cost."

An analysis of the above definitions bringforth the following essential features of office layout:

(*a*) Departmentation of office into a number of sections to facilitate smooth flow of work.

(*b*) Arrangement of furniture and equipment in a systematic and in an orderly way to quicken the flow of work.

(*c*) Placing the right equipment and stationery in their appropriate places so that they are readily available when required.

Importance of office layout

The importance of office layout can be discussed under the following headings:

1. Increases the efficiency of office work: When a proper arrangement of furniture and equipment is provided, it enables the office staff to confine to their places and carry out their activities without moving from place to place. This increases their concentration and the chances of committing errors are very less.

2. Enhances utilisation of office space: By a systematic arrangement of all equipments and furniture, it is possible to utilise the space to the maximum extent as haphazard arrangement will occupy too much of spacc.

3. Facilitates supervision: A good layout of an office enables the office manager to supervise the work of all the staff and to enforce discipline among them. This increases the speed of performing office work.

4. Facilitates inter-communication: Office layout facilitates quick communication of messages, if the departments or sections are properly arranged.

5. Provides good working environment to staff: A well arranged office department permits the utilisation of physical facilities and enables the employees psychologically to feel that they are working in good working conditions.

6. Helps in utilising office assets to maximum extent: By orderly arranging the various sections in an office, it is possible to utilise the available services and assets to the maximum extent. For example, instead of installing a telephone for every room, it may be kept in a common place where it is accessible to every one. Similarly, instead of providing with an adding machine to every staff in the sales and purchase sections, one machine can be provided to be used by both the sections by mutual understanding.

7. Provides flexibility in the use of space: A well planned office will facilitate future expansion and thus avoids the problems arising from non-availability of enough space for future use.

8. To meet statutory requirements: In U.K., Offices, Shops and Railway Premises Act 1963 has a more powerful influence over the functioning of an office. In India, we have Factories Act of 1948 which lays down the provisions relating to area to be provided, floors, passages and stairs, first aid, cleanliness, fire precautions, etc. The layout of office must be such that it meets the legal requirements of a country.

9. To Avoid noisy and distracting departments: As large part of office work relates to mental work, some of the departments of the office must be kept aloof from disturbing sections. Especially typing section and communication department must be segregated from other departments.

10. To offer security and privacy: Office is the place where all confidential matters are dealt with. So, it is necessary that filing sections, cash sections, etc., are to be properly safeguarded.

11. To create favourable impression on customers and visitors: The office is identified with business both by customers and visitors. Hence, the layout of office must be such that it gives better impression on all who visit the office.

12. To provide balanced capacity of equipment and personnel at each stage in work flow: The work to be performed in all sections of an office is not the same. Whereas, some sections require more of space, equipment, furniture and personnel, other sections may require less space and personnel. So a good layout is one which provides balanced capacity of space and equipment in different sections of an office.

Factors to be considered in office layout

The factors to be considered in planning a layout are as follows:

1. Feasibility study: The feasibility study is a useful tool in planning and designing office layout. A feasibility study helps in deciding best layout among various alternatives. The items usually included in a feasibility study are as follows:

(*i*) The financial position of the company and the anticipated growth in the near future.

(*ii*) An analysis of present space available and projection of future space requirements.

(*iii*) The system and procedure of work flow pattern of the organisation.

(*iv*) Relationship among various departments.

(*v*) An analysis of the communication pattern among individuals and groups.

On the basis of the above information, it is possible to select the most appropriate alternative type of layout.

2. Departmental relationship: The relationship between various departments depends upon the flow of work between such departments. Closely related departments such as cash and accounts departments must be located near one another. Similarly, those departments which are frequently visited by customers and others must be located near the entrance of the office building.

3. Flow of work: This is a very crucial factor in determining the efficiency of office layout. It refers to the movement of information either vertically (between superiors and subordinates) or horizontally (between employees of same responsibility).

In order to secure efficient work flow, the personnel and equipment be arranged in such a way that the information flows in a straight line. A most effective means of studying the work flow is to allow the movement of the document through the department. As effective layout depends, upon inter-relationship among equipment, paper and personnel, an analysis must be made in terms of work flow in the organisation.

4. Use of partition walls: The use of movable partitions provide privacy without affecting the flow of work. This facilitates flexibility in providing layout of an office.

5. Space requirements: The space required for office staff depends upon such factors as the equipment to perform a work, type of furniture, structural pillars and columns, nature of work, etc. The total space requirements is known by taking into account, the actual space required for various levels of Office Managers and space for different rooms such as reception room, conference room and so on.

6. The organisation chart: The organisation chart helps in knowing the relationship between superior and subordinates and therefore helps in knowing the space required by superiors and subordinates. In other words, it enables to know the existence of number of departments or sections in an office and how much space is to be provided for each such section.

7. Protection of employees needed in future: The development of an organisation in the near future demands increase in the number of office staff. The recruitment of additional staff requires more space which is to be considered while deciding the layout of an office. The other factors which determine additional staff are increase in size of business, introduction of a new line of products and change in the methods of performing office work. All these factors go to determine the extent of space required for the future.

8. Communication network: Where face to face contact among office staff is considerably involved, it is more appropriate to set up such departments close by to one another. This avoid unnecessary movements from one department to another and thus saves time of office staff.

9. Identifying specialised areas: Yet another factor that is to be considered while planning office layout is identifying the specialised work areas. Some of the important work areas which deserve special consideration are (*i*) reception area (*ii*) conference room (*iii*) computer room (*iv*) secretary's office (*v*) mail room and (*vi*) the records area. The location of each room is in turn determined by other factors.

10. Safety consideration: The design and layout of office should not impede the movement of employees from one area to another. The path ways should not obstruct the movement of employees and force them to take short cut routes, interfering with others' work. The doors and staircases must not hinder the movement of office staff.

11. Expansion potential: Keeping in mind Ihe future expansion potential of office accommodation, it is necessary to prepare a space analysis chart indicating the probable need of additional space in future. This also increases the flexibility in the use of office accommodation.

12. Environment conditions: The layout of an office is also affected by the physical facilities such as lighting, air-conditioning and noise control which are to be provided in office building.

13. Equipment and furniture: The size and number of furniture and equipments to be used also affect the layout of an office. Large sized and more number of furniture and equipments demand more space.

Principles of office layout

While designing the layout of office space, it is necessary to apply certain important principles so as to utilise the available space most effectively. These principles are as follows:

(1) To determine the inter-relationship between equipment, information and staff in the flow of work.

(2) The work flow should move in as straight a line as possible. Criss crossing and back tracking should be avoided.

(3) The work flow should revolve around the major source document.

(4) The organisation chart should be used to determine the hierarchial relationship between individuals.

(5) Communication pattern between individuals must be determined.

(6) Work groups performing similar or related duties should be located near one another.

(7) Individuals or work groups with frequent public contact should be located near the entrance of the premises.

(8) Individuals or work groups whose work require considerable concentration should be placed in a quiet area of building.

(9) Space allocation should be based on the position of the individual, the nature of the work being performed and the amount of special equipment required.

(10) Groups or individuals providing specialised services should be located near those who use such specialised services.

(11) Furniture and equipment should meet the needs of the individuals using them.

(12) Aisles should be sufficiently wide to accomodate the rapid and efficient movement of employees.

(13) Safety considerations must be given utmost importance.

(14) Adequate provisions have to be made for lighting, air-conditioning, humidity control, and noise control.

(15) Concern for future expansion is important.

(16) The arrangement must be such that work should come to the staff but not *vice versa*.

Steps Involved in office layout

The layout of an office involves the following steps:

1. Entrusting the job of office layout to a competent person: In Western countries, the planning and arrangement of office layout is considered as a full time job which is entrusted to a competent person. Such a person must possess complete and comprehensive knowledge of the needs of the organisation. The office manager can take the assistance of a draftsman from the engineering department and an office superintendent in carrying out this responsible job.

2. Planning: The person to whom the job of office layout is entrusted will discuss with the departmental head of each section to know the space required and the direction of work flow on all operations in the office. He will also take into consideration the various principles of office layout discussed earlier.

3. Preparation of a blue print: This step involves measuring the existing arrangement and equipment and showing the exact present location. This also provides for the position of doors, aisles, furniture and equipment at their appropriate places. The tools used in preparing blue print are (*a*) template and (*b*) plastic models. Templates consist of scaled versions of furniture and equipment and are typically constructed of cardboard. The template is used in tracing the various items on the layout. Plastic models are scaled versions of various pieces of office furniture and equipment. As the plastic models can be easily re-positioned on the floor plan, their use facilitate exploring various layout possibilities.

4. Getting approval from the section head: Before the blue print is adopted it is necessary to get the approval of the concerned section head. This avoids unnecessary relayout of office space from time to time.

Location of departments in office

The location of various departments of an office ensures smooth flow of work and efficient functioning of the whole office. The following points must be considered while positioning the different departments or sections of the office:

(*a*) The departments where work pass through between one another are to be established nearby.

(*b*) Where utmost supervision is required, it is better to establish a common room to accommodate all the sections of an office within the same room.

(*c*) The cashier's office must be safeguarded all around and it may be positioned within the general office.

(*d*) The rooms for directors, executives, accountant and personal assistants must be separately established. Direct access by the public to these departments should be restricted.

(*e*) The typing pool is to be set up far away from executive rooms so as to prevent excess noise created by typing pool. Similarly, other departments which use modern office equipment producing excess noise must also be set up away from those departments where work requiring concentration is involved.

(*f*) The filing and the indexing section must be set up near the typing section to facilitate quick filing of documents.

(*g*) If the size of the organisation is too big and the number of visitors are many, it is desirable to have an enquiry counter and a waiting room.

(*h*) Departments such as purchasing and personnel, where too many persons visit, must be set up near the reception room.

(*i*) Conference room, interview room, directors' meeting room must be set up far away from noise producing areas.

(*j*) Toilets and cloakrooms should be set up at a convenient place.

(*k*) Adequate space must be provided in all departments for future expansion.

The check list given below helps in designing the best layout of office:

(1) Avoid overcrowding.

(2) Ease of daily cleaning.

(3) Staff not facing directly into light.

(4) Proximity of cloakrooms and toilets.

(5) Main gangways about 5 feet wide and minor gangways about 3 feet.

(6) Minimise staff movement.

(7) Placing filing cabinets near staff using them.

(8) Adequate space between desks.

(9) Separate noisy machines from staff who are engaged in work requiring high concentration.

(10) Minimise paper movement by designing according to workflow.

Types of layout

Office layout can be designed according to the following two types:

1. Group layout: Under this type of layout, the office staff performing similar type of work are grouped together. For example, all typists performing typing can be grouped into one typing pool. Similarly, all accounting staff using accounting machines can be grouped into another section.

2. Process layout: Under this type of layout, the arrangement of office space is based on the sequence of operations, performed by office staff. For example, typing section, filing section and despatch section can be set up close by as the papers move from one section to another section in a definite sequence.

In practice, it is difficult to have a definite type of layout and hence a combination of both the types of layout may be adopted. For example, we see typists in each and every department of office and not necessarily in the typing pool.

Open office and private offices

An open office, otherwise known as general office, is one large room where several sections or departments work together instead of working in separate rooms. The open offices are becoming quite popular in modern days because of its comparative merits over private offices. Under this type, all the staff will function under the common roof. But each section is demarcated by using movable partitions or by placing almirahs and cabinets between two sections.

Advantages of open office

1. Capital outlay is lower.
2. Maintenance and redecoration are easier.
3. It leads to saving in floor space.
4. It facilitates better supervision.
5. It facilitates greater flexibility in the layout.
6. It leads to economies in lighting, heating, etc.
7. It results in better placing and use of machines and equipments.
8. It minimises movement of staff.
9. It improves communication and flow of work.

Disadvantages of open office

1. It changes the atmosphere drastically.
2. It does not facilitate secrecy of work which is very essential in office work.
3. It leads to excess noise.
4. Workers dislike to work in a large open areas. It results in reduction in the morale of staff.
5. It leads to security problems. No one can be held responsible in a large open office.

6. It may upset the health of workers by the spread of diseases.
7. It may result in overcrowding of staff.
8. It results in distraction of work caused by visitors.
9. It may pose problem of setting ventilation and heating to suit everyone.
10. It leads to the problem of status and prestige among supervisors and managers.

Private office or closed office

A private office refers to the establishment of small rooms for the use of executives such as managing director and various departmental managers. Where it is not possible to have a separate room altogether, they may be separated by one another by using partitioned walls. The use of private offices is justified under the three circumstances, *viz.*, (*a*) where prestige is a matter of utmost importance, (*b*) where the work to be performed is of confidential nature and (*c*) where concentration is required in performing the work. The private office is more expensive in the sense that it is equipped with modern furniture and decorations, carpeting, double glazing, air conditioning, use of curtains and so on.

Advantages

1. They facilitate in maintaining business secrets.
2. It provides good working environment to the managers.
3. It improves efficiency because of the absence of noise.
4. They don't spread diseases from one person to another.

Disadvantages

1. It leads to wastage of space.
2. Work flow is delayed.
3. There will be communication gaps between different departments.
4. It is a rigid form of layout which does not facilitate adaptation to changing conditions.
5. It involves frequent movement of managers and staff from department to department.
6. Supervision becomes ineffective.
7. It does not facilitate utilisation of natural lighting and ventilation.

Recent trends in office layout

The office layout has undergone considerable changes in modern days with many improvements. These latest changes in office layout can be studied under the following headings:

1. Office landscaping: The concept of landscaped office originated first in Germany in 1960 and now used in other countries very frequently. It refers to the planning of office space, free of the traditional permanent wall, corridors and private offices, and the row-after-row arrangement of desks and other furniture. The special features of landscaping are as follows:

(*a*) It utilises only a minimum number of permanent walls.
(*b*) Arrangement of furniture in an asymmetrical order according to the needs, though not in a definite order.
(*c*) Use of carpets, soft lighting, noise control and air-conditioning.
(*d*) Interior decoration.

The office landscape offers the following benefits:

(*a*) It results in savings in cost when changes in layout are required by expansion and organisational changes.
(*b*) The area of floor space available for use is more since only partitioned walls alone are used in place of permanent walls.
(*c*) It improves productivity because of greater efficiency in work flow, improved communication channels, improved worker morale and a greater feeling of worker involvement.

2. Movable partition: Movable partitions are increasingly used in office layout owing to economy over permanent walls. Such partitions are available in variety of sizes and shapes made out of wood, metal, glass or plastic materials. Partitions can also be prewired with telephone and electrical connections and they can be installed with special sound absorbing materials.

3. Modular furniture: The modular furniture is a multipurpose table which consists of desk space, file space and storage space. Such furniture is specially designed to meet specific needs of employees which results in greater productivity and efficiency. They occupy less space when compared to conventional furniture and in some cases, the modular furniture and movable partitions can be purchased as a single component.

Mistakes in layout

It is common to commit the following mistakes in office layout:

1. Adopting the original plan: Although the conditions and circumstances have changed the layout design may not be changed and it may be adopted in its original form. This may not suit the existing situations and, therefore, have to be revised.

2. Use of permanent structure: At the time of designing the layout, due consideration may not be given to future changes or alterations. In times of need this permanent structure will hinder easy alteration and it will also be costly. Further, this also dislocates office activities.

3. Utilisation of more space than required: Some time the accommodation for executives are provided with larger areas than actually required. The work in other sections will suffer because of less space available in such sections. Therefore, careful planning is necessary at the time of designing the office layout.

4. Defective planning: Very often the designing of office layout is taken up by departmental managers who lack proper knowledge about layout design. In such cases it only leads to wastage of place and inefficiency.

Re-layout of office accommodation

Whenever mistakes are committed in designing the layout, it involves re-layout of office accommodation. The following factors also contribute to the re-layout of office:

1. Changes in procedure: Whenever there is any change in the procedure of performing office functions, it invariably leads to the alteration of layout. For example, where modern office equipments are used, it requires additional space than what was provided for.

2. Change in labour force: Whenever the number of office staff increases or decreases owing to transfer, promotions, recruitment or discharge, the layout of office is to be modified.

3. Increase in size of organisation: Owing to increase in size of the business, the office may also have to be rearranged to meet the requirement of expansion in the size of the organisation.

Systems approach to office layout

The system approach to office layout was first developed by one of the famous German Management consulting teams by name *Quickborner Team for Planning and organisation* in the year 1960. In modern days it has attracted widespread attention in the U.S.A. According to this approach, the office should be designed according to the flow of information. In other words, the systems approach to office layout begins with an analysis of the flow of documents and the flow of oral communications in an organisation. Once these two communications flow have been identified and described, an office layout can be determined.

One of the outstanding features of systems approach is the use of open space which was discussed earlier in this chapter. This is so because, it facilitates the communication and work flow through all sections which work together in the office. This also leads to the flexibility in the layout which can be adjusted depending upon the need. However, to achieve flexibility, it is necessary to provide uniform lighting, air-conditioning and noise control measures.

The system approach to office layout results in the following advantages:

(*a*) High efficient work flow.
(*b*) Improved communications.
(*c*) Reduction of movement by staff.
(*d*) Increased feelings of personal involvement in the work of the firm.
(*e*) Increased utilisation of space.
(*f*) Reduction in building and maintenance cost.
(*g*) Flexibility in the arrangement and rearrangement of work areas.

QUESTIONS

Objective Type Questions

(1) What do you mean by Office Accommodation?
(2) What do you mean by centralisation of office accommodation?
(3) Distinguish between centralised and decentralised office accommodation.
(4) Define office layout.
(5) Mention any two tools used in office layout design.
(6) Mention the steps involved in office layout.
(7) What do you mean by group layout?
(8) What do you mean by process layout?
(9) What do you mean by open office?
(10) What do you mean by private office?
(11) Distinguish between open and closed offices.
(12) What do you mean by systems approach to office layout?

Analytical Type Questions

(1) Outline the importance of office accommodation.
(2) Explain the steps involved in shifting an office building to another locality.
(3) Briefly explain the recent trends in office location.
(4) Outline the importance of office layout.
(5) Outline the principles of office layout.
(6) Explain the steps involved in office layout.
(7) What points are to be considered in locating different departments in an office?
(8) What do you mean by open office? State its advantages and disadvantages.

(9) What do you mean by private office? State its advantages and its disadvantages.

(10) Explain the recent trends in office layout.

(11) What are the usual mistakes involved in planning the layout? When does re-layout become necessary?

(12) Explain the concept of system approach to office layout with its advantages.

Essay Type Questions

(1) Explain the factors to be considered while providing office accommodation.

(2) Explain the factors to be considered in designing office layout.

8

Office Environment

INTRODUCTION

The Term *Office Environment* refers to the provision of physical conditions such as lighting, ventilation, air-conditioning, cleanliness, noise level, colour scheme and a wide variety of other factors which improve the efficiency of office staff. The environment of the office has a significant impact on the performance of office staff. There is a direct relationship between the good working condition and the performance of the office employees. Office work is mostly mental work which requires more of concentration. Further, research has proved that office work leads to excess of fatigue than physical work. The office environment must be such that, it must provide more comforts to employees. It must be the duty of office manager to provide such a type of environment which is pleasant, comfortable and conducive to good working habits.

The physical environment of an office relates both to external surroundings and internal physical conditions. The external surroundings relate to (*a*) location of office building which affects the health of the employees when any unhygienic locality is selected, (*b*) structural design of the building as for instance in case of a multi-storey building, if the floors are not connected with lift services, employees have to move from floor to floor wasting their time and (*c*) freed from external dust and noise which again affect the health and when exposed to noise constantly reduces the concentration on work.

The internal physical conditions have a direct bearing among the working staff. The physical discomfort caused to workers will definitely cause strain and fatigue thereby reducing the efficiency and high rate of absenteeism of the employees.

Importance of office environment

The importance of office environment can be enumerated under the following:

1. To fulfil the statutory requirements: In UK, Offices, Shops and Railway Premises Act, 1963 provides for a number of provisions which must be strictly completed with in office department of the business. Similarly, in our country, the Factories Act of 1948 extends some important provisions to be fulfilled when applied to the office.

2. To increase efficiency: Provision of poor lighting, excess of noise and lack of proper ventilation have adverse effect over the efficiency of employees.

3. To improve the health: Health of office staff is affected by dust, bad lighting, excess noise and such other factors. While bad lighting affects the sight, the excess noise has had effect on nerves, the overcrowding on morale and draughts on physical health.

4. To reduce absenteeism and excess labour turnover: When workers are dissatisfied with the working conditions they feel like joining the other offices. This involves loss of efficient and experienced workers in the office.

5. To reduce fatigue: The speed of performing work is hampered due to excess strain when good working conditions are not provided.

6. To improve morale of staff: The surroundings with which office staff work have a psychological impact over their minds. The provision of good working conditions always improve the morale of employees.

7. To protect office equipment and records: Certain costlier equipments such as computers are to be protected from dust and high temperature. Similarly, office records and documents are to be safeguarded from the occurance of fire. Hence, necessary steps must be taken to prevent spoilage of office equipment and records by providing good physical conditions.

In order to achieve the above objectives, the following environmental factors are to be provided for in an office:

Cleanliness

Cleanliness affects the general morale and efficiency of office personnel. Any office which is dirty and untidy will lead to inaccurate performance of work. A clean and well maintained office not only improves the health of workers but also projects good image of the organisation. The common place where dust and dirt accumulates in an office are floors, staircases, walls, ceilings, furniture, windows and doors. This requires frequent cleaning either manually or by such devices as power driven floor polishers and vacuum cleaners. A definite programme of special cleaning should be laid down. The shelves, racks, cupboards, cabinets and desks should be cleaned and all records and papers should be cleaned from time to time so that dust and dirt can be removed. Furniture, windows and doors must be polished and painted from time to time. The walls must be colour washed frequently. All wastes including waste papers, carbons, old magazines and journals must be disposed off from time to time.

Decoration

Good decorations effect the appearance of a room and enhance its value as a place of work. The decoration of an office has a tremendous effect upon the morale of the staff. An ugly surrounding is depressing while pleasant surroundings are conducive to good work. The decoration of office need not be standardised as it differs from building to building and from room to room. While decorating the office buildings, the architectural style and the materials used in construction must be considered. The decoration depends upon the use of building materials such as bricks, wood, metal, glass and plastics. Those rooms which are exposed to direct sun light need decoration with cool colour such as blue whereas those not exposed to sunlight may require decoration with colours such as red or yellow.

The public waiting room and the entrance room must be appropriately decorated as it influences the public about the image of the business. General rooms of the office can be decorated with appropriate colours. A cheerful colour has a cheering effect upon the employees and thus affects efficiency. The study of the reactions of workers to different colours has been referred to as "psychomatics". The psychological impact of colour has either a positive or negative influence on performance of work, fatigue, morale, attitude and tension. It is generally recognised that colours have some effect on human emotions; some are cheering others depressing, some are restful and others stimulating. Colour in an office, therefore, provides not only an aesthetic value but also a functional value.

Colour considerations

In developing a colour scheme for an office, certain important factors are to be considered. These factors are:

1. Colour combination: For the sake of studying colour scheme in an office, colour combination can be of three types *viz.*, primary colour, secondary colour and tertiary colour. Primary colour relates to yellow, red and blue. A combination of the primary colours gives rise to secondary colours as for example mixing of red and yellow will result in orange colour. Tertiary colour is obtained when two parts of one primary colour and one part of another primary colour are mixed. In the above example, the tertiary colours are yellow-orange.

2. Effect of light on colour: There is a close relationship between lighting and colour conditioning so much, that both are considered to be Siamese twins. This is true because, the various types of artificial light have different colour spectrums. The source of light will enhance only those colours that are also within the spectrum of the light source. For example, fluorescent lighting generally repel red or orange colours. Therefore, fluorescent lighting will not enhance red and orange colours.

3. Reflectance value of colour: Certain areas of the office requires colour with higher reflectance values than do other areas. For example, the ceiling requires a colour with a higher reflectance value than does the floor.

4. Impact of colours: Different colours create different impact on employees. For example colours such as blue, green and violet create calm and retiring moods. Whereas colours such as red, orange and yellow create warm and cheerful moods. Other colours such as deep purple and pale violet are considered to create depressed moods.

According to Quible the following principles should be considered in designing a colour scheme for an office area:

(*a*) Colour cannot be considered by itself, but must be considered in terms of its impact on the total environment of the office.

(*b*) Black and white colour can be used to influence other colours. Black will influence another colour by making it lighter and more distinctive. White will influence another colour by making it darker.

(*c*) Any colour used against a darker colour will appear lighter, while any colour used against a lighter one will appear darker.

(*d*) Colours lose their brilliance and "wash out" in bright light, but they darken and lose their intensity in dim light.

(*e*) Warm colours are considered to advance, while cool colours recede.

(*f*) Two colours with greatly contrasting values have the effect of tiring the eyes rather quickly.

(*g*) Small areas of bright, secondary colours that are in balance with large areas are often useful.

(*h*) Light colours will make a small room look larger.

(*i*) A narrow area can be made to appear wider by making the end walls a brighter colour than the side wall.

(*j*) Deep brown is the most preferred dark colour in an office.

(*k*) A low ceiling will appear to be higher if the ceiling is a lighter colour than the walls.

(*l*) In working areas, floors should be darker than walls, and the walls should be darker than the ceiling.

(*m*) In work areas in which the rational light is from the North or East, a warm colour should be used on the wall opposite the window but when the natural light is from the South or West, a cool colour should be used on the wall opposite the window.

Lastly, the cheerful effect of good decoration should not be spoilt by hanging of calenders and notices. They may instead by notified on notice board. However, reproduction of good pictures may be displayed on the office walls with pleasing effect.

Lighting

Provision of adequate light is the most important environmental factor as it increases productivity and adds to employee satisfaction. No person in an office can work efficiently where lighting arrangement are not satisfactory. A good light refers to economical provision of right quantity and quality of light in the right place. The quantity of light required in an office depends upon the type of work to be performed. The quality of light to be supplied is as important as the quantity of light. The quality of light includes its colour, direction, diffusion, steadiness and the glare it produces. Any deviation from the above will impair the vision and add fatigue to employees. In the words of John A. Shubin, an efficient lighting system in an office reduces eye fatigue, helps in preventing accidents and improves morale.

Features of good lighting

The following are the characteristics features of good lighting:

1. Proper intensity: The unit used to measure the intensity of light is known as lumen, one lumen per square foot being equal to a foot candle. As the intensity of light varies from department to department, it is better to classify all departments and work areas according to the number of foot candles necessary for optimum lighting condition. The required intensity of light for different types of work are given below:

Types of office work	Foot candles on work
(*a*) Designing and detailed drafting	200
(*b*) Accounting, Auditing, Tabulating	150
(*c*) Regular office work	100
(*d*) Filing	70
(*e*) Work areas not involving prolonged viewing such as interviewing, wash rooms	30
(*f*) Corridors, elevators, stairways	10

2. Proper diffusion: It means an even spread of light over the working place. When the light is not properly diffused, the reflected light falling on eyes from a glass, working tables or any other equipment will result in poor visibility. Proper diffusion of light is necessary as eyes cannot adjust each time when brightness varies. For uniform distribution of light, the spacing between light units should not exceed their mounting height above the level of the work area.

3. Elimination of glare: The brightness or brilliance produced by light will have certain adverse effects over employees such as discomfort, interference with vision, high fatigue, headache and nervous effect. One of the feature of good lighting system is the avoidance of surface glare completely. There are two types of glare which are observed in lighting system, *viz.*, direct glare and reflected glare. Direct glare which results from sunlight or ceiling light can be eliminated by mechanical devices and appropriate light fixtures. Reflected glare is caused by light striking on highly polished surfaces. Reflected glare can be eliminated by relocating the work and source of light to prevent reflection towards the worker.

4. Right direction and reliability: Light must come from correct direction so as to prevent shadow falling on the object. The supply of light must also be reliable. Frequent power cuts resulting in disruption of lighting facility can be overcome by installing generators.

5. Economical and maintenance cost: The cost of operating and maintenance cost of lighting equipment must be less.

6. Elimination of abrupt contrast: The contrast between two surfaces is measured in terms of foot lambert. A foot lambert is a unit used to measure brightness of light. When the contrast between two surfaces is excessive, eye fatigue results from the frequent expansion and contraction of pupils of the eyes. An acceptable range for a contrast of light is a three to one ratio. This means that the brightness of the surface on which a task is being performed should not be greater than three times the brightness of the background.

7. No Dazzling light: As far as possible, the dazzling light should be avoided because they cannot perceive brightness beyond a certain limit. Otherwise it may lead to problem of eyesight of employees.

8. Light should be cool: The heat emitted by light often makes employees tiresome and this reduces their efficiency. Therefore, the light must not produce excess heat in office.

9. Light should be steady in its flow: Often there will be flickering in light due to objects passing through the source of light or due to sudden change in load. This produces undue eyestrain to employees and so the steady flow of light is essential.

10. Colour combination: The use of colour increases the illumination and helps in comfortable viewing. According to Bethel and others "light and paint are the Siamese twins of illumination. Together they are a team which can banish darkness; one without the other will only half do the job".

Importance of lighting in office

The importance of lighting in office can be realised from the fact that virtually every office task is a seeing task. Lighting in office must facilitate the office staff to seek clearly, quickly and accurately what one is doing. When the lighting facility is inadequate it results in delays and mistakes. The importance of lighting in office is reflected under the following:

1. To increase productivity: A study conducted by public building service of the federal government in an office of the Bureau of the Census revealed that there was an increase in productivity by 3.5 per cent when lighting was changed from 30 foot candles to 50 foot candles. Similarly, it was observed in yet another study conducted by the Bureau of Internal Revenue Office that when illumination was increased from 10 foot candles to 50 foot candles it resulted in 5.5 per cent increase in overall production.

2. To increase quality of work: By providing light upon accepted standard, it is possible to improve accuracy and neatness of office work to a large extent. Inadequacy of light leads to more errors owing to eye strain and fatigue.

3. Better employee morale: Provision of good lighting facility will improve the morale of employees. Good employee morale has many advantages such as higher productivity, reduced labour turnover and lowered absenteeism. It also results in attracting highly skilled employees.

4. To reduce fatigue and eye strain: A good lighting system first of all reduces the eye strain of employees. Secondly, it minimises the fatigue of employees. Thirdly, it helps the older employees from poor eyesight. Fourth, it reduces headache caused by poor light. Thus, it is responsible for maintaining the health of employees.

5. To improve the prestige of the company: An attractive and efficient lighting arrangement creates a favourable impression on visitors who visit the company. It adds to the reputation of the company for progressiveness and efficiency of operation.

Sources of light

There are two sources of light: (1) Natural or day light, (2) Artificial light.

1. Natural light: Light which is obtained from sun through the office roofs, doors and window openings are referred to as natural lighting. Natural lighting is affected by (*a*) the shape and size of windows, the colour of the glass and the extent of its cleanliness, (*b*) outside objects which block out light such as trees and buildings and (*c*) variable weather conditions which depend on time of the day and different seasons of the year.

Advantages of natural light

1. Its supply is plentiful.
2. It is available free of cost.
3. It requires no maintenance.
4. It is always available regularly.
5. Its distribution is uniform.

Disadvantages of natural light

1. It varies from season to season, day to day and sometimes even hour to hour.
2. It varies with the size and position of windows and roofs.
3. Its intensity cannot be altered.
4. It is available only during day time but not in the night.

2. Artificial light: Artificial light is used to supplement day light. In designing artificial lighting system the following steps are to be considered:

(*a*) Ascertain the foot candle illumination required both general and at specific work centre.
(*b*) Decide upon the most suitable type of lamp.
(*c*) Calculate the number of fittings required.
(*d*) Ascertain the voltage of the bulb required.

Types of artificial light

Artificial light suitable for office work can be of two types, (1) filament lamps or incandescent lighting and (2) fluorescent lamps. In choosing a particular type of lamp the following factors are to be considered: (1) initial outlay (2) cost of renewal (3) current consumption and (4) suitability and efficiency.

1. Filament or incandescent lamps: This type of light is produced by filament bulbs. These lamps involve less initial investment. They burn instantaneously when switched on. They require less maintenance and have longer life. But the intensity of light is insufficient for office work. They produce excess heat and do not possess natural day light colour. The filament temperature determines the life and efficiency of filament lamps. If the temperature of filament is high, the efficiency of light will also be high. But the life of the filament bulb will be short with a high temperature.

2. Fluorescent lamps: This types of lamps are very popularly used as it offers many advantages such as (*a*) they consume less power, (*b*) they do not provide shadow and glare, (*c*) they do not produce excess heat, (*d*) the light is distributed uniformly, (*e*) if has day light colour and (*f*) it has long life. But it has two disadvantages, *viz.*, (*a*) its initial investment is high and (*b*) its maintenance charges are high.

Types of lighting system

Lighting system consist of the following types:

1. Direct Lighting: Under this system, approximately 90 to 100 per cent of the lighting is directed downward to the working surface. This results in excessive glare and very little light is diffused. This is responsible for creation of shadows. So unless light fixtures are closely arranged, a uniform light may not be obtained.

2. Semi-direct lighting: Under this system, about 60 to 90 per cent of the light is directed downward, the remainder being directed outward. This system eliminates the shadows that are characteristics of direct lighting.

3. Indirect lighting: Under this system, about 90 to 100 per cent of the light is first directed upwards to the ceiling. The light is then diffused and reflected downward to the working area. As the light is diffused before it reaches the working surface, shadows and glare is eliminated under this system.

4. Semi-indirect lighting: Under this system, about 60 to 90 per cent of the lights is directed towards ceiling and is then reflected downwards. The balance of 40 to 10 per cent light is immediately directed downward.

5. General Diffuse Lighting: Under this system, about 40 to 60 per cent of light is directed to the working surface. The remainder of light is being reflected from ceiling. This system of lighting produces more light for the same voltage when compared to semi-indirect system. But the shadow and glare produced are more when compared to semi-indirect light. This system of light produces more glare and shadows.

Differences between Natural light and Artificial lig Ventilation

Point of differences	Natural ligh	Artificial light
1. Availability of light	It is available only during day time.	It is available both during day and night time.
2. Initial investment	It requires no investment as it is available at a free of cost, being the free gift of Nature.	It requires initial investment for its installation.
3. Cost of operation and aintenance	It does not require maintenance cost and no power cost need be incurred for its operation.	It requires maintenance and consumes power. So cost of operating it is more.
4. Quantity of supply	Its supply is in abundance.	Its supply is limited.
5. Regularity	It is availablethroughout the year. But the intensity varies from season to season.	Its availability depends upon electricity supply and during the period of power cut it is not available unless generators are installed.
6. Alteration of intensit	Its intensity cannot be altered.	Its intensity can be altered by using bulbs of different voltages.
7. Suitability	It is suitable during day time.	It is suitable during night time.
8. Colour	It has natural day light colour	The colour can be changed depending upon its requirmet.

9. Utility	It is used only in place where lightspreads.	It can be extended to interior places where natural light is restricted.
10. Uniformity	Natural light is distributed uniformly.	Articificial light is unevenly distributed.

Ventilation

The term ventilation in relation to office is used in a narrow and broad sense. In its narrow sense, ventilation is basically removal of stale air in the office building by fresh air. Inadequate ventilation results in discomfort and fatigue as the concentration of carbondioxide, humidity and temperature will rise in the office during working hours. To ensure a comfortable and healthy working atmosphere, it is necessary to provide a definite circulation of air throughout the office. As a rule, the ventilation is considered satisfactory where ventilation arrangements provide a change of air 4 to 6 times per hour.

In its broad sense, the term ventilation is used to create controlled environment which includes control of (*a*) ventilation, (*b*) temperature and (*c*) humidity.

Essential requirements of ventilation

In order to provide better working conditions and comfort to office staff, ventilation system should meet the following requirements:

1. Rate of supply of fresh air: The rate of supply of air in office depends upon its size and the number of office staff. The minimum rate of fresh air in the office is estimated at $20m^3$ per person per hour. A ventilation system should be designed so as to provide inflow of minimum air inside the office and flow of ventilated air from the office.

2. Air movement or air changes: For effective working of ventilation system, it is estimated that 5 or 6 air changes per hour is sufficient. Air change per hour is the volume of outside air allowed into a room in one hour compared with the volume of the room. The air movement must be uniform and should not be stagnant at any spot of the work. The free movement of air is secured by providing cross-ventilation in a naturally ventilated building. In a mechanically ventilated building, air movement is achieved by means of fans. Air movement should be ensured not only in terms of velocity but also in direction.

3. Cool air: The incoming air in an offi ce building through ventilation system should be cool in summer and warm in winter. This implies that effective temperature should be maintained with respect to comfortable conditions for different seasons of the year. Investigations undertaken with regard to temperature of air reveal that 20°C and 22°C of temperature is to be maintained during summer and winter respectively in office. However, the value of effective temperature depends upon the type of work to be done, geographical conditions, etc.

4. Purity of air: The ventilation system must provide for pure air which is free from impurities such as bad odours, dust and fumes. To get pure ventilated air, it is necessary that venilators should not be situated near chimneys, latrines and such other places.

Sources of ventilation

Supply of air in office can be provided from two sources, *viz.*, (1) Natural source and (2) Artificial source.

1. Natural source: This is considered to be the best source of ventilation in office as it involves no investment and maintenance cost. However, it is not always a reliable source because blow of wind varies from season to season. In order to derive the maximum ventilation in an office, it is necessary to make adequate provisions in the office building such as provision of required number of windows, constructing the building giving importance to the height of the building, and using building materials such as hollow blocks which permit inflow of air into office building.

2. Artificial ventilation: This source of ventilation involves the use of mechanical arrangement for providing enough ventilation into office building. This source of ventilation is expensive, as it involves initial investment on mechanical equipment, its operating cost and maintenance cost. But it is reliable source of ventilation when compared to artificial source. In this system, the outside air is supplied into office building either by positive ventilation which means the supply of air by means of a mechanical device such as a fan. Whereas the removal of air and its disposal outside by such a device is termed as *exhaust of air*. For positive ventiliation, fans of centrifugal type is used. They are mounted centrally so as to derive maximum air supply. For exhaust of air, propeller type of fans are used.

Heating

The offices, shops and Railways Premises Act 1963 (in U.K.) lays down minimum temperature requirements of an office as 67-70°F (about

19-21°C). A clerk's efficiency is impaired by an atmosphere which is either too cold or too hot. Any temperature of 75°F above brings about a reduction in efficiency by 15 per cent. Dryness of the air, with a temperature higher than 68°F lowers vitality, reduces resistance to infection and renders the individual hypersensitive to change in temperature. The ideal heating system for offices is one which gives an even heat throughout the room. The problems associated with heating are (*a*) the method of generating warmth and (*b*) the method of conserving it.

Method of heating

Heating systems can be classified into two methods; (*a*) Radiation method *i.e.*, by the direct rays of heat from the appliance and (*b*) convection methods, *i.e.*, by setting up warm current air.

The following are the important methods of heating by radiation:

1. Coal fire: Though they give cheerful appearance they leave behind ash which requires cleaning besides posing the problem of storage.

2. Gas fire: They have an improvement over coal fire in the sense that they are more clean and easily controlled when compared to coal fire.

3. Electric fire: This is quite popular and is very convenient for intermittent use.

The following are the important methods of heating by convection:

1. Central heating: This method is used in large buildings. It involves a boiler which is heated by coal, gas or oil. The heat so generated is supplied to different rooms.

2. Electric tubular heater: This apparatus consists of electric heating elements enclosed in thin metal tubes and are fixed on walls. They are connected to electric points and whenever heating facility is needed, by switching on, heat is generated.

3. Electric floor warming: Under this method, electric cables are used beneath the surface of the floor. The cables are heated during nights and switched off during the day. The heat so generated is retained throughout the day. But it involves heavy capital investment initially.

Noise control

It is felt that noise and office executives are enemies of long standing. The effect of excess noise in an office is very distressing and may lead to poor mental and physical health. The chief sources of noise within the office are telephones, typewriters, office machines, conversations and the movement of people. Research has shown that noise can raise the heartbeat, blood pressure, increase muscular tension and decrease the rate of digestion. Intermittent noises are more distracting than constant noise and higher the volume, the more annoying it becomes. Noise bears a direct relationship with the efficiency of office work. Performance is affected through lack of concentration, difficulty in hearing clearly, increased mistakes, lower morale and increased fatigue.

Methods of reducing noise

(*a*) Noise can be reduced by sound proofing with the help of acoustic material. The ceilings and walls are treated with sound absorbent materials.

(*b*) By using automatic door closer and rubber stops noise can be reduced. Further, doors do not slam and thus less wear and tear is caused to doors.

(*c*) By partially controlling telephone bells.

(*d*) Covering floors with rubber or carpets which reduces noise caused by the movement of people.

(*e*) Encouraging employees to speak in ordinary conversational tones and not to speak loudly.

(*f*) Isolating noisy machines in a sound proof room and by using noiseless typewriter.

(*g*) Planning the work routine so that walking distance can be minimised.

(*h*) Arranging for conference or interviews to take place in a special room.

(*i*) If possible siting offices away from noise, *i.e.*, away from noise of machinery or traffic on the outside street. Alternatively double windows may be necessary to reduce noise.

Safety

When compared to accidents that occur in factory, the number of accidents in offices is negligible. However, accidents do occur in office, varying from minor cuts caused by razor blades to a serious fall while climbing up tall filing shelves. Accidents cause both direct and indirect loss to the business. Firstly, the injured person is to be given treatment involving medical expenses. Secondly, there will be a loss of time in work, owing to the inability of the accident victim to work. Thirdly, other workers stop their work to see if they can help the injured person or to discuss about accident. It is the duty of office manager to create a sense of safety—consciousness among office staff. He must also make sure that first-aid kits are available. It is also necessary to train one of the office staff in giving first aid treatment. It is in the interest of management and everyone concerned to know about the fire precautions. At the same time it must be ensured that all fire fighting equipments are made available and operational. Finally, the office manager must ensure that the accidents are reported according to company and legal requirements.

The following are some of the causes of accidents:

(*a*) Loss of concentration through distraction, emotional problem or some form of tension.
(*b*) General apathy created by the situation within the office.
(*c*) Carelessness caused by overconfidence or poor attitude.
(*d*) General indifference.
(*e*) Disobedience of instruction given to avoid accidents.
(*f*) Negligence.
(*g*) Lack of training.
(*h*) An foreseen situation.
(*i*) Poor maintenance of equipment.
(*j*) General fatigue or drowsiness.

Types of office accidents

The following types of office accidents provide for the office manager about various areas of improvement:

(*a*) Slipping on poor flooring.
(*b*) Tripping over obstacles such as parcels, small items and leads from telephones and machines.
(*c*) Tripping over poorly maintained stairs.
(*d*) Catching clothing and the body on sharp edges such as corners of desks, extended drawers and machines.
(*e*) Colliding with other people, with open filing drawers or with clear-glass doors.
(*f*) Electric shocks from poorly maintained points.
(*g*) Fire and small explosions through incorrect use of inflammable liquids or gas.

Steps to control accidents

(1) To keep all gangways clear.
(2) To keep all corridors clear.
(3) To maintain floors and stairs regularly.
(4) To avoid leaving parcels or any items lying around in the office.
(5) To display warning notices of any temporary or permanent hazard.
(6) To encourage tidiness.
(7) To make flow of work between employees easy and rearrange to avoid possible collisions.

(8) Clear-glass doors should be fitted with prominent warnings signs
(9) To avoid placing articles in precarious high positions.
(10) To use step-ladders rather than chairs to reach high positions.
(11) To use scientific loading of store cupboards.
(12) To emphasis through notices and remainders the dangers of lighted cigarettes, inflammable liquids and any other inflammable items used in the office.
(13) To maintain regularly all electrical wiring and points and do not allow misuse.
(14) To ensure that the first-aid kit is ready and well stocked.
(15) To remind supervisors periodically of the importance of accident prevention.

Floor covering

Floor covering has assumed more importance in modern commercial office on account of improving the decoration as well as controlling the noise. The following factors are to be considered while laying down the floor coverings:

1. General comfort under foot: The floor covering should have an even surface, should not produce noise while walking and should retain the same temperature when compared to the rest of the room.

2. Cleanliness: The floor covering should be capable of cleaning and it should not allow accumulation of dirt on it.

3. Durability: It should be durable and should be capable of resisting temperature, decay and disintegration.

4. Sound reflection: It should have sound-absorption qualities.

5. Easy of repair: It should be repaired easily.

6. Fire resistance: It should resist fire to a reasonable extent.

7. Maintenance: It should be easy to keep it in good condition.

8. Good appearance: It should give good appearance.

9. Reasonable cost: The cost of purchasing it should not be excessive.

Some of the important material used as floor covering are tiles, carpet, wood, rubber and so on.

Air-conditioning

By popular usage the term *air-conditioning* is used to describe a system which provides cooling of the atmosphere within a building structure. Technically speaking, air-conditioning refers to simultaneous control of air, temperature humidity, motion, distribution, pressure and purity including such factors as dust, odours, bacteria and toxic gases. A true air-conditioning system must be able to provide control over all these factors both during summer and winter seasons. Air-conditioning in office is important on account of the following:

(*a*) It provides comfort to office staff.
(*b*) It safeguards the health of employees.
(*c*) It increases the efficiency of the office staff.
(*d*) It reduces absenteeism.
(*e*) It reduces the cleaning and redecorating cost by utilising an integrated air-conditioning system.

System of air-conditioning

On the basis of location of air-conditioning equipments, air-conditioning can be classified into three systems. They are:

1. Central system: Under this system, the air-conditioning equipment is installed in one central point instead of providing separate units of air-conditioning unit for every room. There, the conditioned air is distributed to all the rooms by ducts. This system of air-conditioning requires less space for installation, its maintenance is easy and it also economical.

2. Self-contained or unitary system: Under this system, an attractive portable air-conditioning plant is placed inside the room near the ceiling or window. This air-conditioning plant is self-contained in all respects and conditioned air is formed inside the unit itself. This conditioned air is circulated into the room without the help of any ducts.

3. Semi-contained or unitary-central system: Under this system, air-conditioning plant is installed in each and every room. But the conditioned air is supplied from central system. For supplying the conditioned air to each member of air conditioning plant, it requires small sized ducts. Alternatively, conditioned air may be supplied from a central plant but the heating or cooling may be carried in the room itself.

Supply of water

Adequate supply of drinking water is a must in all offices. It is estimated that on an average a person drinks water atleast 5 times a day. And if the distance to be covered is more by an employee for the sake of drinking water, he would waste more of his time. So, water is to be made available at convenient points in office premises. Further, water to be provided must be cool. When adequate supply of water is not available, the cost of acquiring it is to be given more importance. Water for drinking purpose must be pure and without contamination.

Toilet facilities

Adequate number of toilets are to be made available to office staff. In most of the countries, the Law lays down that a minimum of one toilet is to be provided for every 20 persons and a separate toilet for each sex. In addition to toilets, washing facilities must also be provided for. Cleaning substances such as soaps, and towels are equally important ingredients. Proper arrangements must be made to clean all toilets and wash rooms from time to time. It is also necessary to provide toilet and washing facilities near working areas. Otherwise, clerks will spend too much of their time in going to and coming from toilets and wash rooms.

Security and secrecy

The main purpose of office security is to safeguard the (*a*) records, (*b*) cash and (*c*) office equipment. As a precautionary measure in some offices, a stranger is not at all allowed into the office. In most of the offices, as a matter of rule, the visitors are expected to deposit their belongings into the hands of watch and ward staff. To ensure safety and security, all doors are locked and windows and skylights are wire meshed.

The following steps are taken to safeguard the office property:

1. Cash security: Under this type of security, the person who handles cash of the business is expected to deposit certain amount of cash at the time of his appointment. This ensures safety from fraud and misappropriation of each belonging to business.

2. Reference checking: This step is taken at the time of recruitment. The incumbent is expected to furnish the reference of reputed persons who provide the information regarding honesty and integrity of the person who is to be appointed by the employer.

3. Provision of safes: Costly equipment, cash and other confidential matters are always preserved in steel safes and locked. The keys are kept only by responsible persons.

4. Insurance: For loss of property arising out of the theft, burglary, fire, etc., insurance may be taken by the employer.

Secrecy of business on Internal Security

It refers to safeguarding the intangible asset of the office. The secrets of office operations are considered as an intangible assets. The secrets in office may related to accumulated experience, research in production process, quality control reports, routing sheets, names and addresses of suppliers of raw materials, new product development, maintenance schedules, future plans for expansion. All these knowledge should be used exclusively for the company's benefit but not exposed to competitors.

Types of information

Broadly speaking information in office can be classified into two types: (1) Open Information and (2) Confidential Information:

1. Open Information: Open information refers to information which is meant for advertising purpose. Examples of open information are financial statements to be advertised to meet legal requirements, advertisements about the financial prospects to build the image of the company, information regarding the skill and knowledge of prospective employees, the employer is seeking to recruit.

2. Confidential Information: It is a type of information which a company deems it necessary to withhold from being released to unauthorised persons. Examples of confidential information are, changes in the use of technology, costs incurred in production, productivity records and so on.

Educational safeguards

One way of controlling the dissemination of information through employees is to educate them on the following topics:

(*a*) The importance of proprietary information about the company's ability to compete successfully and about its expansion programmes.

(*b*) The need for an employee to avoid discussing confidential topics, technical and professional matters.

(*c*) Employees' responsibilities for maintaining control over documents entrusted to them and for assuring that these documents are returned for storage or destruction when they are no longer required.

(*d*) The need for employees to avoid leaving confidential papers and documents as they may be seen copied or taken away by unauthorised persons.

Dust control

Whenever office buildings are situated near market places and on busy streets, they are prone to excessive dust. Similarly, offices established near certain factories such as cotton mills, jute mills, etc., are also exposed to dust. When dust enters into office buildings it not only affects the health of office staff, but also reduces efficiency. The importance of dust control can be enumerated as follows:

(*a*) To improve efficiency of office staff.

(*b*) To maintain good health of office staff.

(*c*) To maintain efficiency of lighting as accumulated dust on light fixture reduces brightness.

(*d*) To maintain cleanliness in the office which is very important both from the point of view of visitors and office staff.

(*e*) To keep up the life of office records and office equipment.

The following steps are to be taken to prevent accumulation of dust:

1. To clean doors, windows, walls and ceilings frequently.
2. To clean tables, desks, chairs, equipment from time to time.
3. To improve upon illumination, light fixtures are to be cleaned on a regular basis.
4. To use carpets so as to prevent dust due to movement of people.
5. Use of air-conditioning system to avoid adverse effects of dust.
6. Frequent washing of the floors and corridors to avoid accumulation of dust.

QUESTIONS

Objective Type Question

1. What do you mean by office environment?
2. What is meant by psychomatics?
3. Mention four colour considerations which affect office environment.
4. Mention any four advantages of natural lighting.
5. Mention any four disadvantages of artificial lighting.
6. Define office ventilation.
7. Mention four essentials of office ventilation.
8. Distinguish between ventilation and air-conditioning.
9. Mention three methods of heating in office building.
10. Mention three systems of air-conditioning.
11. Distinguish between office security and secrecy.

Analytical Type Questions

1. Explain the importance of office environment.
2. Briefly explain the role of cleanliness as a factor of office environment.
3. Explain the impact of interior decoration of an office over visitors and office staff.
4. Briefly explain the characteristic feature of good lighting in office building.
5. Explain the importance of lighting in office.
6. State the merits and demerits of natural and artificial lighting used in office.

7. Distinguish between natural and artificial lighting.
8. Briefly explain the different types of lighting system applicable in an office.
9. Briefly explain the essential requirements of office ventilation.
10. Explain the sources of office ventilation.
11. Explain the need for and methods of noise control in an office.
12. State the various causes of accidents in an office.
13. State the steps to be taken to prevent office accidents.
14. Outline the factors to be considered in laying down floor covering.
15. Outline the importance of air-conditioning in an office.
16. Explain briefly the systems of air-conditioning in an office.
17. Explain the significance of water and toilet facilities as environmental factors in an office.
18. What are the security measures that are to be taken to safeguard office property?
19. Outline the importance of dust control and steps to be taken to control dust in an office.

Essay Type Question

1. Explain the various environmental factors which improve efficiency of workers in an office.

9

Office Supervision

INTRODUCTION

The Term *Supervisor* has its roots in the *master* whose counterpart in the olden days happened to be the master craftsman. He served as a real boss with autocratic power in respect of recruitment, training, entrusting work, remunerating and controlling the subordinate. However, according to Peter Drucker, the supervisor's job arose from the position of foreman who is concerned with getting the work done through employees. Today's supervisor combines some of the qualities of both *foreman* and the *master*. A Supervisor is a mediator between top level management, on the one hand, and rank-and-file workers, on the other. According to Viteles M.I. supervision refers to the direct immediate guidance and control of subordinates in the performance of their task.

Definition of supervisor

Littlefield and Peterson define a supervisor as "a person who carries out lower level responsibilities for higher level management and has direct control over personnel."

Terry defines supervisor as a "management member working at an organisational level where personal oversight of tasks assigned to small groups is assumed in order to assure satisfactory performance."

Supervision includes three elements. They are:

1. Commanding: In the process of commanding, the supervisor assigns work among his subordinates and gives them orders and directions for its performance. He also provides them with amenities needed for performance of work.

2. Guidance: The second important element of supervision is guidance of subordinates. If need be, the supervisor has to train them also. The process of guidance includes telling the subordinate about methods and procedures of doing work and solving their difficulties.

3. Controlling: The third element of supervision is the control process. A supervisor has to ensure that the work is carried out according to plans and in the desired manner. He has to take corrective action if he sees that the work is not progressing according to plans. For exercising control, the supervisor is given power to reward or punish his subordinate.

Importance of supervision

(1) It is necessary for effective direction.
(2) It ensures workers perform their duties satisfactorily.
(3) It facilitates co-operation and co-ordination among staff.
(4) It helps in implementing the policies.
(5) It facilitates systematic performance of work in the office. In the absence of supervision, each worker will do what he likes.
(6) It makes sure that the quality of work is maintained and the wastage is eliminated.
(7) It maintains discipline in the office.

Principles of effective supervision

Supervision will be effective if the following principles are borne in mind:

1. Proper organisational climate: The most essential aspect of management is that the managers must realise the importance of a supervisor and due respect must be granted to his position. In addition to this, the supervisor must be paid attractive salary and he must be conferred with certain rights and powers. To enhance his prestige and efficiency, his suggestions, recommendations and ideas should be given due consideration.

2. The supervisor must be informed about the nature and scope of his work: A supervisor can efficiently function and guide his subordinates only when he clearly knows the exact nature and scope of his job.

3. Delegating sufficient freedom and direction to subordinates: Effective supervision is based on granting maximum freedom to the subordinates. Once the subordinates have been properly, motivated and explained about his work and objectives to be achieved, they should be left free to achieve it according to their own ability and skill.

4. Developing good human relations with subordinates: Pressure tactics do not work well in the long run. The supervisor should treat his subordinates as human beings and should pay regard to their difficulties so that he develops a team of willing workers rather than crowd of hostile slaves.

5. Supervisors should not be required to do production work: As far as possible, a supervisor must serve only as a friend, philosopher and guide to workers. He should not substitute himself to the employees.

6. Ensuring effective communication: A supervisor is connecting link between management and employees. He must translate the decisions of management properly for the common understanding of the employees. Similarly, the problems of employees must be properly represented to the management for taking actions promptly.

7. Close supervision should be avoided: Supervision can be of two types (*a*) close and (*b*) general. When each and every activity of the subordinate is keenly and continuously watched, it is known as close supervision. This type of supervision is less effective as it reduces the freedom and kills the initiative of his subordinates.

General supervision means granting more freedom to subordinates in his methods of work. Here the subordinate is only told what he is to do. How he is to do and the manner in which he has to do is left to him. General supervision motivates workers and creates a sense of responsibility in them.

Types of office supervisors

Based on the degree of supervision, supervisors are classified as first line supervisors, second-line supervisors, and third-line supervisors. The first-line supervisor is concerned with the supervision of workers at the bottom of the organisation directly. Thus, he comes into contact directly with the employees and besides supervising the work of such employees, he guides, assists and controls their activities. This type of a supervisor is seen in relatively small sized business establishments. The second-line supervisor is concerned with supervision of one or more first-line supervisors. Such type of supervisors are found in medium size business organisations. Often they are called by other names such as office superintendent. The third-line supervisor supervises one or more second-line supervisors. Such supervisors are found in large sized organisations and are often called by the name office manager. The following are various types of supervisors found in an organisation:

1. Autocratic or authoritarian supervisor: An autocratic supervisor reserves the authority with himself in terms of his area of supervision. He will take a decision without consulting others. Though he plans the future course of action, he will not let others know the future plans. Instead, he will inform his subordinates what immediate steps they must take. The subordinates have to strictly obey the command of the supervisor without questioning the authority. He does not consult his subordinates on any matters and he remains aloof from the group for most of the time.

2. Free Rein or independent supervisor: A free rein supervisor avoids using his powers indiscriminately. Instead of dictating the terms to the subordinates, he leaves the problem for them to deal with. He gives the power to his subordinates to establish goals and to carryout the activities to achieve the goals. The free rein supervisor assists his subordinates to solve any problem they face with. The role of free rein supervisor is a passive one as he does not interfere with his subordinates. In fact he does not lead his subordinates but merely provides resources required by them. This type of supervisor is also known as *Laissez Faire* supervisor.

3. Democratic or participative supervisor: A democratic supervisor consults his subordinates before taking a decision and issuing the orders. He allows his subordinates to participate in the group discussions and contribute their ideas for the attainment of the group objective. He will chalk out the plan on the long term basis and informs in advance the future course of action to be taken by his subordinates. He trusts them in terms of their abilities and capacities and reposes full confidence with them. He gives an opportunity to his subordinates to take initiative and to use their judgement in solving some of the problems.

4. Task-centered supervisor: A task centered supervisor is mostly concerned with the performance of the task assigned using standard methods and procedure. He has firm belief in getting the work done by devising better method, by keeping his subordinates ever busy and rewarding or punishing to get the work done.

5. Employee-centred supervisor: An employee centred supervisor gives utmost importance to his subordinates rather than the work to be performed by them. He infact looks after the welfare of his subordinates by solving their problems. He gives more emphasis to improve the human relations within the group of subordinates.

Position of office supervisors

The industrial revolution which is characterised by mass production by mechanical means and division of labour, has changed the position of supervisor to one of bewildering and often frustrating complexity. Today's supervisor is a vigorous leader of men, a shrewd and effective planner of work and source of technical know-how. The position of the supervisor is correctly viewed as "the supervisor occupies a twilight position between the manager above him and workers below him and is squeezed between them." This statement implies that supervisor is a man in the middle—a buffer between the management and labour, a grass root of management as well as an agent of management. In a bid to span the two different groups, he often falls in between. He is in an unenviable position belonging to both the groups or neither of them. He cannot identify himself totally with either the category of management or employees.

Though manager above him expect him to function as their spokesman in relation to workers and also to be the transmitter of information and instructions from management to labour but he is accepted as part of the management. He is not taken into confidence by higher level managers. He is not given enough authority to make operational goal and to enforce discipline amongst workers. His authority position in the organisation decisions, to accomplish organisational position in the organisation is weak and vague. There is much rigidity the regimentation in his job situation with the result, he may feel suffocated. He often tends to get confused. Often managers, above him come down heavily upon him whenever they feel that he failed in meeting the production schedules, keeping up production and keeping down costs. Managers above him brand him as disloyal and as one who lets down the management. They view him as the chief culprit, responsible for conspiring with his group members to sabotage the goals of the organisation. His group members also expect him to behave in a supportive manner to function as their representative in the council of management, to champion their cause, to uphold and protect their interests. Sometimes they question his authority and power by implication and brand him as pro-managerial and anti-worker. They even develop feelings of suspicion, hostility and ill-will towards him.

The supervisor's position is such that he is often in a dilemma as to whom to please. If he pleases one group, he is bound to incur the displeasure of the other. If he tries to please both the groups, he tends to incur the displeasure of both. He cannot establish adequate and enduring relations with either the managers or the workers because of such conflicts in the role expectations.

Since the supervisor is face to face with the rank and file workers, he is often confronted with the problem of labour union pressures and interference in the normal working of his unit.

The supervisor also gets continuous stream of advice, suggestions, etc., from several specialised staff and it is a problem for him to decide whether he is being advised or helped or is being interfered with. In most cases, the supervisor's much time is wasted in paper work, *i.e.*, filing, etc.

This leaves inadequate time for his supervisory work. Supervisors also look for job security because in times of down turn, management may resort to pulling down the supervisors rank in the hierarchy. Thus, in view of all these problems, the supervisor generally feels handicapped and helpless in carrying his job satisfactorily.

Essentials of good supervision

The essentials of good supervision can be classified into two categories *viz.*, (*a*) characteristics of good supervisors and (*b*) skills of supervisors. This is shown in the following chart:

Essentials of good supervision

Characteristics of good supervisors	**Special skills of supervisors**
Achieving cooperation	Human relations skills
Listening	Teaching skills
Making decision	Communications skills
Delegating	
Understanding others	
Fairness	

Characteristics of good supervisors

Among the various characteristics which make a good supervisor, the following are the important ones:

1. Achieving cooperation: It may be said that without the cooperation of subordinates, the supervisors' job becomes very difficult. Cooperation can be achieved by showing an interest in considering subordinates as individuals and also in the work they do. Another way of achieving it is to make subordinates aware of the fact that top-level management depends upon the workers for their ideas and suggestions. Thirdly, by providing as much variety as possible in the daily routine activities, cooperation can be achieved by the supervisor. It is difficult for a supervisor to have the full cooperation of subordinates who lack interest in their job. Fourthly, by solving all the problems which the subordinates face, the supervisor can get cooperation from them.

2. Listening: This is considered to be another important characteristic of the supervisor. The relationship between the supervisor and subordinates depends upon the extent of listening to the subordinates by the supervisor. Often the supervisor is guilty of not listening to subordinates who wish to discuss a situation. Such a habit reflects negatively on a supervisor since the subordinate is likely to have an impression that the supervisor has little concern for him. Apart from listening to subordinates, the supervisor must also pay attention to or concentrate on what the subordinate has to say for establishing a good relationship. The supervisor can become a more effective listener in many ways. One way is to pay full attention to the subordinates and prevent their comments from being blocked out. The second way of listening is to evaluate the merits of the subordinates' suggestions. The third way is by maintaining an open mind rather than an emotional or biased feelings. Effective listening involves more than understanding the words. Understanding the discussion also includes facial expressions, gestures and so on.

3. Making decisions: The third characteristic of a good supervisor is the ability to take a prompt decision at the grass root level. Inefficient decision making is on account of wrong identification of the problem or vague identification of the situations surrounding the problems. Very often supervisors fail to distinguish properly between the problems and their symptoms. Unless the symptoms are clearly analysed, decisions may be somewhat ineffective. The supervisor must consider the impact of the decision on future course of activities. The future impact should be considered especially if the decisions are likely to have a significant effect on employees, work process or financial resources.

Having taken a decision, it is to be communicated to those who will be affected by the decision. Communication of decisions is very important as its acceptability is greatly affected by the manner in which the details of the decisions are communicated.

Some decisions are affected by certain techniques. Such devices may be in the form of progress reports, briefing sessions and other types of follow-up measure. Where corrective measures are needed the supervisor must consider such suitable measures.

4. Delegating: Effective and meaningful delegation of tasks to subordinates is yet another characteristic of a good supervisor. However, in practice, the supervisor hesitates to delegate the authority to subordinates for several reasons. The following guidelines are of immense use to supervisors in this context:

(i) Select the appropriate person to whom a task is being delegated.
(ii) Select tasks that can be delegated.
(iii) Help the person to whom tasks have been delegated.
(iv) To make sure that work assignments are fully understood.

But the process of delegation is subject to one limitation, that is, the delegated task can be performed in more than one method, other than the one suggested by the supervisor. In this regard, there must be good understanding between a supervisor and subordinates as to the best method that can be followed in discharging the delegated task.

5. Understanding others: As one of the characteristics, it is necessary for the supervisor to have a thorough understanding of the needs, drives, interests and attitudes of every subordinate in order to motivate them. The following aspects of the subordinates deserve special understanding by the supervisor:

(*i*) *Social Traits*: In order to understand the subordinates, an awareness of the social traits of the subordinates is needed. Some of the social traits that are to be understood are subordinates' aggressiveness; his tendency to withdraw, or to dominate the situation or to put others at ease.

(*ii*) *Personality traits*: Personality understanding is necessary to gain confidence of the subordinates by the supervisor. Such an understanding is also used to assess the emotional needs of subordinates.

(*iii*) *Character*: The understanding of the character of subordinates is essential to entrust work of high responsibility to such person whose character is sound.

(*iv*) *Work habits*: The understanding of work habits of subordinates relates to the interest, initiative, integrity. Such an understanding is necessary to determine the degree of supervision that subordinates require.

(*v*) *Relations with others*: Such as understanding helps the supervisor in knowing the cooperative spirit of subordinates. Again involvement of such persons on group work and utilising them for public relations can also be decided on the basis of this understanding.

(*vi*) *Fairness*: Fairness, as one of the characteristic of the supervisor is essential to establish a good relationship between himself and his boss. Very often subordinates towards whom supervisor has negative feelings are ill-treated, whereas with those on whom he is having positive feelings are favoured. The best practice for supervisors is to treat all subordinates equally in similar situations.

Special skills of the supervisor

Apart from the above discussed characteristics, a supervisor must also possess some of the skills to be effective. These skills are as follows:

1. Human relation skills: A supervisor must acquire human relation skill in order to secure full cooperation of the subordinates. Once the superior-subordinate relationship is spoilt, it becomes difficult to expect the subordinates to be loyal to the office functions. It is the human relation skills which enable the supervisor to get better ideas as to how to treat each subordinate. Human relation skills can be learnt either through on-the-job training or through courses designed by universities.

2. Teaching skills: As supervisors are expected to train or teach subordinates, they must necessarily possess teaching skills. The areas in which the supervisor needs training for effective teaching are in demonstrating, explaining, and in evaluating subordinates' performance. Teaching skills can be acquired both by experience and by attending to the courses run by professional institutions.

3. Communication skills: The success of supervisory function, to a large extent, depends upon communication skills. A supervisor must be aware of factors that are responsible for impeding the communication process. Communication also involves the ability to show empathy and concern for others.

Functions of supervisor

The following are the important functions of supervisor:

1. Planning: This is considered to be the most important function of supervisor as considerable amount of time is spent on this function. Some of the functions relating to planning are (*i*) determining the objects to be attained by the office staff, (*ii*) determining the policies through which the objective could be achieved and (*iii*) prepare time schedules for performing different types of work in office.

2. Organising: Organising function of a supervisor involves fitting in the best employee for each and every job in the office and thereby assigning such jobs to the appropriate subordinates. This function also involves development of an environment in which subordinates can be productive and efficient.

3. Staffing: The staffing function of a supervisor is limited but not extensive. However, higher-level supervisors exercise more control while selecting new employees. Some of the staffing functions of a supervisor are (*i*) orienting new employees, (*ii*) training new employees and (*iii*) counselling employees.

4. Directing: The directing function of a supervisor includes (*i*) leading, (*ii*) motivating, (*iii*) developing, (*iv*) recognising and (*v*) criticising subordinates. In order to make directing, functions more effective, a supervisor must not only be concerned with the goals and objectives of the organisation but also with how well the needs of each subordinate are related to the organisation's goals and objectives.

5. Controlling: The supervisor is concerned with comparing actual results with anticipated results. The supervisor is responsible for taking corrective action if the actuals are less than the expected results. It is also the responsibility of the supervisors to determine the validity of the standards that are set and to develop work measurement methods.

Duties and responsibilities of office supervisor

More specifically, the duties of office supervisor can be listed as under:

General duties

(1) To establish the climate of human relationship at the departmental level of the organisation.

(2) To shape the attitudes that motivates employees towards better performance on their jobs.

(3) To interpret and apply company policies, work specifications and job orders.

(4) To train new employees and instruct the existing employees to work effectively and safely.

(5) To counsel and exercise discipline over employees.

(6) To initiate or recommend personnel actions such as promotions, transfers, and discharges.

(7) To plan and maintain time and work schedules.

(8) To adjust and improve work procedures, using his knowledge of equipment capacities.

(9) To take necessary steps to improve quality of office work.

(10) To coordinate the activities of his department in such a way as to meet its goals economically.

Main duties

(1) Giving instruction to the subordinates to do the work.

(2) Controlling the staff to see that it is done.

(3) Maintaining good human relations with staff.

In relation to the work

(1) Plan the work of the section.

(2) See that work is done on time.

(3) Secure accuracy.

(4) Coordinate the work with other sections or departments.

(5) Distribute work fairly.

(6) Develop new methods of doing the work.

In relation to subordinates

(1) Delegates responsibilities.

(2) Settle personal frictions, jealousies etc.

(3) Give credit where it is due.
(4) Maintain discipline and reprimand when necessary.

In relation to superiors and associates

(1) Accept responsibilities for the work of the office.
(2) Cooperate with other supervisors.
(3) Permit and encourage interchange of staff.

A supervisor is responsible for the following personnel in an organisation:

1. Higher Management (Office manager): The supervisor is responsible for implementing the policy and philosophy of the management in the office department of the business enterprise. He has to ensure strict maintenance of discipline on the employees in respect of their arrival and departure and smooth working in the office. He is responsible for carrying out the orders as issued by the top management in terms of executing the work.

2. Co-Supervisor: An office supervisor has to work in liaison with the supervisors of other departments. A supervisor is a member of a peer group, and many of his successes or failures depend upon the way in which he can influence or is influenced by his associates.

3. Employee: The supervisor is responsible for providing all the furniture and stationery required by the employees. He must also arrange for the provision of good physical facilities required in the office such as lighting, ventilation, air-conditioning and so on. He is responsible for settling the grievances of office staff. He is also responsible for the induction, training, and motivation of office staff.

4. Unions: The office supervisor is responsible for negotiating both with union leaders as well as with management to settle any problems that may creep in the office.

Training office supervisors

One of the most important factors in designing training programmes for supervisors is determining the areas in which they need training. Some of the topics frequently covered in supervisory training programme include.

(1) Delegating work
(2) Disciplining employees
(3) Training Employees
(4) Hiring, orienting and promoting employees
(5) Handling grievances
(6) Scheduling work

(7) Quality control of work
(8) Developing effective work procedures
(9) Developing effective human relation skills
(10) Developing effective communication skills
(11) Developing effective counselling skills

Those supervisory training programmes which are more intensive are conducted over a short period of time, while less intensive programmes lasts for a longer period of time.

Supervisory committee

This is considered to be one of the recent developments in the office management. It is a forum under which the supervisors discuss matters of common interest among themselves. This committee is constituted in addition to representation given by office manager to the main committees set up at top level management. A supervisors' committee is formed to discuss the problems faced by them so that the management can solve such problems on representation. The committee also provides an opportunity to solve various problems faced by supervisors by the combined efforts and judgement of the committee.

Span of supervision

The phrase *span of supervision* refers to the number of subordinates who can be successfully directed by a supervisor. This is based on the theory of relationship, which gives theoretical ground for limiting the number of subordinates who can be directed and controlled by a supervisor. It has been the experience all along in the business world that too many subordinates attached to a single supervisor leads to friction, delay and confusion. It is estimated that the ideal number of subordinates to be attached to a supervisor can be 9 or 10.This is so because every supervisor has limited capacity to supervise his subordinates. When too many subordinates are attached to a supervisor, it becomes difficult to assign tasks, answer their questions, motivate and coordinate the work of all the subordinates.

The concept of span of management was first developed by V.A. Graicunes, a French management consultant in 1953. The span of control varies from organisation to organisation. The following factors determine the span of supervision:

1. Ability of the supervisor: The leadership qualities such as initiative, enthusiasm, ability to make quick decision and effect communication, possessed by the supervisor determine the span of supervision. The span will be wider if the supervisor possess these skills in greater degree when compared to others.

2. Time available for supervision: The span of supervision will be narrow at the top level as top management has less time to supervise. Instead, they have to spend more time in planning, directing, organising, decision making and controlling. Whereas the bottom level management can spread more time in supervising as they are not overburdened with all managerial functions.

3. Duties and responsibilities of the executives: The duties of a chief executive is more complicated when compared to departmental managers or even the lower level managers, hence, the span of supervision will be less at the level of managing directors and more at the stage of middle and lower level management.

4. Ability of subordinates: An experienced subordinate requires less of supervisors' time when compared to a new entrant to the job. Similarly, subordinates with good judgement, sense of responsibility, knowledge, experience, etc., need less help from a supervisor.

5. Repetitiveness of activities: Routine and repetitive types of problems can be solved more easily than complicated problems which arise occasionally. Similarly, familiar job can be performed more easily and with less effort. In this case, the span of supervision will be wider.

6. Degree of decentralisation: If the degree of centralisation is high, the span of supervision will be narrow. On the other hand, if the degree of decentralisation is high, the span of supervision will be wide.

7. Availability of staff assistance: If the assistance provided by the staff officers are more, the span of supervision will be narrow. Such assistance may be in the form of guidance on methods, routing schedules, quality standards, attending to personnel problems, etc.

Impact of span of supervision on organisation structure

The span of supervision has a close relationship with the organisation structure of an enterprise. A narrow span of supervision will cause a tall structure and a wide span will involve a flat one. Further, a narrow span of supervision will involve more levels of management and *vice versa*.

Impact of wide span of supervision

A wide span of supervision involves less supervisors to supervise the subordinates. This will naturally involve less supervision cost. It also involves less number of levels of management through which communication can take place more effectively. It also leads to better coordination of work. However, the performance of work may not be equal to the expected standard because of supervising a large number of subordinates. It may not be possible to give individual attention by the supervisor to each and every subordinate.

Impact of narrow span of supervision

A narrow span of supervision will involve increased cost of supervision. With the increase in the levels of management, the communication process will be more complicated, both upwards and downwards. There will be the problems of coordination because of increased number of levels in management. But it has the advantage of establishing better contacts between the supervisors and subordinate. It also facilitates strict control and ensures closer supervision.

QUESTIONS

Objective Type Questions

1. Define a Supervisor.
2. State three elements of supervision.
3. Distinguish between first-line and second-line supervisors.
4. What do you mean by third-line supervisor?
5. What is a supervisors' committee?
6. What is meant by span of supervision?

Analytical Type Questions

1. Outline the importance of supervision in an office.
2. Briefly discuss the principles of effective supervision.
3. Explain the different types of office supervisor.
4. Discuss the position of office supervisor.
5. Explain the functions of office supervisor.
6. Outline the duties of office supervisor.

Essay Type Questions

1. Explain fully the essentials of good supervision.
2. What is span of supervision? Explain the factors which determine the span of supervision. What is the impact of span of supervision on organisation structure?

10

Records Management—Filing and Indexing

INTRODUCTION

Maintenance of important documents and records is one of the most important aspects of office management. The management of every organisation will have to refer to various correspondence both incoming and outgoing relating to sales, purchases, credit, employee work history, equipment and other company assets and multitude of other items. If these records are not systematically maintained, it will lead to confusion and delay in locating them. Much of the time is lost in searching documents which have not been maintained scientifically. In order to enable the management to act promptly, it is very essential for ready tracing and identification of records. Records management is thus an aspect of office management which is concerned with receiving, handling, preserving and destruction of old records.

Definition and types of records

Records refer to the informational documents utilised by an organisation to carry out its various functions.

According to Ricks and Gow, "Records refers to all books, papers, photographs, maps or other documentary materials, regardless of physical form or characteristic, made or received for legal purposes in connection with the transaction of business".

Records contain information about and evidence of organisational functions, policies, decision, procedures, operations, and other activities. A record may take different forms such as paper, microfilms, computer type, video disk and so on.

Types of records

The records dealt within an office can be classified on the following basis: (*i*) Importance of records and (*ii*) Its contents.

1. On the Basis of importance of records: According to this basis, records can be classified into four types. They are:

(*a*) *Vital records*: Vital Records are very essential for the continued existence of a business. Such records need to be preserved permanently and as such their protection and storage is of utmost importance. As a precautionary measure, the duplicate copies of such documents are maintained in different places other than the filing section. Some of the examples of vital records are production records, accounting records, personnel records, contract deeds and so on.

(*b*) *Important records*: These records are not used regularly but felt essential in the long run. Once the end use of record is derived they may even be disposed off. Some examples of important records are redeemable debentures, loan documents, etc.

(*c*) *Useful Records*: These records are useful for the short period of time and after their use they are destroyed. Examples of such records relate to enquiry letter, settlement of claim, follow-up actions, placing orders and such other documents.

(*d*) *Non-Essential records*: These Records have little value and hence destroyed once they serve the purpose for which they are intended. Some of these records will not be filed because of its least importance to the organisation. Examples of non-essential records are brochures, inter office memorandum, advertising letters, etc.

2. Contents of records: Depending upon the contents, records can be classified into the following:

(*a*) *Correspondence records:* These records include documents such as letter, notices, circulars, memoranda, etc., sent or received by the organisation.

(*b*) *Accounting Records*: Accounting records involve documents relating to purchases, sales, stock reports, assets and liabilities statements. Some of the documents relating to purchases are tender statements, purchase orders, material received report, material inspection report, debit notes and credit notes, invoices, etc. The documents relating to sales relates to price list, catalogues, invoices, etc.

(*c*) *Legal records*: These records include documents relating to contract deeds, registration of charges created, lease agreement, etc.

(*d*) *Personnel Records:* These documents contain particulars about the employees of the company such as employment history card, labour placement record, labour turnover record, accident reports, performance reports, etc.

(*e*) *Statutory Records:* Such records are to be maintained according to the requirements of various statutes such as Companies Act, Income Tax, Workman's Compensation Act, Factories Act, MRTP Act and other Acts which have a close bearing upon the activities of a company.

Purposes of Records

A well classified and preserved records serve the following purposes:

1. Facilitates future reference: A business deals with numerous transactions supported by a number of documents. Such documents constitute memory of the business which are useful for future reference in order to take decisions.

2. Serves as an evidence: Records serve as a useful evidence in times of disputes. The settlement of such disputes is based on written records.

3. It serves as an yard stick for measurement of progress of business: This is considered as historical function of record keeping. Records help to evaluate the performance of the business over a period of time. It can also be used to compare the performance achieved in relation to similar business in the neighbourhood.

4. It portrays the existing state of affairs of the business: The records relating to the assets and liabilities show the state of affairs of a business. Similarly, the records relating to trading and profit and loss accounts show the profitability or otherwise of the business.

5. It facilitates in detecting errors and omissions: A regular review of records shows the accuracy of all the transactions in a business. Steps can be taken to eliminate errors and omissions by developing a control design such as standard cost. This reflects the efficiency or otherwise of a business.

6. It meets the legal obligations: A large number of books and records are to be compulsorily maintained by companies as per the Companies Act of 1956. Failure to meet this statutory requirement leads the officers of the company to pay penalty as well as to undergo imprisonment. Some such records to be maintained in a company are the Register of members, Register of Debenture holders, Minutes books, Register of charges and Mortgages created, Books of Accounts and Audit Report and so on.

Essentials of record keeping

In order to achieve the above objects, the following essentials of a record keeping are to be ensured:

1. Simplicity: The system of record keeping must suit the requirements of the business but not complicate the procedure. It should be within the comprehension of all concerned in the organisation.

2. Accuracy: The records to be maintained should reduce mistakes and errors of all types.

3. Economy: It must involve less cost in terms of investment and maintenance in respect of money, time, energy, efforts and materials.

4. Usefulness: The record keeping must secure the facts needed for the management and avoid collecting unnecessary details.

Recent trends in record keeping

Record keeping has undergone the following changes in modern days:

1. Use of loose-leaf and card system: The traditionally maintained bound-book records are substituted with loose leaf documents and cards. This facilitates simplicity and economy in record keeping.

2. Avoiding useless copying: There is a tendency to avoid unnecessary copying of details to avoid waste of time and efforts. For example, by maintaining all the invoices of customers systematically either on chronological or numerical basis, the need to prepare and maintain a sales journal is avoided.

3. Discontinuation or destruction of records: In the process of record keeping, the real need for keeping a particular record is questioned and investigated. Only those records which are useful alone are retained and such records not being used are discontinued or destroyed. This is as compared to traditional system where all records were maintained irrespective of their need or otherwise.

4. Coordination of record keeping: The traditional system of record keeping consisted of maintaining a separate document or a file for each and every subject matter. This involved more expenses on documents and it was a time consuming process. Today, record keeping is coordinated in such a way that one record may serve different purpose.

5. Eliminating unnecessary efforts of staff: There is a considerable change noticed in respect of simplifying the efforts of office staff by means of reducing the unnecessary work relating to record keeping. In addition to eliminating unnecessary work, a practice of using standard abbreviation, use of printed forms leaving blank columns to be recorded on the basis of transactions are widely used to reduce the efforts of staff.

Principles of record keeping

The following are the important principles of Record Keeping:

1. The purpose of record keeping must be justified: The records to be maintained must serve any of the purposes discussed earlier. Where the record keeping fails to meet any of its objectives, then record keeping is a waste. The record keeping function should not be undertaken for the sake of simply preserving the records. If the records of an office are examined one by one in the light of this principle, it will be noticed that atleast some records may not be justified in terms of its maintenance.

2. A record must be capable of verification: Unless records are capable of verification, it should not be taken up for preserving. The records to be maintained must be capable of serving as an evidence in a court of law but not based on mere hearsay which is of no value in making a wise decision.

3. Classification of records for its full use: The records to be maintained in the office are to be classified on some basis for quick identification. The two bases of classifying the records are as follows:

(*a*) *Chronological classification*: This is an old basis of classifying the records. Under this basis, records are maintained on the basis of time. Its chief merit is that it facilitates easy identification for verification purpose. Its chief drawback is it takes more time to identify if the volume of records is large.

(*b*) *Subject classification:* Under this classification, records are maintained on the basis of a subject matter. By arranging all documents of related subject, the time wasted on searching such documents can be avoided.

4. Ready availability of information: As the purpose of keeping records is to furnish information it must ensure that all information is made available instantly at all times. Sometimes information from certain records need to be verified by management frequently. Such records must be preserved so as to locate them easily and supply them promptly. The record keeping system must be designed in such a way that it meets the immediate needs of all those who rely upon records.

5. Records must be produced at a reasonable cost: The cost of collecting, storing and presenting them must be reasonable but not expensive.

6. Better utilisation of storage space: The system of preserving the record must occupy little space. Records must be kept in a concise form so as to involve less space in maintaining them.

7. Preservation of records for the period required: Certain records need not be retained once they serve the purpose. Otherwise they accumulate into a big heap and pose problems both in respect of space and time involved in searching out other important document. In other words, only permanent records alone need to be preserved while destroying all unwanted records.

Definition and need for record management

According to Ricks and Gow[1] "Records management is the systematic control of records from creating to final disposition."

Zare. K. Quible[2] defines records management as "the activities designed to control the life cycle of a record from its creation to its ultimate disposition".

The life cycle of a record has the following stages:

1. Creation stage: The function of a creation stage involves preparation of new forms, its maintenance and control of records. New Forms are to be prepared only when a need arises and justified. This stage is also concerned with developing efficient methods of recording data on documents for ensuring accuracy and completeness of data. Under this stage, the length of time for which records are to be stored is determined before its destruction.

2. Utilisation stage: This stage is concerned with developing efficient procedure for storing and supplying the records to the needy person at the right time.

3. Storage stage: The stage involves efficient utilisation of filing equipment and the space occupied by it. To enable quick reference, records must be stored in a place which is accessible to those who utilise them. This stage is also concerned with protecting records against disaster or unauthorised use.

4. **Retrieval stage:** This step involves locating the required records rapidly.

5. Disposition stage: This stage involves preserving only valuable documents which are considered vital for the successful and smooth working of an organisation. In other words, documents not required any longer are disposed or destroyed.

Need for records management

Zare Quible summarises the need for records management thus:

(*a*) To provide control over the record cycle, *i.e.*, the creation, utilisation, storage, retrieval and disposition of records.

1. Information Resource Management-p. 3.
2. Introduction to Administrative Office Management-p. 431

(*b*) To develop efficient procedures for each stage of the cycle.
(*c*) To eliminate needless storage of duplicate records.
(*d*) To reduce cost in each stage of the records cycle.
(*e*) To develop realistic standards for employee performance and evaluation programme.
(*f*) To standardise procedures and equipment in the records management programme.
(*g*) To develop throughout the organisation an awareness and an appreciation for the value of a records management programme.

Filing as a form of record keeping

Filing is the basis of record keeping. It entails the process of arranging and storing records so that they can be located when required.

Filing has been defined by Mills and Standingford as "the process of so arranging and storing original records, or copies of them, that they can be readily located when required."

Zane Quible defines filing as "one of the activities in the records management programme, which involves systematically classifying, coding, arranging and placing records in storage so that they can be quickly and easily retrieved when needed."

An efficient filing system is one in which (*a*) the records required at any time can be produced without unreasonable delay, (*b*) the records are adequately protected during the period over which they are retained for reference and (*c*) the cost of installing and maintaining the system is reasonable having regard to the service which is required.

Essentials of good filing system

The essentials of a good filing system can be summarised under the following points:

1. Accessibility: This is a vital requirement in a good filing system. There must always be an easy access so that records required can be produced promptly.

2. **Simplicity:** The filing system must be simple to operate. In other words, the system should not be overcomplicated. Instead, it must be simple to understand.

3. Suitability: The filing system must fit in with the requirements of the firm. A centralised system of filing suitable to one organisation may not be suitable for other organisations.

4. Adaptability: The filing system must be capable of meeting the changing circumstances and also to cope with expansion of the business.

5. Economical: The filing system must be economical in terms of investment, labour, consumable equipment and overheads.

6. Safety: The fling system must be safeguarded against fire, dust and dirt.

7. Cross-reference: Cross-reference should be provided where necessary, so that a document can be found under different headings.

8. Upto date filing: Records should always be filed upto date, although this may depend on the staffing and on control exercised over them.

9. Use of Tracers: A system of using Outguides or Tracers should indicate which documents have been removed when and by whom.

10. Reference: The system of filing must locate the records easily without involving delay.

11. Retention: Only those records which are considered essential alone need be filed permanently. All useless and other records not required for future reference are to be discarded.

12. Classification: There must be a suitable method of classification for filing records. The number of miscellaneous files is to be kept to minimum.

Planning a new filing system

Before establishing a suitable filing system in an organisation, it should be planned properly so as to meet the objectives of filing, keeping in mind the nature of records. The following factors are to be considered while planning a new filing system in any organisation:

1. Choosing or selection of a system of filing: The word *System* in this connection refers to the method of arrangement or classification, the type of equipment used, the organisation of staffing and the methods used in filing process. The following factors in turn determine the selection of an appropriate system of filing:

(*a*) Features, *i.e.*, which system possess most of the essential features of a good filing system.

(*b*) Classification, *i.e.*, which method of classification is most suitable for the present situation.

(*c*) Permanence, *i.e.*, are the records to be filed permanently or to be destroyed after short interval.

(*d*) Space, *i.e.*, the area required for a filling department.

(*e*) Initial cost, *i.e.*, the investment required for filing equipment is to be considered.

- (*f*) Operating cost, *i.e.*, cost of the various alternative system must be compared and considered.
- (*g*) System, *i.e.*, having regard to all the above points; centralised or decentralised system is to be decided.

2. Deciding the equipment to be purchased: The following points are to be considered while deciding the equipments to be purchased:

(*a*) *Quantity*: This is based on documents to be handled over a period of time and the period of its retention.

(*b*) Comparative cost of various equipment must be considered.

(*c*) *The risk of loss*: To avoid this, wooden filing cabinets are substituted with steel cabinets.

(*d*) *Choice of equipment*: This depends upon the size and shape of documents for which storage is to be provided.

(*e*) *Indexing*: The form and method of indexing is also to be decided.

3. Training: The required number of staff is to be recruited and trained in the basic principles of filing and indexing.

4. Formulation of rules and procedures: A set of rules and procedures is laid down and strictly enforced to the efficient system of filing. The following points are worth noting in this regard:

- (*a*) Fixation of responsibilities on the senior staff for filing of records and documents.
- (*b*) Classification of records for the sake of filing.
- (*c*) Devising clear cut method for recording the issue and return of documents.
- (*d*) Deciding the retention period for the documents.
- (*e*) Responsibility for the disposal of old records.

Organisation of filing

After planning a new system of filing, it must be properly organised under any of the following systems:

I. Centralised System: The centralised filing system may mean keeping (*a*) all files in one place (*b*) all files of general interest centrally, while those of purely departmental interest are kept by respective department and (*c*) keeping most of the files in departments but controlled and staffed from one central point. A centralised filing system provides for the housing of all important records in one location within the organisation. In other words, it means that all papers about the same subjects from different departments are filed together on common files in the central filing department. All records that need to be retained are forwarded by each department to a central records area. Those departments wishing to refer to papers then borrow the files from the central filing department. Centralised filing is not suitable for a large sized organisation because placing the central records in a location convenient for all departments is virtually impossible. However, for smaller organisations, a centralised system is more appropriate.

Advantages of centralised filing

1. Effective Control: Control is exercised more effectively because of fixation of responsibility on one individual. Effective control is also possible because of closer supervision within the department.

2. Specialisation: Specialisation of staff results in efficiency in the filing system.

3. Uniformity: It leads to uniformity of equipment and filing procedure.

4. Elimination of duplication: Duplication is eliminated as single copy of each document is required for the central file.

5. Economy: This system results in the economy in terms of operating cost, equipment, space and overhead expenses.

6. Continuity: This programme operates continuously even in the absence of some employees.

Disadvantages of centralised filing

1. Delay: There is considerable delay involved in obtaining the required documents because of the distance involved between various departments and central filing system.

2. Unsuitable classification: Because of adoption of standard classification of records under a centralised filing system, it may be entirely unsuitable for documents received for filing from other departments. For example, correspondence from sales department might be more suitably filed by geographical classification, but the centralised system of classification is an alphabetical one.

3. Accumulation of records: Over a period of time, all unwanted documents accumulate into a big heap.

4. Lack of secrecy: The confidentiality of records may be very difficult to maintain.

II. Decentralised system: A decentralised filing system is one in which the records of each department are housed within that department until it is finally disposed off. This system is more widely used because it allows control over them and have immediate access to their own records.

(*a*) *Convenience:* It facilitates independent filing system involving a single filing cabinet which has easy access to the documents.

(*b*) *Savings in time*: As it does not involve searching of documents (as in the case with central filing system), it saves time in locating the records.

(*c*) *Flexibility in classification:* Depending upon the need of the departments, the system of filing and classification can be adopted.

(*d*) *Maintenance of secrecy:* As records are not exposed to others, it is possible to maintain secrecy within every department of the organisation.

Disadvantages of decentralised filing

1. Duplication of equipment: It leads to excess investment on equipment as each and every department must have its own filing equipment.

2. Occupies more space: As filing function is involved in every department it occupies more space. Thus, the available space is wasted under decentralised filing.

3. Lack of uniformity: As each department has its own record system, a lack of uniformity exists in the total records system.

4. Duplication of records: As each department may retain copies of the same record, this practice encourages duplication in records.

III. Combination records system: It is a compromise between centralised and decentralised filing system. Under this system, a central filing department is used for all documents of a general nature. All other documents will be filed in the departments with which they are specially concerned. Under this system of filing, the responsibility is assigned to the records manager who establishes the network for the operational procedures of the system. This system combines the advantages of both the centralised and decentralised system of filing.

The choice of a particular system of filing depends upon certain important factors such as (*a*) attitude of top management towards the storage of records, (*b*) competence of personnel, (*c*) size and type of the organisation, (*d*) philosophy of the organisation with regard to centralisation and decentralisation and (*e*) the number and types of records stored.

Basis of filing

There are three methods of filing. They are:

1. Horizontal filing: This method is the oldest method of filing. This method is also known as flat filing as the papers or folders are filed one on top of the other on shelves or in shallow drawers. The chief advantages of this method are:

(*a*) It is simple and has easy access to the documents.

(*b*) There is less risk of losing or misplacing the documents filed.

However, horizontal filing suffers from the following disadvantages:

(*a*) It involves wastage of space when compared to vertical method.

(*b*) It lacks flexibility as it does not allow for expansion.

(*c*) Reference becomes difficult.

2. Vertical filing: This is the most popular method of filing. Under this method, the papers are stacked on edge, one behind another in drawers. The advantages of this method are as follows:

(*a*) It facilitates speed of location through the system of indexing.

(*b*) It is easy to remove and reinsert the documents.

(*c*) This method is adaptable to different types of cabinets such as steel, wooden and also of different shapes and mechanisms such as circular, mechanical and electrical equipment.

3. Lateral filing: This is a modified method of vertical filing in the sense that the papers and other documents are again staked on edge. The term lateral is used to mean that they are arranged side by side, usually on shelves or racks.

System of classification or forms of classification

A classification system is a logical and systematic arrangement of records which uses numbers, letters or a combination of numbers and letters for record identification. There are six methods of classifying records. They are (1) alphabetic, (2) numerical, (3) alpha-numerical, (4) geographical, (5) chronological and (6) subject classification.

1. Alphabetic system: Under this system, record are classified on the basis of alphabetic letter, word or unit. A separate file can be maintained for people, organisations or agencies. This filing system provides for the grouping of records pertaining to the same individual or organisation. This system resembles to listing out names in the telephone directory. This system is particularly suitable under two circumstances, *viz.*, (*a*) where the headings of classification can be adequately expressed in one main word and (*b*) where the volume is small and the need for expansion is limited. Its chief merits are:

(*a*) It is easily understood by clerks without much training.

(*b*) It is flexible in the sense that new headings can be introduced any time without disturbing the classification.

(*c*) No separate index is required as it is self-indexed.

But this system is subject to the following demerits:

(*a*) It is difficult to forecast the space required for different letters.

(*b*) Where the names very closely resemble, it leads to confusion.

(*c*) Large volumes of records cannot be accomodated.

2. Numerical System: Under this system, record are arranged in order by number rather than by name. This system can be adopted under two ways; numbers can be assigned to the documents or records which require filing. In other words, the number becomes part of the record itself. Secondly, the numbers can be assigned to files that are to be kept in a specific order. Where numbers become part of the document, reference will be made by the document number. In case number is assigned to the files, reference will be made by subject or name. For example, when a number is assigned to an invoice it will be referred to by its number when enquired by concerned person. On the other hand, where a number is assigned to a file consisting of a case history of an employee, a person outside the filing department would not know the number of the file and the enquiry will be made by the name of the person whose case history is under reference.

Numerical classifications are of three types, *viz.*, (*a*) serial or consecutive numerical classification, (*b*) duplex numerical classification (number separated into parts) and (*c*) decimal-numerical-classification.

(*a*) *Serial or consecutive numerical classification:* Under this arrangement, documents are filed consecutively beginning with 1, 2, 3, 4 and so on. In some case the number may even begin with 10 or 100 or 1000 and increase consecutively. This system is more suitable when numbers are pre-printed on the original record as in the case of purchase orders, cheques, etc. The missing numbered documents amount to its loss or misplacement. The same thing holds good in case of numbering files containing various documents.

(*b*) *Duplex numberial classification*: It is a system of classification which consists of two or more parts, separated either by a dash or a comma. This system is more useful where a large number of records (say more than 10,000 records) are to be filed. The parts or groups of numbers comprising the duplex numbers are referred to as the primary, secondary and tertiary or final numbers. The primary number serves as the guide to the filing section drawer or self, the secondary number indicates the guide location within the file system and tertiary number indicates the classification in which the file is located behind the secondary guide.

(*c*) *Decimal-numerical classification*: This system is used in libraries, government agencies and organisations.

Advantages of numerical classification

(1) It ensures accuracy in filing.
(2) It is possible to use file numbers as a source of reference.
(3) It accommodates unlimited expansions of documents.

Disadvantages of numerical classification

(1) It involves more time in referring to the index.
(2) Files carrying miscallaneous papers are not too easy to arrange under this classification.
(3) It takes more space in indexing.
(4) It may lead to errors in filing owing to transposition of figures.

3. Alpha-Numeric classification: Under this system of classification arrangement of records are based on a combination of words and numbers. Alpha-numeric files may be based either on subject or phonetic arrangement.

In the subject alpha-numeric system the subject is indicated by its name and related elements are denoted by numbers. For example, if the subject matter of filing relates to advertising through various media, advertisement is denoted as a subject by writing its media as A, to indicate advertisement by television A_2 advertisement by Radio and A_3 advertisement through newspapers.

In the phonetic arrangement the classification is based on the sound of the name. This system is more suitable where certain problems such as wrong spelling, mispronunciation, different spellings of similar names are involved. A separate number is given to the subject and names for the variations. For example, it indicates the names of different persons who deal with the company may be classified according to this method as follows:

1 — C. Chand Maheswar
2 — C. Chanda Maheswar
3 — C. Chandra Maheswar

4. Geographical classification: This system of classification is based on a location or an area. The area or location can be grouped on the basis of state, district or city. This basis of classification is more suitable for filing sales records, customers, files belonging to institutions such as banks, branch offices, etc. Geographical filing has the advantages of adding, deleting or rearranging the files easily. Its chief drawback is it involves more time to use a geographical file as it required consultation of alphabetic index.

5. Chronological classification: It is an arrangement in which records are stored in the order of date they are received. Some of the documents that are filed under this classification are sales records, purchase records, personnel records, etc. This type of classification does not require an index. Under this system, records are arranged in reverse chronological order *i.e.*, the recent record or the last received document is placed first or in the front and the first received record is placed at the back.

6. Subject classification: Under this system, all documents relating to a subject are brought together in one file. The subject can in turn be classified into main heading and sub-heading. For example, when a subject deals with employees, the classification of record can be as follows:

Employee	(Main Headings)
Recruitment	(Sub-heading)
Remuneration	(—"—)
Training	(—"—)
Transfers	(—"—)

This system of classification is time consuming because each document must be read before the subject matter is decided.

Filing Equipment

The selection of filing equipment depends upon the following factors:

1. It should serve the purpose of filing: The first important factor that determines the filing equipment is to meet the purpose of filing. The following are the important purposes that should be taken into account before deciding about the filing equipment.

(*i*) Protection of documents against:
- (*a*) Loss through careless handling.
- (*b*) Loss or damage by fire.
- (*c*) Deterioration through dust.

(*ii*) Prevention of theft or unauthorised reference.

(*iii*) Reduction of physical efforts of the concerned clerks in respect of inserting, or locating and extracting documents.

2. Ease of filing: The equipment to be used must be simple to operate, supported by indices, guides and folders.

3. Transfer facility: The equipment must facilitate free transfer of documents and easy reference.

4. Quality of equipment: The quality of equipment used must be good so as to be durable in nature.

5. Economical in space: The equipment should occupy less space.

Methods of filing

The equipment used for filing can be presented in the chart shown at next page.

1. Manual Methods: Under this method, the filing equipments are positioned at a particular place and the clerks have to go to the equipment for filing or removing the records. The following equipment fall under this category:

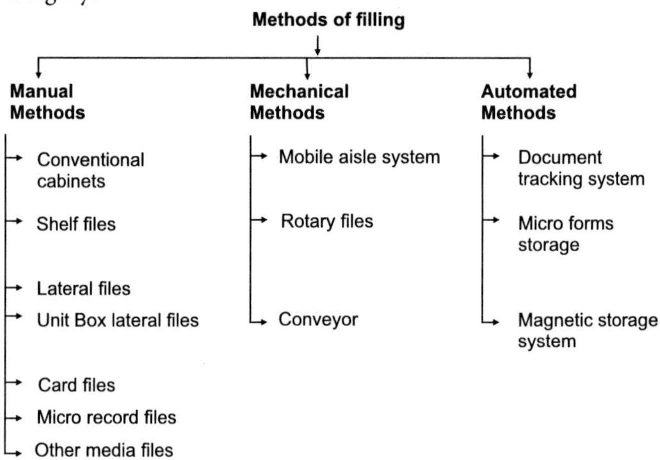

(*a*) *Conventional or vertical cabinets*: This method consists of cabinets which may have drawers varying from 2 to 5. This cabinet with drawers depends upon the number of documents that are to be preserved. The holders are maintained in a vertical position in the drawers which is usually provided with steel rods on which the folders are suspended.

(*b*) *Shelf files cabinet*: Under this method, a shelf of 3 feet in width and 2 feet in height is used. The documents are stored in folders which are suspended as in the case of above method. This method is an improvement over the previous method in terms of speed of storage because of absence of drawers which requires opening and closing.

(*c*) *Lateral files cabinet*: The lateral file cabinet is upright in term of its position with a height of about 7 feet. The folders containing the various documents are filed laterally along the shelves of the cabinet. The contents of each folder are clearly indicated on an index strip attached to the spin of the folder.

(*d*) *Unit Box lateral files*: This is a modified lateral filing cabinet under which a number of lateral filing cabinets are fitted on mobile bases and mounted on a prefabricated polished hardwood floor. This method is more economical in terms of floor space and provides full visibility of documents.

(*e*) *Card files*: Under this method, cards of uniform size is used to serve (*i*) as quick reference, (*ii*) as an index for different files and (*iii*) as a record of activities such as bills receivable and bills payable. Varieties of manual storage equipment are used for cards such as cabinet withdrawers, boxes, trays, etc.

(*f*) *Micro record files*: This method of filing involves storage of microfilms. The equipment mostly resembles a cabinet with a difference that drawers are shallow when compared to drawers under vertical filing.

(*g*) *Other media files*: Some of the equipment that fall under this category are:

(*i*) Audio visual media. This equipment is used to store films, tape recordings, etc.

(*ii*) Magnetic media. This equipment is used to store computer tape reels, cartridges, etc. Magnetic cards are usually stored in sleeves and then housed in boxes or card holders.

(*iii*) Maps or engineering drawings. Maps and engineering documents are large in size so the equipment for storage is also a quite different and may be designed specially so as to include vertical or horozontal pigeon holes.

(*iv*) Publications. Racks are chiefly used to preserve all journals and magazines.

2. Mechanical Methods: Mechanical method of filing ensures speed of access to records. They save space and reduce storage space. Some of the equipment used are as follows:

(*a*) *Mobile file system*: This is a form of space conserving cabinet with shelves which move on tracks to create aisles for accessing records.

(*b*) *Rotary files*: A Rotary file is a single or multiple tier unit in which each tier rotates individually for quick storage of records. They provide multiple access to stored material and ensure full use of storage space.

(*c*) *Conveyor System*: Under this system the desired folder is brought to the user in response to dialling or by key in the folder number. A record user pushes a button wherein a rack of records move around to the desired location for access.

3. Automatic Method: Automatic method of filing involves computer assisted storage and retrieval. Some of the systems used under this method are:

(*a*) *Document tracking system*: Under this system, essential data in each folder stored in a central location are recorded in memory. This enables the system to track folders as they leave storage or when passed from person to person.

(*b*) *Microforms storage system*: This system provides computer assisted file control, storage and retrieval. It functions on the analogy of a computer. It consists of key board which the operator uses to direct the functioning of the equipment and to indicate the particular document to be viewed.

(*c*) *Magnetic storage system:* This system uses a scanning and storing technology in which documents are converted into code and stored on magnetic tape and retrieved when needed on a screen. This system provides speedy access, requires less space and increases security of files.

Filing materials

Filing materials are items which aid in storing and retrieving records. Materials used in storing records include guides, folders, labels and binders. These are explained briefly hereunder:

1. Guides: Guides are used in segregating records into sections with a view to facilitate storage and for separating folders by keeping them upright in a cabinet or on a shelf. An extension of the guide either from the top or side edge provides for easy identification of the file sections. The quality of paper plays an important role in selecting a guide. The chief forms of materials from which guides are prepared are fibre, manila, plastic or any light metal.

2. Folders: A folder is a container used for preserving documents within the storage equipment. It is always convenient to keep documents in folders when they are of different sizes. A folder can also be marked with guides to help in location. The folders used are of the following types:

(*a*) *Plain folders*: It consists of a thick sheet of paper which is folded so as to form a cover.

(*b*) *Suspension folders*: This type of folders are used under vertical system of filing.

(*c*) *Labels*: A label is used to identify the contents of folders, drawers, shelves, trays and boxes. It may take the form of a card, pad or sheet.

(*d*) *Binders*: Binders are used to preserve cassette tapes, micro film jackets and computer prints.

(*e*) *Fasteners*: Fasteners are used to hold the documents tightly while removing or inserting a particular record. A clip is a typical example of a fastener. Fasteners used may be a strip fastener. Ring fastner and paper fastner.

Filing routine or filing procedure

The filing routine or procedure involves the following steps:

(*a*) The documents that are to be filed must be instructed by a competent authority so as to enable the clerk to file all the documents. The instruction usually will be to write "file" at the bottom of the document along with the initial and date.

(*b*) The documents to be filed must be classified according to the file number or any other suitable basis so that the documents are not wrongly filed. Again by giving serial numbers to each document, it can also be ensured that no document is lost by ensuring the continuity in the number of documents.

(*c*) If the number of documents is large, then an index may be maintained for easy reference.

(*d*) If centralised system is followed, the documents are to be sent to the filing department. Otherwise, the departmental clerk will file the document in the same department.

(*e*) When the documents need reference in future they may be issued on the basis of a requisition slip. An *out-slip* is maintained to record all the outgoing document so that if any other person wants to refer to the same document he can be directed to place where such document is already sent. Once the issued document comes back again the *out-slip* may be cancelled.

(*f*) When the documents serve the purpose of filing and where it is no longer needed for future reference it may be transferred to another room known as secondary filing section. Alternatively they may be destroyed on getting authorisation from a competent person.

Record retention and destruction of old records

Very often unnecessary records are retained and important ones thrown out. This has given rise to record retention policy. The record retention programme is to be decided, keeping in view of the space available, legal requirements, and the cost involved in record retention. Once the records get overloaded, three courses of action can be resorted to *viz*., (*a*) transfer records to secondary rooms, (*b*) destroy unwanted files and (*c*) micro film the record and destroy the originals. The following factors determine the record rention programme:

1. The space available: If more space is available, records can be retained for longer duration.

2. Volume of individual record: If it is small, they may be kept for longer duration.

3. Legal requirements: If records are to be retained to meet statutory requirement, they are kept for longer duration.

4. Frequency of reference: If the documents are to be referred frequently, it has to be retained for longer duration.

5. Historical Interest: If the documents are of historical importance they are retained for long duration.

A retention programme would list out all the records in the office under headings 1 year, 2 years, 6 years, indefinitely, etc. The following is a classified list of documents and their respective rention period.

	Documents		Suggested retention period
1.	Accounting and Audit reports	—	Indefinitely
2.	Investment schedules	—	10 years
3.	Stock inventories	—	10 years
4.	Cancelled cheques	—	6 years
5.	Articles of associates	—	Indefinitely
6.	Annual return	—	Indefinitely
7.	Certificate of Incorporation	—	Indefinitely
8.	Debenture and debenture Interest	—	12 years
9.	Meetings, documents such as polls cards, proxy forms voting sheets, etc.	—	3 years
10.	Statutory books	—	Indefinitely
11.	Agreements	—	6 years after termination
12.	Licensing agreements	—	6 years after expiration
13.	Purchasing contracts	—	6 years after termination
14.	Sales contracts	—	6 years after termination
15.	Contact of employment	—	7 years after leaving
16.	Tax returns	—	Indefinitely
17.	Lease	—	12 years after completion
18.	Vehicle license	—	2 years after disposal

Once the purpose for which the documents are filed comes to an end, it need not be stored any longer. In other words, the unwanted records can be disposed off in a convenient manner possible. There are four methods of records disposition. They are:

1. Protection: Certain records are considered to be of vital importance to the business. They are, therefore, bound and can be preserved in safe vaults. Often they can be duplicated and the copies are stored in different places.

2. Transfers: Transfer refers to disposal of records from a high-cost storage area to a low-cost storage area. The frequency of use is the basic factor which determines the transfers of records. For example, if a record is referred twice in a month, it may be stored in the less accessible area of the storage centre (for example, in the lower drawer of a file cabinet) when compared to records which are referred thrice a month.

3. Micro recording: Micro recording as a form of record disposal serves two purpose, *viz.*, (*i*) it reduces the space required to store records and (*ii*) it enables to take multiple copies when needed.

4. Destruction: Those records which have been retained upto the stipulated period of record retention schedule may be destroyed. When records are destroyed a certificate of destruction is prepared which identifies the date on which the document is destroyed.

Micro filming

Micro filming is a process under which records are photographed on a narrow safety film in order to reduce the size of the records so that they occupy less space in storage and facilitate indefinite period of retention. It serves the following purposes:

1. Saving of space: By filming the documents, they can be viewed when needed. This saves filing space and time of filing clerk.

2. Security: It facilities safeguarding the original important documents and thus avoids handling of original documents by reproducing them on the reader. Important documents such as statutory books and contract deeds require precaution against loss by fire. Such documents can be preserved by micro filming them.

3. Audit: Documents are micro filmed to ensure continuity of audit of original documents.

4. Micro filming of large documents: Certain documents such as blue prints, drawings, etc., will be drawn on large sheets of paper. Such documents can be micro filmed for better view and easy storage.

The micro film equipment consists of:

1. Filming unit: In this unit, the documents are fed and filmed on 35 mm or 77 mm film. The film is obtained in the form of a reel. A 100 feet reel of 16 mm film will accomodate approximately 8000 documents of quartz size.

2. Reader: It reproduces the magnified image on a screen. Sometimes the reader is combined with the filming unit to form one machine.

3. Processor: It is a continuous film developing unit designed for day light.

Advantages of micro filming

1. Savings in space: This is the most important advantage of micro filming. It is estimated that 98 per cent of storage space can be saved by micro film documents.

2. Adaptability: Micro filming can be adjusted to suit the requirement of the business.

3. Accessibility: It requires about 15 seconds to locate a document and if a print of the document is required it can be obtained in a further 6 seconds.

4. Portability: It condenses a large volume and weight of papers to a reel of negligible size and weight. This again results in the saving of physical effort and transport cost.

5. Completeness: It is possible to get the compact and complete information by microfilming as compared to a typewritten copy.

6. Elimination of errors: Errors that occur in copying from one document to another, say, by typing can be eliminated by microfilming.

7. Protection: Original documents can be safely preserved by micro filming them. Micro filmed records serve as a substitute to the original documents.

8. Non-deterioration: The micro filmed documents are not subject to deterioration when compared to ordinary papers.

9. Non-inflammable: Microfilm is non-inflammable. Thus, it overcomes the risk of fire.

10. Tamper-proof: While it is possible to make an unauthorised change in the original documents, it is not possible to do it on micro films as they are tamper proof.

Disadvantages of micro filming

1. Illegibility: When the equipment is misused or when not operated properly, the film may become illegible.

2. Difficulty of location: If classification or indexing is not made properly it becomes difficult to locate a particular document.

3. Inadequacy as evidence: Very often microfilm copy is not accepted as evidence in legal cases.

4. It is expensive: Microfilming is a costly method of storage and small units cannot afford to microfilm their documents.

Records management manual

It serves as a guide to the functioning of the records management system. It contains information relating to the person concerned with the records, the time of filing, the place of filing, the method of filing and how the records management system has to function. The records management manual serves four important purposes. They are (1) It establishes the standard procedure relating to determining records retention periods, selecting equipment and transferring records to the record centre, (2) It establishes responsibility as to which individual is responsible for completing the tasks, (3) It assists employee training in office and (4) It provides necessary information in updating the procedures.

The preparation of records management manual requires a thorough knowledge of the organisation, its goals and the manner in which the records section is organised to attain such goals. The preparation of manual involves the following steps:

(*a*) Obtain the approval of top executives preparing a manual.
(*b*) Determine the type of manual needed.
(*c*) Assign authorship responsibility.
(*d*) Identify sources of information for the manual.
(*e*) Determine the content of the manual.
(*f*) Collect and analyse data.
(*g*) Write the manual.
(*h*) Publish the manual.

Contents of records management manual

The records management manual contains the following:

(*a*) The objectives of records management programme.
(*b*) Statement of the policy of the programme.
(*c*) Organisation structure of the programme.
(*d*) Filing system and the type of records filed under each system.
(*e*) Personnel involved in the records management programme.
(*f*) Records retention schedule.
(*g*) Procedure for records retrieval.
(*h*) Disposition of records.
(*i*) Procedure for evaluating the programme.

Indexing

An index is a locating tool. As a tool it indicates or points out the place where exactly the files are maintained. Its function is to act as a guide to identify where exactly a particular document or a file is stored. Just as an index in a book directs the reader to a page within the book, a record index directs the records clerk to a particular file where the required information may be located. The object of an index is to make it easy to refer to any particular record in a system. In the present day business world, where the number of transactions have become numerous, it becomes very difficult to handle all types of documents. Especially when there is an urgent need to refer to any document, its tracing out becomes difficult. So an appropriate system of Indexing helps in locating the document easily and thus save time which otherwise would have been wasted by way of searching. Thus, it can be said that indexing is an aid to a good filing system. Indexing can be maintained separately when the documents are large in number. Alternatively self-indexing is also possible when documents are less in number. Telephone directory is an example of self-indexing wherein the names are arranged in alphabetic order of the subscriber and reference to the names directly leads to the telephone number. When a separate index is maintained, it involves two steps, *viz.*, (*a*) consultation of index as a first step and (*b*) locating the records as the second step. So, as far as possible self-indexing is resorted to by most of the offices.

Types of index

The following are some of the important types of index used in offices:

1. Book or ordinary page index: This type of index will be in the form of a bound book or register which is divided into alphabetic sections in which the names of correspondents are entered into. Each section of the book is carved at the right hand side of the page and the alphabetic letters are written on this carved (cut out portion) pages. Where the names beginning with a particular alphabet is more in number, more number of pages can be allotted for such correspondents. For example, names beginning with A, N, M, R, S,V, etc., are more in number compared to the alphabets, X, Y, Z, O, U. All names commencing with the same alphabet is arranged on the pages reserved for the particular alphabet. Sometimes the first page of the book itself can be used to serve as an index. Under such circumstances, the various page numbers are allotted to cover the names of different correspondents. For example, the first 10 pages of the book can be reserved for all those persons whose name begin with A, the second five pages for all those names which begin with B and so on. This type of index is used in the banks to locate the account numbers of various customers.

The chief advantages of a bound book index are (*i*) It is inexpensive and it can be maintained for a long duration and (*ii*) As the pages of books are bound, the pages cannot be lost or misplaced. But its disadvantages are (*i*) It is not possible to write new names which may require rewriting of the index, (*ii*) It cannot be expanded beyond a certain limit because it can not accommodate all the names.

2. Loose-leaf book index or vertical card index: In order to overcome the disadvantages of bound book form of index, a loose-leaf book is used. Under this type of index, the loose-leaf papers or cards are held vertically by a device which facilitates the removal and insertion of paper or card when necessary. The papers or cards are tightly fitted on metal hinges and screwed. By unscrewing the process, it is possible to take out any paper and have it inserted and screwed again for a firm hold. This type is more flexible than bound book type as it facilitates addition to any number of papers or cards. But this system takes more time to locate the paper and the chances of misplacing them is also more. Further, the constant use of paper or card is subject to wear and tear over a period of time.

3. Vowel index: Where the number of correspondents, is large, as in the case of a large sized business a vowel index is used. This is in fact a modified type of book index. Under this type, the various sections provided in the index book are subdivided into six sections to include the five vowels of English language *viz.*, a, e, i, o and u. The name beginning with an alphabet is first entered under the corresponding alphabet and then by the vowel occuring after the initial letter. For example, the name Vinod will be recorded in the section 'V' and vowel sub-section 'i'.

4. Card index: This is considered to be an improvement over book index. Under this type, instead of using a sheet of paper, cards of uniform size, say 4" × 2½ are being made use of. These cards contain the names and other particulars to be indices such as file number, etc. The cards are arranged in trays of boxes either according to alphabetic order or numerically. Card indices are mostly seen in libraries, hospitals and offices to maintain the records of employees, sales and materials.

5. Visible card index: Under this type, a series of cards are arranged in such a way as to overlap, leaving each card exposed. This exposed edge is used for the reference purposes while the remainder of the card is used for recording purposes. These cards are arranged in such a way that they can be withdrawn, replaced or rearranged as and when necessary.

6. Stripe index: This type of index is more suitable when a list of data such as names, telephone numbers, and addresses are involved. Under this type, a frame is used under which stripes made out of thick paper or card are fitted and subsequently withdrawn or rearranged when necessary. Each stripe is meant for one item usually consisting of two or three lines. The frame used for this purpose differs depending upon the purpose which it has to serve. Some frames are fixed on walls, while others take the form of a book or they can be arranged on a rotary stand which when turned gives reference to any desired portion of the index.

7. Wheel index: Under this type of index, cards are arranged on the circumference of a wheel which may be fixed or portable. Hundreds of cards can be attached to a wheel and about six wheels can be set up so as to be accessible to every clerk who is concerned with the job of indexing. The capacity of cards can be increased by increasing the diameter of the wheel.

8. Slotted cards: Slotting is a process (a device) by which cards can be selected or sorted. The cards are punched with holes at one or more points, each hole or points represents a classification in a code number. The information in terms of which it is required to select or sort is recorded around the edge of the card by cutting the appropriate holes into slots. These cards are inserted into a metal needle. Only those cards which require reference do not pass through the metal needle. When the metal needle is lifted, the cards lie behind, thereby separated from others.

QUESTIONS

Objective Type Questions

1. Define Record as used in an office.
2. Mention four types of records classified on the basis of its importance.
3. List out four types of records classified on the basis of its contents.
4. Define records management.
5. Define filing.
6. Distinguish between centralised and decentralised filing.
7. Distinguish between horizontal filing and vertical filing.
8. What do you mean by lateral filing?
9. List out the various systems of classifying the records.
10. What do you mean by alphabetic system of classification?
11. What do you mean by numerical system of classification?
12. What is meant by alpha-numerical classification?

13. What do you mean by chronological classification?
14. What do you mean by subject classification?
15. List out any four manual methods of filing.
16. List out any two mechanical and automated methods of filing.
17. What do you mean by a *guide*?
18. What do you meant by a *folder?*
19. What do you mean by a *label?* You mean by a
20. What do you mean by a *fastener?*
21. List out four methods of records disposition.
22. Define micro filing.
23. What do you mean by records management manual?
24. Define indexing.

Analytical Type Question

1. Explain briefly the different types of records used in an office.
2. Briefly explain the purposes served by records in a business.
3. What are the essentials of record keeping? What are the recent trends of record keeping?
4. Explain briefly the principles of record keeping.
5. Define records management. Outline the need for records managements.
6. Outline the essentials of a good filing system.
7. Explain how you would plan a new filing system in an office.
8. What is centralised system of filing? State its merits and demerits.
9. What is decentralised system of filing? State its merits and demerits.
10. Briefly explain some of filing materials used in a modern office.
11. Explain briefly the steps involved in filing procedure.
12. Write a note on record retention and destruction.
13. State the advantages and disadvantages of micro-filming.
14. How is record management manual prepared? State its contents.
15. Briefly explain different methods of Indexing.

Essay Type Questions

1. Explain the different bases of classifying office records.
2. Define filing. State is purposes. Explain the various methods of filing.

11

Office Stationery

INTRODUCTION

Office Stationery is an essential input with the help of which the office staff work effectively and efficiently. Though office stationery did no receive much importance in the olden days, it has assumed more importance in modern days. The quantity of stationery and the amount spent on it depends upon nature and size of the business. For example, stationery used and the investment on it is more in banks, insurance companies and in big joint stock companies. On the other hand, its use is restricted in job order industries as in the case of furniture making. It has been estimated that the average expenditure incurred on office stationery and supplies in USA varies from $50 to $200 annually on each clerk on the payroll. This goes to suggest that utmost control is to be exercised to reduce cost incurred on office stationery. By the strict control, the cost of ordering, storage and issuing stationery in the office can be reduced by 25 per cent. Office stationery does not form part of finished product but they certainly render service essential to actual operations in the organisation.

Meaning and types of stationery

Stationery means all papers, records and all small office consumables such as ink, pencils, rubbers, blotting papers, etc. In other words, it means those expendable items which are necessary for consumption in the daily operations but do not generally enter into the finished product.

Office stationery is used throughout the organisation ranging from clerical workers upto the executives. According to Terry, the lack of stationery would cause serious delay in getting out serious office work. Stationery when not provided in time reduces the efficiency of clerks, wastes their valuable time, and delays submission of records and reports. Some of the important types of stationery used in office are as follows:

1. Letter heads of different sizes.
2. Papers for typing.
3. Carbon papers.
4. Duplicating papers.
5. Stencils.
6. Pen.
7. Ink for pen and for duplicating machines.
8. Refill and nibs.
9. Stamp pads.
10. Typewriting ribbons.
11. Pencil eraser and pencil sharpener.
12. Cellotape, stapler, pins, clippers, tags & rubber bands.
13. Sealing wax, gum.
14. Registers, files, file boards.
15. Envelops.
16. Office forms printed with blank spaces.

Selection of stationery and other office supplies

Selection of stationery is the process of choosing the right type of supplies which suits the purpose for which they are meant. Two important factors which govern selection of office stationery are quality and price. Fixation of standards or specification would guide the selection process of stationery. Standards are also useful to compare the quality of the materials actually purchased. The selection of stationery is by no means an ordinary task. This is because varieties of stationery offered keep changing continuously with change in technology and increase in the number of competitors. The selection of materials is also often based upon the samples. The selection of stationery is to be decided between the standardised branded product which is superior in quality and non-standardised products which are inferior in quality. It is always better to select standardised stationery as they offer the following advantages; (*a*) It enables the purchase of good quality materials, (*b*) It helps in uniformity in the purchase of stationery which results in bulk buying (*c*) It helps in simplicity and reduction of varieties and (*d*) It helps in purchasing the required quantity of stationery at the required time. As against selecting the standardised stationery, a non-standard product may appear to be economical and prove costlier in terms of efficiency and waste. For example, selection of a low quality duplicating paper cannot be used to stencil on both sides, though its cost is less. So, it is always recommended to select only standardised stationery though it is costly.

Stationery control — Its purpose

The purpose of stationery control is as follows:

1. To reduce the cost related to stationery: Office stationery involves incurring expenses in its acquisition, storage and issue. When it is not properly checked at all these stages, it involves incurring additional expenses. Such expenses are as follows:

(*a*) Rent payable together with lighting, ventilation, heating and air-conditioning of store room where stationery is stored.

(*b*) Investment on storage equipment and its depreciation.

(*c*) Investment on the stationery handling equipment such as ladders, elevators, etc., and depreciation thereon.

(*d*) Interest on capital tied up in stationery.

(*e*) The wages & salaries payable to office staff dealing with stationery.

(*f*) Loss of materials due to faulty stock keeping methods.

2. To avoid wastage in stationery: Wastage in stationery could be prevented by (*i*) not purchasing excess quantity of stationery, (*ii*) preventing the deterioration in the quality of stationery owing to sun, heat or exposure to bad weather and (*iii*) preventing the loss arising out of theft.

3. Right type of selection: In order to purchase good quality of stationery and supplies, it is essential to select the best supplier. To take full advantage arising out of purchasing the stationery, different methods of purchasing can be resorted to such as (*i*) spot purchases, (*ii*) contract purchasing and (*iii*) inviting tenders from the most competitive suppliers.

4. Regular availability of stationery: One of the important reasons for exercising control over stationery is to avoid overstocking and understocking of it. In this process, what is more important is the arrangement to be made for getting the supplies of stationery in adequate quantity at all times. While overstocking leads to blocking up the investment and increased storage cost, understocking hampers the speed of office work and reduces the efficiency of office staff.

5. Payment of reasonable prices: Though purchase of standardised stationery is advocated, it is also essential to consider the cost factor. The benefit derived from the use of stationery must outweight the expenses incurred in its purchase. It is better on the part of office manager to keep a constant touch over the various dealers as well as the market conditions to take benefit from favourable circumstances.

Essentials of stationery control

The essentials of stationery control are as follows:

(*a*) Checking what is ordered, buying in economical quantities, and using the best buying methods.
(*b*) Purchasing in required stock to avoid deterioration and obsolescence.
(*c*) Storage of stationery in the best possible way to avoid deterioration.
(*d*) Following a good system of issues, so as to reduce wastage in consumption process.

Purchase of office stationery

The purchase and supply of stationery poses a problem especially in a large sized factory. According to Brech "buying is very much a specialist activity. It calls for commercial acumen....". Before purchasing the stationery, the following factors should be considered:

(*a*) The quantity should be sufficiently large to obtain the benefit of a lower price.
(*b*) Cost of storage space.
(*c*) Usage of particular items ordered.
(*d*) Current market price and estimated price in future.
(*e*) Quality.
(*f*) Coordination of the requirements of all departments.
(*g*) Possible obsolescence.
(*h*) Availability of funds in the business.

Purchase of stationery is a matter of policy to be decided by the management. This can be organised under the principle of centralisation and decentralisation.

Centralisation of purchases

Centralisation of purchases is followed where a company has a number of departments within.

The requirements of all the departments are pooled and all purchases are made under the supervision of a specialist. Centralisation also implies purchases by a head office all stationery required by branch offices. This system of purchasing has the following advantages:

(*a*) It avoids duplication in the purchase of stationery.
(*b*) It fixes responsibility on a single individual for the purchase of all stationery and supplies.
(*c*) It relieves others from the botheration of purchases.

(*d*) Purchasing in bulk leads to several advantages in the form of discount, home delivery service, etc.

(*e*) The purchase officer can acquire better skill and knowledge in purchasing the stationery.

(*f*) It involves less capital outlay on stationery.

However, centralisation of purchases has certain disadvantages:

(*a*) It lacks flexibility in the sense that the purchase officer alone has to purchase a fixed quality and quantity of stationery.

(*b*) When the departments or branch offices are scattered, distribution of stationery poses a problem.

Decentralised purchasing

Under this principle, the individual branch offices or departmental heads are given freedom to purchase the required stationery for their use. Most of the disadvantages of centralised system can be overcome by decentralised system. However, in practice it would be desirable to combine these two systems to derive the combined advantages of both the system.

Methods of purchasing stationery

In a small sized office, purchase of stationery is purely based on its requirement. But in a large sized company, the purchase officer can follow any of the following methods of purchases:

1. Issue of Tender: Under this method, the quantity of stationery required for a year is estimated. An advertisement is given inviting the manufacturers or dealers to quote their prices for the supply of stationery. The manufacturer or dealer who quotes the lowest price is selected for placing the order and an order is issued for the supply of stationery either in bulk or at frequent intervals.

2. Purchase of stationery from the existing suppliers: This method is followed when the existing supplier supplies good quality of stationery at reasonable prices. The supplier could be a local dealer or may be from a distant place. However, this method should not be blindly followed for a long time because other competitors may supply with better terms and conditions of sale.

3. Contract purchases: Under this method, the supplier is informed to supply the stationery at regular intervals. A contract is specifically entered as to the quantity and type of stationery required by the company. Best example in this connection would be contract entered into with the printer to print and supply bill books, printed forms etc., at regular intervals.

Objectives of purchasing stationery

All purchases of stationery must aim at achieving the following objectives:

1. Selection of outstation supplier: Generally speaking, suppliers can be chosen from local area or outstation locality. The cost of stationery differs between these two types of suppliers. Further, the quality and other terms and conditions of supply differ. The time taken to deliver the stationery also differs. The right supplier is one who could supply the stationery at the lowest possible price, the required quality and at the required time. The selection of suppliers can also be based upon the suggestions of sales representatives of many manufacturing companies such as Kores India, Gestetner, etc.

2. Purchase at reasonable price: Purchase at a reasonable price is possible by (*a*) buying stationery in bulk as bulk purchases are priced less after allowance of discount, (*b*) by taking advantage of market conditions, (*c*) by placing orders directly with manufacturers rather than buying through wholesalers and other middlemen.

3. Purchase of required quantity of stationery: The purchase of stationery in the required quantity is necessary to ensure smooth functioning of office by eliminating delays and stoppage of work. Neither it is desirable to overstock or understock stationery. Overstocking involves excess investments, risk of obsolescence, more storage space, deterioration in quality and more losses and wastages. It is always desirable to fix a reorder level, the level on reaching which fresh purchase of stationery is made.

4. Purchase of required quality: The purchase of good quality stationery ensures efficiency in office work and also ensures less wastages of stationery.

5. Purchase at the right time: In order to eliminate undue delay in the office work, it is necessary to buy the stationery at the required time. It would be advisable to prepare a schedule for all requirements of stationery and place a single order for its supply. Whenever there is any delay in getting the supplies, it is necessary to take follow up action.

Procedure involved in purchasing stationery

The following steps are involved in a scientific purchase procedure:

1. Receiving purchase requisition: Whenever the stationery in all the departments including office reaches reorder level, a request is made to the purchase manager (or office manager) to arrange for the purchase of all stationery by preparing a document known as a purchase requisition slip. However, the preparation and placement of this slip does not arise when the management of the organisation decides to buy once or twice a year all the stationery required by it.

2. Deciding about the quantity, quality and price: Before the stationery is actually purchased, the purchase manager (or office manager) will decide upon the quantity, quality and price of the stationery. Some of the factors which determine these requirements were discussed already. However, the purchase manager can consult the various departmental managers to decide these aspects of purchasing the stationery.

3. Selection of a supplier: As discussed earlier, the supplier can be selected by calling for tenders, or by meeting sales representatives or selecting the existing supplier for the supply of stationery. Other matters to be decided in this regard are (*a*) whether to select a local dealer or an outstation dealer and (*b*) whether to select a manufacturer or a wholesaler for placing the order.

4. Placing the purchase order: It is an order on the basis of which the supplier undertakes to supply the stationery. It serves as a contractual agreement which cannot ordinarily be revoked unless circumstances force it. The purchase order consists of the following details (*i*) the name and address of buying concern, (*ii*) the name and address of selling concern, (*iii*) the quantity of supply, (*iv*) the quality, (*v*) the duration within which it is to be supplied, (*vi*) the rate of stationery and (*vii*) the signature of purchasing authority. It is the duty of supplier to supply the stationery as per the specification of purchase order.

5. Follow-up action: When the stationery is not supplied as per the promised date, it would be worth while to take follow up action by reminding the supplier to expedite the order quickly. In case of inordinate delay, the order can even be cancelled and alternate arrangement can be made to procure stationery and supplies from a different and reliable supplier. It is desirable to maintain a list of prompt suppliers so that orders can be placed in times of urgency.

6. Receipt and supply of stationery: Usually the incoming stationery is received by the office manager and he will make sure that the stationery supplied conforms to quantity and quality ordered. A note known as *stationery received note* is prepared and a copy of which is sent to storekeeper along with the stationery received. Intimation to various departments which require stationery urgently is also given.

7. Settlement of bill: On ensuring that the stationery supplied is in accordance with the purchase order *i.e.*, in respect of quantity, quality and price, the accounts department would settle the payment with the supplier.

Storage of office stationery

Storage of stationery is an important aspect of stationery control. Unless the stationery is properly stored, it leads to considerable losses in the following ways:

1. Deterioration: Stationery may get deteriorated by careless handling and also by exposure to atmospheric conditions such as sunlight, heat and moisture.

2. Disorderly arrangement: Any unsystematic storage of stationery may not be available when they are urgently wanted. Sometimes it may lead to duplication of purchases when it is not traced or identified. This will lead to unnecessary investment on the purchase of such stationery.

3. Defective storekeeping: When proper attention is not given to the stocking of stationery, it may give rise to overstocking and understocking. The disadvantages of this are already discussed earlier.

4. Careless use: Very often the stationery is misused as for example, using a letter head for rough calculation, discarding a pen or pencil which is half used, throwing excess stationery instead of returning to be store room. All these losses arise on account of defective store practice.

Organisation of store room

The organisation of storekeeping department depends upon:

(*a*) Design and layout of the office.
(*b*) The degree of centralisation required.
(*c*) Need for departmental storeroom. Generally speaking, storekeeping department can be organised under centralised system and decentralised system.

Centralised system

Under this system, all the stationery is received and issued from the single stores department. The advantages of centralised storing are as follows:

(*a*) Few clerks are required in the storeroom.
(*b*) Better control is exercised over stationery.
(*c*) Less equipment for storage.
(*d*) Space occupied is less.

The disadvantages of centralised system of storing are:

(*a*) The centralised store room may be far away from other departments. Often it may cause delay in issuing stationery.
(b) The chance of risk of loss on account of fire is high.

Problems of storekeeping

The following factors are generally applicable to all the organisations in the problem on handling stationery:

1. Location of store room: As far as possible the location of store room must be in the central place of the office. The location to be selected must have the facility of natural lighting. Otherwise supply of artificial lighting will involve heavy expenses. Other factor that are to be considered in locating the store room are (*i*) theft prevention, (*ii*) avoidance of fire and (*iii*) facility of supervision.

2. Physical arrangement of the stationery: All stationery must be systematically arranged so as to facilitate quick issue to the various department. This requires purchase of various types of equipment such as cabinets, racks, and almirahs. Adequate space must be left in between every storage equipment. All unwrapped packages should be removed and stationery neatly arranged. New packages must be opened only when the old stock is exhausted. The arrangement must facilitate easy counting of packages, bottles or any other containers. If possible the quantity contained in the package must be visible. This helps in getting the fresh stock well in time.

3. Classification of stock of stationery: It is desirable to classify the stationery on some suitable basis instead of treating it as a miscellaneous item. Having classified, it is to be stored in the classified segment on the equipment.

4. Issue of stock of stationery: The issue of stationery must be taken up at a specified time so as to avoid unnecessary work. Issue must be based on a written document rather than on oral request.

5. Stock taking: In order to avoid overstocking and understocking the stationery, it is necessary to verify the stock at frequent intervals. This can be undertaken on a continuous basis to know the fast moving, slow moving and dormant stock of stationery. This helps in investing only the required amount on the purchase of stationery.

6. Control of consumption of stationery: Very often it is observed that some items of stationery such as pens, pencils, erasers, etc., are being carried away to homes from the office. Hence, it is necessary to assess the actual need of stationery and purchase only the required quantities. It is also necessary to check the quantity of stationery frequently to know that the stock is intact and not shrinked.

Issue of stationery

As a matter of rule, no stationery should be issued unless a written authorisation is produced before the storekeeper. Further, the issue of stationery should be only on a specified date and at a specified time so that store keeper can keep his records upto date. All issues of stores are recorded in the priced stores ledger and must be made in fixed quantities. It is better to fix a maximum quantity of issue at a time and beyond this no issue is to be made. This helps in reducing excess losses and wastages. The storekeeper must maintain the records for receiving and issuing stationery. Whenever any transaction occurs, it is the duty of storekeeper to make the necessary entries in the store records. Further, the stationery found to be in surplus should be sent back to the store room. The interdepartmental transfers of stationery are to be discouraged.

Reducing stationery cost

Stationery cost can be reduced by:

(*a*) Instituting the best systems of buying for different stock of stationery.

(*b*) Using best method of storage in such a way that:

- (*i*) The storeroom should be clean and dry; it must be well lit, it must be under lock and key.
- (*ii*) The physical arrangement of stationery must be neat to prevent spoilage.
- (*iii*) Shelves should be numbered and stationery classified so as to enable easy identification of stationery.

(*c*) Exercising control over the method of making issues.

(*d*) Ensuring that departments do not build up their own stock.

(*e*) Instituting a system of costing and charging stationery to each department.

(*f*) Having a responsible person in charge of issues and to exercise discretion in making issues.

(*g*) Proper forms control to keep printing to a minimum.

Continuous stationery

Continuous stationery is a device by which office forms are produced in a continuous strip; individual forms are usually divided from each other by perforations and several copies of each form are produced simulatenously.

Methods of obtaining forms by continuous stationery

The following are some of the methods through which forms are produced by continuous stationery:

1. One-time carbon backing: Under this method, a carbon sheet is inserted under every document so as to get a duplicate copy of the original.

2. Multiple carbon pocket: Where more than one set of carbon copy is required then number of carbon sheets are inserted under every paper which enables in getting many copies. However, the number of copies to be taken depends upon the type of paper used. Usually thin sheets of papers are used to get about 8 to 10 copies at a time. But the impression got on the last few copies will not be so clear when compared to first few copies.

3. 'N C R' (No Carbon Required): It is a type of paper, the inside of which is coated with a chemical and the uppermost side of the paper beneath is similarly treated with the chemical. When the top copy is typed on it, automatically creates a carbon copy on the sheet beneath by the interaction of these two chemicals. This method is expensive and requires careful handling.

Importance of continuous stationery

Continuous stationery saves labour cost where a large volume of work is involved on standard business firm. Further, making use of modern office equipment depend upon continuous stationery. Again continuous stationery is also a method of obtaining several copies of a document simulatenously. Its specific uses are felt in:

1. Sales invoice sets: Wherein copies are to be sent to accounts department, warehouse department, transport department and sales representatives.

2. Purchase order sets: Wherein copies are to be sent to the supplier to be retained for the reference of purchase manager, to the receiving clerk and to the storekeeper.

3. Wage preparations: Under this category, continuous stationery is useful in the preparation of pay-roll, pay slips and pay-envelopes.

4. Transfer of shares: Under this category, continuous stationery is useful in preparing different sets to be sent to transferee as an acknowledgment for having received the instrument to transfer, preparation of new share certificate, etc.

Types of continuous stationery

1. Roll stationery: Its consists of forms in a continuous roll. This type of continuous stationery is used in typewriters or teleprinters. They may be perforated in between the forms to separate out one form from another.

2. Inter fold stationery: Under this type, the stationery is folded flat and is more popular than the roll type.

3. Fan fold: Under this type, the forms are joined from end to end and also horizontally and folded so as to give the shape of a 'concertina' fashion. If opened out, the stationery would resemble a fan.

Advantages and disadvantages of continuous stationery

The advantages of continuous stationery are as follows:

(*a*) It saves time involved in feeding separate forms into a typewriter, tabulator, etc.

(*b*) It saves time in inserting and removing carbons as in the case of NCR.

(*c*) It facilitates the speedy use of accounting machines, addressing machines, etc.

Its disadvantages are as follows:

(*a*) It is expensive.

(*b*) The impression of last few copies may not be good.

(*c*) The process will be delayed if the continuous stationery is out of stock.

(*d*) The mistake on original copy leads to mistakes on all copies. So, it is somewhat difficult to set right mistakes in all copies.

QUESTIONS

Objective Type Questions

1. What do you mean by office stationery?
2. Distinguish between the office stationery and office supplies.
3. Distinguish between the centralised and decentralised stationery purchase.
4. Distinguish between the centralised and decentralised store keeping of stationery.
5. List out the objectives of purchase of stationery.
6. List out the losses arising out of bad storekeeping of stationery.
7. Define continuous stationery.
8. Mention three types of continuous stationery.
9. Mention four uses of continuous stationery.
10. State the essentials of stationery controls.

Analytical Type Questions

1. State the purposes of stationery control.
2. State the factors to be considered while purchasing office stationery. Explain any two methods of buying the office stationery.

3. State the advantages and disadvantages of centralised and decentralised buying of stationery.
4. State the advantages and disadvantages of centralised and decentralised storekeeping.
5. Explain the purchase procedure of office stationery.
6. State the methods of obtaining forms by continuous stationery. What are the advantage and disadvantages of the same?

12

Office Furniture

INTRODUCTION

Office Furniture is one of the most important assets which cannot, be dispensed with. It consists of desks, tables, benches, chairs, racks, cabinets, almirahs, trays and other equipment allotted to the individual clerks or meant for general use. As office work considerably involves preparation and preservation of records, it is very essential to provide adequate furniture to every clerk to enable him to do his work smoothly and speedily. The adequacy of furniture depends upon the size of the organisations, the number of departments and the number of employees. To derive maximum efficiency in the work, it is necessary to design, locate and arrange furniture in the most systematic manner. Some furniture such as desks and tables help in writing, referring, checking, sorting and examining the documents. Other furniture such as cabinets, racks, almirahs are used for storing the records, reports and other documents. Chairs and stools help in sitting and doing the work and thus eliminating fatigue of employees. Sometimes, desk and table tops are used to lay thing on such as a typewriter. The drawers of some tables are used as a temporary storage place for the records which are under the process of preparation. Above all the variety and quality of furniture add to goodwill of the company by projecting a good image on the visitors. In order to utilise the furniture to the maximum extent, it is necessary to acquire them in the required size and dimension. As office furniture constitute an important property, it involves heavy investment and hence careful planning and selection is to be made at the time of its purchase.

Meaning and features of furniture and fixtures

According to Webster's dictionary furniture means equipments that is necessary, useful and desirable as movable articles, used in making a room ready for occupancy or use. According to this meaning, office furniture will have the following characteristics:

(*a*) A furniture though taken to mean an equipment may best be regarded as an assets. It is a durable asset or a fixed asset which is used to perform office work easily and comfortably.

(*b*) Office furniture is very essential as it serves many purposes such as writing, storing, checking of records. Without office furniture it would be highly impossible to carry out any of the task either by the executives or by the clerks.

(*c*) Office furniture is a useful property of the organisation as it increases the efficiency of workers both in the production and office departments of the business undertaking.

(*d*) Though office furniture is considered to be fixed, in some cases they can be moved from one place to another so as to meet the requirements of the office. This will take place when the relay-out of office is contemplated upon.

(*e*) An office without adequate furniture is considered to be a hallow room in itself not fit for use. It is only when office is equipped with adequate furniture it becomes a complete department capable of being used by office staff.

The term fixture according to the dictionary means something that is fixed in a place as a permanent appendage or structural part. Some of the fixtures usually found in an office are in the form of electrical fittings, carpets on the floors, shelves on the walls, projector fixed on a table for transcribing microfilms and so on. However, there is a difference between furniture and fixture. Furniture is a movable asset while fixture is a fixed asset. Both furniture and fixture are essential tools used for the performance of office work.

Need for and importance of office furniture

The need for and importance of office furniture cannot be under estimated in the present day business world, be it a small size or large sized one. Enormous capital is invested on furniture and fixtures in organisations such as banks, insurance and other big companies. Its importance can be summed up under the following points:

(*a*) They serve as an important tool to perform day to day work in various departments of the business.

(*b*) It enhances the speed and accuracy of work.

(*c*) It gives better and attractive look and thus improves the reputation of the business.

(*d*) They make good appeal to the employees and thus motivate them to work.

The utility of furniture in a modern commercial office can be outlined under the following points:

(*a*) They help in drawing, verifying, checking, calculating and writing various documents.

(*b*) They help in carrying on them some of the important office equipment such as telephone, typewriter, calculator and various other machines.

(*c*) They help in storing important documents and thus help in maintaining the secrets of the business.

(*d*) They reduce the strain of office staff by offering comfortable place to work.

(*e*) They increase speed and accuracy of work by providing different types of office equipment.

(*f*) By means of providing the cupboards within the walls, it saves space as well as investment that would otherwise have been made for its purchase.

Classification of office furniture

Furniture used in an office can be classified into five types on the basis of use, quality, the person to whom it is meant and the material used in furniture making. They are:

1. Executive furniture: This type of furniture is exclusively meant for the executives *viz.*, the managing director or the manager and the board of directors. Such type of furniture can also be used in the reception room in order to add prestige to the company. Usually the furniture used under this classification will be made of superior quality wood with attractive design and innovation style. There is no standardisation in the size and shape of such furniture. Some furniture may be rectangular while other may be semi-circular so that people occupying the chairs in front of the executive are equidistant from him. The surface of the table is usually covered by thick glass material. The furniture is also designed in such a way so as to keep a tray, telephone, table lamp and other stationery and equipment. The chairs are of cushion type and revolving.

2. Special-purpose furniture: A special purpose furniture is meant for performing a special type of work as for example typing, duplicating of records, calculation, etc., the most common special purpose furniture relates to typist desk or table. This table is specially meant for typing purpose and is about 4 feet in width 2 feet 3 inches in depth and 30 inches high. The table may also be provided with drawers in order to store stationery, carbon papers and such other materials. Where the typist also has to perform certain other clerical work such as auditing or sorting out of documents, it is better to have a large sized table which is about 4 feet width, 3 inches deep. Keeping sufficient space for typewriter, the drawers can be provided on either side of the table.

3. Built-in furniture: This is a type of furniture which is devised in order to save space as well as investment on furniture. While constructing office building, necessary provisions are made according to the requirement for a cupboard or a shelf. This portion is later converted into a storage space by using wood or any other form of material such as laminated plastic. Similarly, while ordering, a typist table necessary drawers can be arranged for to accommodate typewriter when work is over.

4. General furniture: This type of furniture is meant for common use for performing routine work by the clerical staff. In the olden days, general furniture was made out of wood. Today steel furniture is used, by and large on account of its durability. The chairs to be used are of standard size so as to offer comforts to the staff. The size, height and shape of furniture is also of a standard type. The table top is usually covered by rexine or glass to avoid spoilage of the surface of table.

5. Modular furniture: This type is also known as system furniture. The purpose of such furniture is to provide greater desk area and covering less floor space. Under this type, one set of furniture is interlocked with another set so that the total frame becomes smaller. By this process of interlocking the furniture, it is estimated that the desk area can be increased by about 25 per cent thereby reducing the total floor space occupied by the furniture by 33 per cent. One disadvantage of this type of furniture is that is gives scope for the clerks sitting close by to talk to each other and thereby wasting time.

Factors to be considered while selecting office furniture

The selection of office furniture should receive the same attention when compared to the selection of any other asset. Any wrong selection of asset will have adverse effects over the functioning of the office. The selection of office furniture is based on the following factors:

1. Design. The design of the furniture refers to the size, height, number of drawers, the make and the quality and type of material to be used in making the furniture. The size of furniture must suit the area of the room. A large sized furniture obstructs easy movement of staff.

2. Investment of capital: This is one of the important factors which decide the quantity and quality of furniture.

3. Durability: Steel furniture is more durable compared to wooden furniture. The plastic laminated-surfaced furniture is very long lasting. In addition to material, the method of making the furniture also decides the durability of furniture.

4. Conservation of space: The furniture to be selected must be such that it must save space in the office. A modular type of furniture discussed already serves this purpose.

5. Fire risk: The metal furniture is not susceptible to the occurrence of fire and can resist it for a longer duration when compared to wooden furniture.

6. Weight: Where the re-layout of furniture is felt necessary at frequent intervals as in the case of a large sized organisation, it is better to go in for a light weight furniture.

7. Cleanliness: Often the furniture as well as the floor area under it need to be cleaned to eliminate the accumulation of dust. The type of furniture selected must give scope for such a cleaning process.

8. Appearance: The furniture must be attractive to the eyes and add further to the interior decoration of the office.

9. To suit the requirement of the staff: The furniture must provide the required comfort to the staff. This factor will in fact overcome the problem of fatigue faced by the clerks.

10. Finish: The use of highly polished surface and use of glass give rise to the problem of glare. Care must be taken to avoid production of glare by the furniture selected.

11. Saving in labour: By making necessary provisions such as drawers, etc., within the tables, the time involved in movement by the clerks from one place to another can be saved.

12. The versatility of the furniture: The furniture to be selected must serve more than one purpose for which it is intended.

13. Meet hierarchal level of the individual: The office furniture to be selected must suit the hierarchal level of the individual concerned. A prestigious furniture must be provided for the chief executive whereas an ordinary one will be sufficient for a typist.

14. Supervision: The type of furniture selected must enable supervision of work by the office manager.

15. Provision for storing the personal belonging of staff: Sometimes, the office staff have to safeguard their personal belonging such as purses, tiffin carriers, and hand bags. To avoid theft, necessary provisions must be made within the furniture for the safe keeping of such belongings of office staff.

Type of office furniture

A modern commercial office makes use of a variety of furniture. They are as follows:

1. Desks: A desk is a work bench provided to the office staff to carry out their work. It provides a working surface whereon the clerical work such as writing, operating the office machines, sorting out of documents take place. It also acts as storage place for various records. The size and shape of desks depend upon the type of work to be performed and also the status of the clerks. The desk should be of a size which fits into the available floor space. It should give good appearance. It should serve more than one purpose as it is very costly to have variety of desks. The following are some of the features of a good desk:

(*a*) It should be simple and light in colour. It should not have highly polished surface.
(*b*) A desk should have less number of drawers. The drawers must be capable of accommodating standard sizes of paper.
(*c*) Desks' top to be covered by linoleum for its long life.
(*d*) The height and size of the desk should suit the person working on it. The normal desk height is 2 ft. 4½ inches from the ground to provide a comfortable working position.

The following are some of the varieties of desks used in an office:

(*a*) *'L' Shaped desk or work stations*: This type of desk resembles the letter 'L' as regard the surface of the desk is concerned. On the vertical side of the desk top, a typist can carry on typing work and on the horizontal side some other activity such as records reference, or by using an adding machine or a calculator, required calculations can be made.

(*b*) *'Z' Shaped desk or Spine table*: This type of desk has a single pedestal desk top attached at each side. A number of 'Z' formations are placed together to form a working group. This type of desk is used where work is regularly passed from one desk to another.

(*c*) *Interchangeable desk or Convertible desk*: Under this type of desk, it is possible to interchange its parts for separate use. It serves the following purposes: (*i*) Reduces space occupied by the desk, (*ii*) makes it more adaptable to changing requirements, (*iii*) provides standardisation with beauty of design and greater comfort for staff and (*iv*) reduces cost of desk as a substitute to another variety.

2. Tables: While desks are found more useful in large sized offices, tables are best suited to small offices. Tables are used for writing, sorting, checking, and for storing equipments such as telephone, typewriter, etc. Usually tables are provided with drawers so as to preserve stationery and other typed papers. A large sized table is used in conference hall where meetings are held frequently.

3. Chairs: Where a large part of the work is to be performed by sitting posture, chairs assume utmost importance as a form of furniture. Comfortable sitting reduces fatigue, improves health, reduces absenteeism and increases productivity. Investigation has shown that bad seating posture has adverse effects over heart and chest. The chairs for office purpose should be well designed according to the stature of the clerks using it. Revolving chairs are more useful where a clerk has to move back and forth frequently. The back of a seat must also support the person using it. The saddle seat is considered to be the best form of seat.

It is desirable to set standards for different types of chairs. The important factors to be considered are (*a*) adjustable height, (*b*) adjustable back rest and (*c*) shape of seat. Each seat may be labelled with the name of the person using it so that it is not used by another person. Chairs can be made out of wood, aluminum, steel, and fibre glass. Chairs for executives are made out of special material with all comforts. The recent trend is towards the use of fibre glass and plastics for the bases of chairs because these materials resist scratches and scuffs.

As regards the dimensions of chairs, the British Standards Institution for Office Furniture has laid down the following:

(*i*) Seat height—17 inches
(*ii*) Maximum effective depth—15 inches
(*iii*) Minimum width when no arms are provided—16 inches
(*iv*) Minimum distance between arms—19 inches
(*v*) Height of elbow rest above chair seat 8½ inches.

4. Almirahs: Almirahs are used to preserve office records. These are made out of wood, steel, etc. Each section of the office is provided with an almirah to keep all documents safely. However, in cash department, almirah can be replaced by a iron safe to keep cash safely. The size of almirahs also differs from sections to section. Steel almirahs are very popular because of the following reasons:

(*i*) It is durable and cannot be easily damaged.
(*ii*) It does not shrink or swell or crack.
(*iii*) Steel almirahs are safe against fire, rats, mice or insects.
(*iv*) It has resistance to fire.

5. Miscellaneous items: In addition to the above discussed furniture, the following miscellaneous items are also to be provided for every clerk to perform his activities satisfactorily:

(1) Desk trays
(2) Desk calender
(3) Scale or ruler
(4) One set of pens black or blue and red with ink
(5) One pen stand
(6) One pencil and eraser
(7) Stapler and pins
(8) Clip box
(9) Stamp pad with Ink
(10) One pad of rough paper and ream of white papers
(11) Dustbin

Recent trends in office furniture

The rapid changes in shaping and sizing of furniture to avoid fatigue of workers is increasingly taking place since 1949. These changes are referred to as 'Ergonomics'. According to Websters' *Third International Dictionary*, ergonomics is "that aspect of technology concerned with the application of biological and engineering data to problems relating to the mutual adjustment of man and machines." This accounts for many of the changes which have taken place in respect of desks, tables, chairs and stools in recent years. The main trends in the field of office furniture are as follows:

1. Use of special purpose furniture: Special purpose furniture is designed to ensure physical comfort for clerks in order to increase their efficiency. Two examples can be cited in this regard:

(*a*) *Posture chairs:* This is specially made for typists which allows for adjustable heights, self-adjusting back and a pivotal seat.

(*b*) *Drop-action desks for typists:* This type of desk provides for a place which can hold a typewriter. When the typist wants to do any clerical work, he can put back the typewriter into this place. Thus, a flat working surface is formed on the top.

2. Saving in space: Office furniture is now designed in such a way as to save maximum space as possible. Few example in this regard are as follows:

(*a*) Modular furniture (this is already discussed earlier).
(*b*) Mobile filing units.

3. Flexibility in the use of furniture: Office furniture is arranged so as to facilitate rearrangement of them easily and readily. To facilitate this, the furniture used in modern days are comparatively light in weight and fully inter-locking.

4. Interchangeability: This is achieved by the use of standard base units together with an interchangeable desk tops which are easily assembled.

5. Prestige furniture: A wide variety of furniture is used to suit the status of different staff and executives of the business. They are decorative ones which also attract the attention of everybody, particularly visitors.

6. Colours: The material used in making the furniture, the make, and use of different colours are some of the outstanding trends seen in office furniture.

7. Portable furniture: To facilitate the rearrangement of an office area, portable furniture is increasingly used. Movable partitions are an example of portable furniture which are often used widely.

QUESTIONS

Objective Type Questions

1. What do you mean by furniture?
2. State the features of office furniture.
3. Mention five classes of office furniture.
4. Mention six types of office furniture.
5. What do you mean by a desk?
6. Distinguish between a desk and a table.
7. Mention any eight miscellaneous items used along with office furniture.
8. What do you mean by Ergonomics?

Analytical Type Questions

1. Examine the need for and importance of office furniture.
2. Briefly explain the various classes of furniture used in an office.
3. Explain briefly the various factors to be considered while selecting office furniture.
4. Explain the recent trends in office furniture.

Essay Type Question

1. Explain the various types of furniture used in a modern commercial office.

13

Office Equipments and Machines

INTRODUCTION

Office Machines constitute one of modern methods of performing office work. It is an improvement over manual method in the sense that it performs the job more quickly and efficiently. However, use of machines need operation and supervision by office staff. As the investment on office equipment and machinery is high, it is the responsibility of office manager to select the right type of equipment. Any wrong selection of machines may fail to meet the purpose for which it is meant. Today, a wide variety of machines are available to perform different types of office work. Though the entry of mechanisation is considered to be late in office when compared to production process in factories, it is now increasing at a pace which seems likely to surpass its progress in the factory. The increased importance of office mechanisation is felt by the management of most of the organisations and many sophisticated machines have been introduced to simplify the mental work of the organisation. This is evident from the fact that in the last 30 years, the office equipment industry has become one of the leading industries.

Policies guiding mechanisation

The following aspects serve as guiding principles of office mechanisation:

(1) Volume of work, (2) Savings in time, (3) Bottlenecks in the mechanisation process, (4) Training the operator, (5) Resistance to changes, (6) Cost of the machine, (7) Maintenance and service cost, (8) Speed of maintenance and availability of spare parts, (9) Operating costs, (10) Special paper work required, (11) Space available, (12) Accuracy and quality required, (13) Less risk of fraud with built-in

checking, (14) Relief (or creation) of boredom and monotony, (15) Obsolescence factor (16) Reaction from other, staff and the staff union, (17) Fear of redundancy and lowering of morale, (18) Output of machine, (19) Lower fatigue factor, (20) Degree of Supervision, (21) Information requirements of Management.

Factors Influencing Office Machines

Equipmont Consideration

1. Need of the machine
2. Determination of appropriate machine
3. Dependability of machine
4. Specification of machine
5. Cost of machine
6. Operational process of machine
7. Safety features
8. Flexibility of machine
9. Ease of machine operation
11. Cost of machine operation
11. Staff

Vendor Consideration

1. Reputation of machine vendor
2. Training provided by the manufacturer
3. Purchasing options
4. Delivery of the new equipment

Maintenance Consideration

1. Servicing the machines
2. Machine maintenance

Factors to be considered before introducing office machines

Before introducing office machinery certain important factors as shown in the above chart ought to be taken into consideration.

Equipment consideration

The following are some of the factors which fall under this category:

1. Need for the machine: The need for machines in the office may be felt for of the reasons such as replacing manual labour (with a view to reduce cost), to overcome shortage of staff or to improve management-staff communication.

2. Determination of appropriate machine: Different machines serve different purposes and hence right choice must be made to serve a definite purpose. Suppliers can be relied upon to suggest the right equipment for performing a right job.

3. Dependability of machine: As only reputed suppliers can manufacture durable machines, it is desirable to select only from reputed concerns. Different buyers can be contacted in order to know from which supplier they buy the equipment for this purpose.

4. Specification of the machines: The specification of machines may relate to size, installation requirements and special structural requirements. Though the machines may satisfy most of the requirements, yet it is often discarded owing to inappropriate specification.

5. Cost of the machine: The investment of office machine is an important factor to be considered as it has a profound impact on the financial policy of the business. Before the machines are bought, quotations are to be invited and the most competitive supplier is to be chosen.

6. Operational process of machines: Certain equipments need consumable as for example, a typewriter needs carbon copies, stencil papers, typing papers, ribbons. It is necessary to determine all such requirements in advance as without such supplies, the machines cannot be used.

7. Safety features: Though most of the office machines are safe in terms of its operation, certain machines used in printing and duplicating processes are not safe when employees are careless. So, the nature of the safety features on the equipment should be evaluated.

8. Flexibility of machines: Certain machines can be used for performing different types of work when compared to other machines. Hence, the extent of flexibility of the machines should be thoroughly evaluated.

9. Ease of machine operation: Some machines are easy to operate while others require complete knowledge about their functioning. It is better to learn about the use of machines when they are demonstrated by the suppliers.

10. Cost of machine operation: The cost of operating the machine which includes the power and labour and stationery cost is to be taken into account before selecting the machine. Where the cost of operating the machine is more than manual labour, it should be dispensed with.

11. Co-operation of Staff: Before installing machines in the office, it is necessary to seek co-operation of the staff. The attitude of staff to mechanisation is to be considered to avoid antagonism towards introduction of machinery.

Vendor consideration

1. Reputation of machine vendor: In order to purchase best type of machines, it is necessary to consider the reputation of the vendor. This depends upon the age of the vendor firm, size of the firm, services provided by the firm, financial stability of the firm, range of machines sold and community attitude towards the firm. Reputation of vendor is essentially considered when purchasing specialised and costly equipment.

2. Training provided by the manufacturer: Some of the machines are of complicated type which require training of the operators. This facility of training to be offered must be ensured both at the time of installation of machines and also when a new operator uses the equipment.

3. Purchasing option: Some suppliers sell the machines while others lease as well as sell. Depending upon the decision taken by the management, this factor is to be considered.

4. Delivery of the new machine: Only those suppliers who can deliver the machines immediately alone is to be selected. This factor is more important when machines ar e to be replaced frequently.

Maintenance considerations

1. Servicing the machine: Only those vendors who can offer service in times of need are to be selected. Those suppliers located at a far off place may not be able to come and repair whenever the need arises.

2. Machine maintenance: The maintenance of machines is yet another factor that is to be considered while selecting the machine. Some machines require more maintenance compared to others.

Objects or importance of office machines

The object of office machines are as follows:

1. It saves labour: The use of machines in offices reduces the number of office staff and consequently results in savings in the payment of wages and salaries. Further machines perform increased volume of work as compared to manual labour.

2. It saves time: Office machines considerably saves, the time of clerks. For example, to convey a message from one to another at a distance of say, a furlong, it takes atleast ten minutes. But using a telephones, the message can be conveyed at the earliest. Office machines are particularly used in those sections of the office where work is to be performed speedily as for example, calculations, preparation of invoices, etc.

3. It perforins the work more accurately: Where accuracy is most needed in the performance of office work, machines are considered as best suited. It overcomes the usual errors committed by the clerks and avoids cross checking.

4. It relieves monotony: Office work, to a large extent, is considered as monotonous and hence constitutes drudgery. If machines are used in such situations, it helps in eliminating monotony and makes office work more interesting.

5. It lessens the chance of fraud: Sometimes, office machines help in avoiding fraud being committed by unscrupulous persons. The best example that can be cited is writing of wrong amount on cheques which can be eliminated by using a cheque writing machine.

6. It provides work of better appearance as for example, a typed invoice.

7. It lessens the fatigue of office staff and thus improves the quality of work.

8. It provides management with more information speedily as for example, with an electronic computer.

Preliminary arrangements to be made before installation of office machines

In order to derive maximum benefits from the installation of office machines, certain preliminary arrangements are essential. These are as follows:

1. Preliminary notice to the staff: In order to seek cooperation from the staff, they must be convinced that machines are introduced only to increases their efficiency and it does not result in dismissal of staff thereby creating unemployment.

2. Gradual introduction: The office machines must be introduced gradually but not all of sudden.

3. Flow of work: There must be careful planning of office mechanisation so as to ensure a smooth flow of work from one machine to another instead of creating a bottleneck.

4. Training: Wherever necessary, it is essential to train the existing staff or to recruit trained operator before the machines are installed.

5. Allocation of machines to departments or personnel: It is desirable to decide in advance what machines are to be used by different departments and which employees are to operate the machine.

6. Accommodation: Sufficient space must be made available for the installation of machines as well as for the operators. Necessary arrangements must also be made to isolate noise producing machines so as to avoid distraction.

7. Maintenance: Proper arrangements must be made for the regular maintenance of machines.

8. Communication: The information relating to the following is to be communicated as and when it is applicable:

(*a*) Personnel entitled to use the machines.
(*b*) Instructions regarding care and maintenance.
(*c*) Procedural changes to be made in the respective departments resulting from the introduction of the new machines.

After satisfying that all the above mentioned factors are within the reach of the organisation, the actual installation of machines is to be considered. The actual installation of machines is in turn governed by the following:

(*a*) Size and weight of the machine for the sake of allocation of space.
(*b*) Availability of suitable power point.
(*c*) Vibration caused by the machine
(*d*) Noise created by the machine demanding a separate room to avoid distraction.
(*e*) Mounting the machine in the correct position so as to facilitate easy operation of machines.
(*f*) Focussing light so as to facilitate correct visibility of papers.
(*g*) Space for keeping service tools and storage facilities.

Purchase *Vs* lease of equipment

Whenever the need for mechanising the office arises, it involves a decision to be taken between out-right purchasing or leasing. However, the following factors are to be considered in determining whether leasing or purchasing is more advantageous.

1. Rapidity of technological development: When the machines are subject to significant changes because of technological development, it is better to acquire such machines on a lease basis. This helps in using the most upto date machines.

2. Investment involved: When the initial investment is heavy, it is desirable to lease the equipment than to purchase it.

3. Special provisions in the lease agreement: If the lease agreement proves more favourable, machines can be acquired on lease basis.

4. Stability of work process: If the work process changes radically, it is better to acquire machines on lease basis.

5. Cost per unit of work: If the cost per unit of work is less under lease basis then machines can be acquired on lease basis.

Types of leasing office machines

Leasing may be of two types: (*a*) Time lease and (*b*) Lease with the option to purchase. Under the time lease agreement, the lessee will never intend to buy the equipment being leased. Under lease with option to buy, lessee may exercise an option to purchase at some time in the future.

Advantages of leasing

(1) It conserves capital which otherwise would have been invested in purchasing the machines.
(2) It facilitates the purchase of up-to-date machines.
(3) It is best suited for short-term needs of office work especially where work involved is of a temporary nature.
(4) It provides for servicing the equipment leased.

Disadvantages of leasing

(1) It is more costly when compared to purchasing the machines.
(2) Lease agreement may make lessee responsible for the repairs and maintenance.
(3) It leads to more paper work.

Advantages and disadvantages of office machines

The advantages derived from the installation of office machines may be classified under the following:

1. To Employers: Employers benefit from office machines in respect of the following:

(*a*) Economies, reflected in cost reduction due to increased productivity and greater efficiency.
(*b*) It results in earning increased profits.
(*c*) It results in preparation of accurate and upto date records.
(*d*) It leads to better communication between management and staff, customer and shareholders.
(*e*) It enhances the prestige with the customers and public.

2. To Staff

(*a*) It reduces the physical fatigue by reducing the working hours.
(*b*) It reduces the mental strain of the staff.
(*c*) It improves the relationship between staff and management.

3. To Public: Customers and public at large will benefit in the following ways:

(*a*) It provides better and quicker service and information as for example, preparation of invoice promptly and in legible forms.

(*b*) Economies effected by mechanisation will result in cheaper goods and services to the public.

The following are the disadvantages of office machines:

1. *Capital Expenditure:* Office machine involves heavy investment and when the required amount is not available, it may even force to borrow loans. This involves repayment of both loan and interest which proves to be burdensome to the organisation.

2. *Depreciation*: If a high rate of depreciation is charged on machines, it reduces the profit available for distribution.

3. *Obsolescence:* Due to advanced technological development, some machines are liable to become obsolete in a relatively short span of time.

4. *Operating cost:* The operating cost of machine together with other consumables adds to the cost of production.

5. *Breakdown of machine:* Whenever there is breakdown of machines, it leads to disruption of work until it is set right.

6. *Training:* Training of staff often poses a problem.

7. *Noise:* Noise produced by machines distracts the attention of others thereby often forcing them to commit mistakes.

8. It cannot substitute experts or specialist.

A machine cannot do work requiring great intelligence as for example an accountant is still required even when an accounting machine is used. In other words, machines do not dispense with the human factor. Often they create more human problems than before.

Types of office machines

A wide range of machines are used in a modern commercial office. This is presented in the following chart:

TYPE OF OFFICE COUNTING MACHINES

Accounting Machines	Correspondence Machine	Data Processing Machine	Time Recording Machine	Reprographic Service Machine
Accounting machine Adding machine and Calculator	Dictating equipment Mail Room equipment Telephone Typewriters	Punched card equipment Computers	Card Time Recorders Autographic Time Recorder Dial Recorders	Photo Copying Machines Duplicating Machine

Accounting machines

The chief machines used in the process of accounting are:

I. Definition of accounting machines: Denyer in his book *Office Administration* has defined accounting machines as "machines electrically operated and used primarily for posting to ledger accounts; they may be filled with a number of adding registers for analysis purposes; have special key board facilities for entering details when posting and usually have a special front-feed device to give speed when feeding ledger cards to the machine."

Features of accounting machines

(*a*) It has automatic movement for the carriage of each entry, (*b*) Automatic calculation and printing of new account balance at each entry, (*c*) If the machine is fitted with a memory or circulating register, automatic totalling of all entries can be made to different accounts, (*d*) Automatic printing of the date when details are entered, (*e*) Ordinary back feed and front feed for ledger cards, (*f*) The more expensive machines have programme bars or control bars which automatically convert the machines for different purposes. Accounting machines may be divided broadly into two types, *viz.,* (*i*) Key-operated (or key board machine) and (*ii*) Punched card machine.

Description of the key operated accounting machines

The key operated accounting machine resembles to a large typewriter. In fact, it is a development of the typewriter as it combines both typewriter and adding machine. It has the following parts:

1. Keyboard: The keyboard may be of two types (*i*) commercial or non-descriptive which consists of only a numerical keyboard and (*ii*) alpha-numerical or descriptive with both typewriter and numerical board.

2. Feed: This portion of the key board machine is used for feeding forms, cards etc., and its position may vary so as to facilitate front feed, back feed and flexible form feed which permits both front and back feeding into the machine.

3. Automatic controls: This part of the equipment is used to control typing, recording etc.

4. Register: This is a mechanism which is capable of storing the amount set up on the key board.

5. Paper tape as a by-product: It is found in some accounting machines, *i.e.,* they have built in paper tape punches. The paper tape produced serves as input data for a computer.

Applications of accounting machines. The following are some of the purpose for which accounting machines are used:

(*a*) Purchase ledger accounts
(*b*) Sales ledger accounts
(*c*) Pay-roll records
(*d*) Shares and stock ledger accounts
(*e*) Cash book writing
(*f*) Cost accounting
(*g*) Hire purchase accounts
(*h*) Preparation of invoice

Advantages of accounting machines

(*a*) It facilitates increased speed of operation when compared with hand written system.
(*b*) It ensures greater accuracy because of making entries simultaneously on a number of documents. This obviates the mistakes which often occur when copying from one document to another.
(*c*) It leads to improved legibility and neat presentation of information. This is beneficial both to management, employees and customers. Management will receive the reports, accounts and statistics in an easily understandable form. Customers will appreciate the improvement in the invoices, debit notes, credit notes, etc,
(*d*) It results in economy owing to reduced number of staff.
(*e*) If facilitates ready reference by means of keeping accounts upto date. Moreover, they are more legible and easier to understand. Thus, it is possible to ascertain the current balance of any account at any time.
(*f*) It facilitates simultaneous posting and preparation of documents. For example, in the payroll accounting it is possible not only to prepare wage statement but also tax records.
(*g*) The introduction of accounting machines will result in an allround increase in efficiency in the accounting and related departments.

Disadvantages of accounting machines

Truly speaking, there are two disadvantages of accounting machines. It is often criticised not because of the fault of the machine but in the manner of planning its work or in its misuse. However, the following constitute the drawbacks of accounting machines:

(*a*) It involves heavy capital investment which small business enterprises cannot afford to invest.

(*b*) The noise produced by an accounting machine distracts the attention of others.

(*c*) Breakdown of the machine may disrupt the accounting work.

(*d*) It is not possible to write, lengthy description through accounting machines for clear understanding.

(*e*) The cost of training is often considerable in a large office.

II. Adding machine and calculator: An adding machine is one which facilitates the process of addition and subtraction. The result of addition and deduction is shown on a roll of paper.

Types of adding machines

The adding machines may be classified under the following categories:

1. Listing and non-listing variety: A listing adding machine is one which gives a printed record of all figures put in the machine on a paper strip called a "tally roll". A non-listing adding machine is one which records only the totals in dials on the machines.

2. Full-bank and simplified keyboard machines: A full bank adding machine has columns of keys numbered 1 to 9 for each position depending upon the capacity of the machine. For example, a machine on which ₹ 9,999,999.99 can be entered, there are nine columns of numbered keys corresponding to the number of digits. The operator has to press the keys required in the various columns and then pull the crank.

A simplified keyboard accounting machine has ten keys numbered 0 to 9. It is operated by pressing the keys consecutively in the order in which they appear. For example, if the key for 2 and 1 is pressed and the machine operated, 21 will appear on the tally roll.

Features of adding machines

(*a*) It has a portion or a part known as non-print key by means of which the machine adds or subtracts without printing but will only print the answer when required.

(*b*) It has addition and subtraction keys which perform the function of adding and deducting the numbers.

(*c*) Sub-total key by pressing which sub-total can be obtained and then addition can be continued further.

(*d*) It has a total key which when pressed gives the net total.

(*e*) A repeat key which can be used to repeat the same number.

(*f*) Correction key to correct if a wrong key is pressed.

(*g*) Dials showing digits entered on the machine.

Applications of adding machines

(*a*) It is used in preparing Trial Balance after balancing every ledger account.

(*b*) It is helpful in preparing Trading and Profit and Loss Account and Balance Sheet.

(*c*) It is helpful in the preparation of wage sheets.

(*d*) It helps in the preparation of statistics relating to sales, purchases, production etc.

Advantages of adding machines

1. **Speed of operation:** In a short span of time millions of figures can be added and subtracted and the result can be known.
2. **Facility of checking:** It facilitates checking and crosschecking easily in case of doubt or discrepancy.
3. **Relieves strain:** It eliminates the mental strain of clerks as continuous adding and deducing is a monotonous work.
4. **Accuracy:** It ensures cent per cent accuracy, provided it is operated correctly.

Disadvantages of adding machines

1. **Noise:** It produces noise which disturbs other clerks.
2. **Breakdown of machine:** When machine goes out of order, the work is held up and to that extent work will be delayed.

Calculators

A calculator is basically used to perform the function of multiplication and division although addition and subtraction can also be performed on them.

Types of calculating machines

1. Printing calculator: A printing calculator resembles an adding listing machine and is the most simplest of all calculators. Calculations are made by setting up the figures required and then pressing the appropriate multiplication or division key wherein the answer is printed automatically on a roll of paper.

2. Key-Driven calculator: It is described as 'Key driven' since no lever is required for its operation. In this machine, keys are arranged in columns in the same way as in the case of the full key board adding machine. When the keys are pressed, the digits they represent are automatically added and the answers are shown on dials on the machine.

3. Rotary calculator: This type of calculator can be of two types, *viz.*, lever set or key set, though the method of operation is same. When calculation relates to multiplication of numbers, the handle is to be turned clockwise and for division by turning anticlock wise.

4. Electric automatic calculator: Its operations are performed with the help of electricity. They have separate sections on the keyboard for multiplicand and multiplier and on pressing the keys it performs calculations automatically.

5. Electronic calculator: This machine is similar in operation to the key-driven calculator, but the answers are shown in the lighted figure in dials and the calculations are performed electronically instead of mechanically.

Applications

There is practically no field where calculators are not used. Some of the areas where they are used are mentioned below:

(*a*) Construction and Engineering calculations
(*b*) Estimating
(*c*) Interest calculations
(*d*) Invoice preparation
(*e*) Pay-roll calculations
(*f*) Percentage calculations
(*g*) Scientific calculations
(*h*) Statistical work

Advantages

(*a*) The outstanding advantage of a calculator lies in its speed of calculations.
(*b*) In addition to arithmetical calculations such as addition, subraction, division and multiplication, some machines are capable of calculating percentages, squares roots and many such calculations.
(*c*) It is simple to operate.
(*d*) It is portable and some can be even carried in pockets.
(*e*) It gives accurate results.

Disadvantages

(*a*) It involves investment at the initial stage.
(*b*) It requires checking of results.
(*c*) Electrically operated calculators cannot be operated during the period of power failure.

Correspondence machines

The following are the important machines used in the process of correspondence:

1. Dictating machines: Denyer in his book *Office Administration* defines dictating machine as "an electronic machine which records speech on one of various possible recording media so that a typist can play back the recording and transcribe it on his typewriter.

Features

(*a*) It uses a suitable medium such as plastic tape, disc or wire to record a human voice.

(*b*) The dictator is provided with a microphone with which he can dictate his letters, reports, etc.

(*c*) There is an arrangement to playback the recording at any time. It has the arrangement of hand controls to start and stop the machine besides control adjustments to regulate speed, volume and tone.

Applications

(*a*) It is used in dictation of correspondence.

(*b*) Its application is found in recording telephone conversation messages and interviews, etc.

(*c*) Its necessity is felt in recording the meeting or conference held in the office.

(*d*) Its other special uses are:

(*i*) Recording engine noise caused by mechanical faults.

(*ii*) Speech training

(*iii*) To record on the spot commentaries of accidents.

Advantages

(*a*) The cost of typing can be reduced as number of typists can be minimised to a lesser number.

(*b*) The grade of employee can be reduced as for example, shorthand typist can be replaced by audio-typist.

(*c*) The machine saves correspondent's time as he need not wait for the stenographer.

(*d*) It is more convenient in the sense that correspondent can dictate at his convenience and regulate the speed at which he dictates, stop and restart the machine depending upon the need.

(*e*) It is portable as pocket models are also available.

Disadvantages

(*a*) The personal contact between correspondent and typist may be lost because of use of this machine.

(*b*) It may require clarity of speech and skill in communication which some correspondents may lack.

Mail room equipment

In a well equipped mail room, a number of machines such as letter opening machine, envelope sealing machine, paper folding machine, stamp affixing machine, franking machine and addressing machine. A brief description of these machines is given below:

1. Letter opening machine: A letter opening machine may be operated by hand or electrically. An electrically operated machine with automatic feed can open at a speed of 500 envelope per minute. It involves a process by which envelopes are opened by means of cutting a narrow strip from the edge of the envelope.

2. Envelope sealing machine: This can again be operated by hand or electrically. A standard electrically operated machine can seal envelops and letters at a speed of 25,000 per hour. The letter and envelops are automatically fed and operator is required merely to feed and remove them after ejection.

3. Stamp affixing machine: This machine is designed to hold a roll of about 500 stamps, to moisten the surface of each stamp as required, feed the stamp into the machine and guillotime it from the roll. For this purpose, stamps in the rolls of about 500 are bought from the post office. The roll is then inserted into the machine which counts and records the number of stamps used. In modern days, this machine is replaced by franking machine.

4. Franking machines: It is a hand or electrically operated machine which prints a form of postage stamp on an envelope. This machine dispenses with the ordinary adhesive postage stamp.

Initially, the franking machine is either hired or purchased from the manufacturers. The machine is then taken to the post office. Once the value franking is determined it is locked and sealed.

Secondly, the required ink is to be filled in the ink container and to set the data printing mechanism every day.

Thirdly, sort out the letters and envelops according to the postage required in order to save constant resetting of the dial.

Fourthly, feed the envelope or letter into the machine one at a time.

Fifthly, in case of parcels and bulky letters, a piece of paper is franked and then pasted on the parcels of bulky letters.

Lastly, all franked letters are put into the post bag provided.

Advantages

(*a*) It avoids spending more time on affixing the stamps on the outward mail.

(*b*) The misuse of stamps by the office staff can be avoided.

(*c*) It ensures easy delivery.

(*d*) Advertising slogans can also be used while franking.

Disadvantages

(*a*) The machine may be issued by unauthorised persons unless it is carefully supervised.

(*b*) Wastage may occur if the operator franks the wrong amount or fails to replenish the ink container.

Addressing machine

An addressing machine is an office machine which is designed to address labels, etc., by duplicating the information from the original copy.

Features

(*a*) It involves the preparation of original or master copy with the help of embossed metal plates or stencils.

(*b*) Additional information such as 'urgent' or 'personal' may also be obtained in addition to the actual address to be printed.

(*c*) It may have a numbering device which can be used to print the same number throughout.

(*d*) A dating device may be used for entering the data simultaneously with the printing of the address.

(*e*) Fascimile signature may be printed by the use of suitable attachment.

Applications

Addressing machines are used for the following purposes:

(*a*) Addressing envelops which are to be sent on a routine basis involving circulars, invoices and statements to customers, notices of meetings to shareholders, payment of dividends and interest.

(*b*) Helps in the preparation of dividend list, dividend warrant, etc.

(*c*) It is used to prepare documents such as notices, proxy forms, etc., to holding meetings.

(*d*) It is helpful in the preparation of payroll and tax returns.

Advantages

(*a*) It ensures speed of operation. It can produce addresses to the extent of 7,000 per hour.
(*b*) It results in economy in the sense, mail room staff can be reduced.
(*c*) It results in accuracy, once the original copy is accurately prepared.
(*d*) It is simple to operate and does not requite much training.

Disadvantages

(*a*) It is costly, especially when embossing of plates is used.
(*b*) Alterations cannot be made easily.

Telephone

Telephone

This is one of the most common office equipments used in the offices of almost all business enterprises. It is a direct, personal and immediate means of communication. It is a line which connects the telephone exchange to the subscribes' instrument. The principles involved in a telephone are as follows:

(*a*) The voice makes sound waves which strike the diaphragm of the microphone in the telephone hand-set.
(*b*) The pressure waves cause the diaphragm alternatively to compress and release the carbon granules behind it. This alternatively increases and decreases the flow of current in the circuit passing through the telephone network to the earpiece of the caller's hand-set.
(*c*) In the earpiece, the current is led around an electro-magnet which becomes magnetised as the current varies. The strong current

attracts the earpiece diaphragm strongly, while the weaker current releases the diaphragm.

(*d*) This movement of the diaphragm imitates the movement of the voice box miles away which causes the current to vary; and we hear the same sounds the speaker is making.

Advantages

(*a*) It is a speedy means of communication, which takes hardly few minutes to bridge gaps of hundreds of miles.

(*b*) It establishes person to person contact.

(*c*) It is a cheap means of communication if control is exercised over the user.

(*d*) Its facility is available continuously at all times.

Disadvantages

(*a*) It does not facilitate written records and hence cannot serve the purpose of reference.

(*b*) It may be misused by the office staff for their personal use.

(*c*) Though personal contact is established, the caller cannot be seen. The person has to be identified only by the voice.

Procedure

(*a*) To find out the telephone number of person to whom call is to be made through Telephone Directory.

(*b*) To find out the code number of exchange, if it is an out station locality.

(*c*) Dial the number after lifting the receiver.

(*d*) Listen to the ringing tone or engaged tone.

(e) At the end of the call replace the receiver carefully.

Typewriter

Perhaps there is no office which does not use typewriter in modern days. While in the olden days most of the letters were handwritten, the typewriter has come as one of the important equipment known to everyone. The typewriter produces letters of good appearance, neat, legible and well displayed. The following points are worth noting in this connection:

1. Type: In most of typewriter the Roman type is fitted.

2. Spacing: The spacing of lines to be typed may be single spacing, double spacing or treble spacing. This can be adjusted by the operation of a lever.

3. Carriage size: The carriage size of the roller in a standard size of the typewriter varies between 10 to 11 inches wide which can practically hold varieties of sizes of papers.

4. Tabulating mechanism: The tabulator consists of rack at the back of the carriage on which small forked 'stops' can be filled at any required point. This is to enable the typist to stop the carriage at predetermined positions to assist in setting out work accurately and quickly. The typist has to press a key to make the carriage move and stop at the point required.

Typewriter

Type of typewriters

1. Noiseless typewriters: As the name itself suggests, this type of equipment is quiter in operation when compared to other types. This type is used where work requiring more concentration is involved.

2. Electric typewriter: This is becoming more popular both from the employers' point of view on account of increased output and from employees' point of view owing to less effort involved in typing. This machine is electrically operated but the typist has to press the keys gently in order to operate the typewriter. Its chief advantages are as follows:

(*i*) It appearance resembles to that of printed matter.

(*ii*) As many as 20 copies can be taken at a time.

(*iii*) Stencil typing can be done best in this typewriter.

Its disadvantages are:

(*i*) It takes some time for the typist in getting used to light touch.

(*ii*) It is expensive when compared to other typewriters.

3. Variable-type typewriters: This typewriter facilitates interchange of type blocks so as to provide variety of sizes and styles of type. The change of size or style can be made without removing the paper from the machine. This type of typewriter is useful for typing price lists, catalogues, etc., where prominent headings are necessary.

4. Automatic typewriters: This machine is used to type a standard letter automatically either single or in large numbers. It is a machine in which plain paper is fed on which standard letters or paragraphs are typed at the rate of 150 words per minute. They are usually operated by a prepared reel of punched paper tape which can be stored and used again for automatic re-typing of the matter when required.

Typing pool

A typing pool refers to a system under which all or most of the typists in an organisation work in one central place together instead of typing in different rooms. Under this system, the work is shared among all the typists instead of typing individually.

Advantages of typing pools

(*a*) It ensures economical use of typist labour as for example, the idle time arising while managers are at meeting can be filled by other work.

(*b*) It facilitates even distribution of work *i.e.*, no typist is overburdened under this systems.

(*c*) Difficulties arising out of sickness and holidays can be overcome by allocating work to other typists.

(*d*) It is easy to train typists under a typing pool in various fields.

(*e*) The noise of typing is confined to one room only.

(*f*) It is easier to supervise all typists under a typing pool.

Disadvantages of typing pools

(*a*) The personal contact between the executive and typist is lost.

(*b*) It is not useful when personal secretaries are employed.

(*c*) It may result in gossiping among all typists.

(*d*) It may lead to delays when typists are frequently called from the central room.

Data Processing Machine

Data processing machine

The two important data processing machines are (1) Punched card equipment and (2) Computers.

1. Punched card equipment: This is the first equipment to apply automatic data processing. The most important feature of a punched card machine lies in the common language provided by the punched card. The card can be used to record alphabetic information, numerical information and special symbols such as "₹", "%", etc.

Equipment used in punchcard system

1. Key punch machine: A key punch machine is used to punch the holes in the punched card. The data for punching the holes can be obtained from various documents such as purchase orders, invoices, payment vouchers, inventory reports, etc. This equipment has a key-board which resembles to a typewriter keyboard. The operator after reading the information from the various documents mentioned above enters the same data (information) on the card.

The key punch machine has a feeding mechanism which permits the automatic feeding of a new card. This equipment is also capable of programming which means several operating functions can be performed automatically. It can also be used to interpret the information contained on the card which means that the letters, numbers or symbols are printed at the top of the card. This can be used to verify the accuracy of the information punched in the cards.

2. Card verifier: The purpose of the card verifier is to verify the accuracy of the information contained on the card so punched by the key punch machine. The operator using the keyboard, punches the same card for the second time based on the same information. If the punched hole this time is in a different position (not coinciding on the hole originally punched) then an electrical contact is lost and the machine automatically stops. This indicates the errors in punching. The operator then ascertains whether the fault lies in the first or in the repeat punching.

3. Interpreter: The function of the interpreter is to print on the cards the data that is contained in the punches on the card. In other words, it translates the punched data into alpha, numeric or special character and prints it on the card. This is so because the key punch machines do not have a printing mechanism. Interpreting the punched data is necessary when the cards are to be used for filing purposes.

4. Reproducer: This equipment is used to duplicate the data contained on one set of card to another set of cards. This is useful when the original set becomes worn out.

5. Sorter: The function of the sorter is to arrange the card into alphabetic or numerical order. For example, sales invoice cards have to be sorted out on the basis of territories.

6. Tabulating or Accounting machine: After sorting out the cards they are fed into a tabulator which sense the information punched in the cards, automatically adds up the various totals and prints the totals at the end of each section. The tabulator has a plugged programme.

Applications

Punched card equipment are put to the following uses:

1. **Bank transactions:** The usual purposes served in the bank transactions are preparation of cheques, standing orders, reconciliation statements, payment of dividend, interest, etc.

2. **Budgetary control:** In preparing departmental budgets and master budget.

3. **Cost accounting:** In ascertaining the total cost of production.

4. **General accounting:** In preparing invoice, sales and purchase ledger and depreciation accounting.

5. **Sales analysis:** In preparing market and advertising research copies.

6. **Stores accounting:** In preparing stock verification report.

7. **Wage accounting:** In preparing wage sheets, wage slips etc.

8. **Statistical records:** In analysing and tabulating the facts and figures.

Advantages

1. **Speed of operation:** This is considered to be an outstanding advantage of punched card machine.

2. **Accuracy:** The card verifier ensures 100 per cent accuracy of the results.

3. **Simplicity of operation:** Once the person is trained, it is very simple to operate.

4. **Economy of labour:** As most of the work is performed by the machine labour, cost is saved to a large extent.

5. **Adaptability:** It is suitable to all types of business, big or small.

6. **Production of computer input:** The cards produced by punched card machine may be used as input for a computer.

7. **Information to management:** It provides accurate and upto date information which is very essential to management.

Disadvantages

1. **Cost:** The initial investment is heavy.

2. **Operating cost:** The cost involved in punching and verifying the card increases the operating cost.

3. **Noise:** The equipment produces excessive noise which disturbs people working in the same room.

4. **Break down of equipment:** This is a serious disadvantage as the processing of punched card machine relies upon its continuous operation. If one component, say, the sorter breaks down, the results may be chaotic.

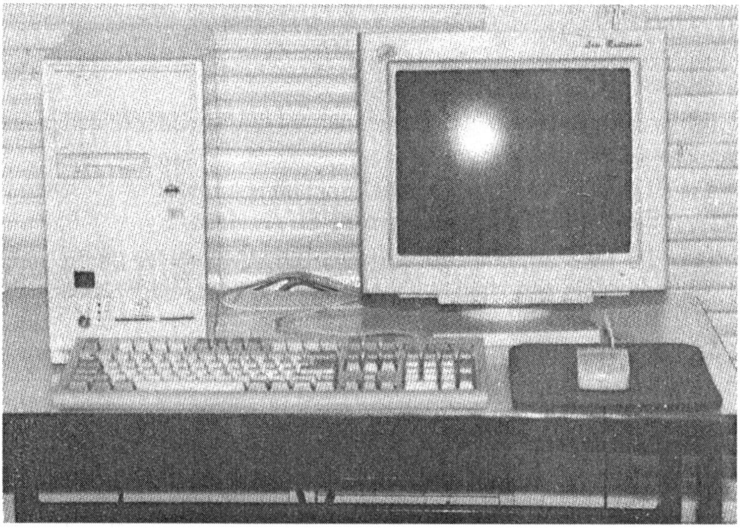

Computer

Computers

The introduction of computers has revolutionised the management function of most of the business enterprises. An electronic computer is an office machine by which office data is processed electronically at great speed which means the performance of calculations, analysis and printing results. A computer differs from a calculator in respect of a 'memory' the capacity being higher in the case of a computer.

Characteristic of computers

(*a*) A computer is capable of performing only such functions which are instructed. In other words, it will not undertake anything other than what is instructed by its programme.

(*b*) It is capable of performing complex calculations rather than simple calculations. Its great capacity enables large volumes of data to be processed very quickly with greater accuracy.

(*c*) For programming the data in computers it is a pre-requisite that the data is capable of representation in an alphabetic or numerical pattern recognised by the computer.

(*d*) Performing the work and presenting the results in a very short span of time is one of the distinctive features of computers.

(*e*) The magnetic storage devices which are part of computers enable a considerable degree of integration between systems to be achieved.

Functions

Mills and Standingford have summarised the functions of computers thus:

(*a*) To receive one or several programmes of instructions, store these and obey them as may be required.

(*b*) To take in new information through one or more input channels and store it for reference as required by any of the programmes.

(*c*) To perform any arithmetical operation as required by a programme.

(*d*) According to the state of information, it produces, selects and carries out alternative courses of action.

(*e*) To apply checks to data it receives or produces and if the test indicates a failure, produce a record or a signal to obtain human intervention and meanwhile proceed to next transaction or to another job.

(*f*) To store data produced for further reference.

(*g*) To select information from the store, arrange it in any sequence, and discharge it through one or more output channels to be printed for human use or to be recorded for subsequent computer use.

The Computer system

The computer system can be studied under two headings, *viz.*, (*a*) hardware and (*b*) software.

Hardware

The term hardware is used to denote the actual computer and its associated equipment. A computer consists of five components. They are as follows:

1. Input unit: This component receives the data in an appropriate form such as punched cards, perforated paper tape and magnetic tape. In this equipment the data is converted into electrical pulses, which represent the 'language' of the computer.

2. Storage unit: This component is also known as memory unit. The data which is in computer language is related in this unit which may consist of magnetic tape, magnetic discs, plated wire, etc. This equipment holds standing information, new information and the programmed instructions.

3. Control unit: This is also known as coordination unit which directs and brings into operation the various circuits required to carry out the programmed instructions.

4. Arithmetic and logic unit: This is also known as the function or process unit which performs all the arithmetical calculations at high speed.

5. Output unit: This equipment converts the results from the language of computer to the ordinary language.

Working of a computer

The working of a computer can be discussed under the following steps:

1. Programming: As a computer is capable of performing all the work relating to almost all the functions of a business such as purchase accounting, sales accounting, wages accounting, cost accounting, etc. It is necessary for the programmer at the first instance to prepare a programme for a particular task.

2. Input: Having prepared a program this is fed into the computer through any of the input media such as punched cards, paper tape, etc.

3. Storage: The data complied earlier and the information related to the current task is held on storage unit to facilitate further operation.

4. Processing: This stage involves in the following sub-stages:

(*i*) Transmission of data contained in the punched card to the central processing unit.

(*ii*) The existing data from the storage unit is fed simultaneously along with current data into central processing unit.

(*iii*) Acting upon the data supplied by the two sources, the processor performs the necessary calculations and assembles information.

(*iv*) The processor then passes the results of its work to the output devices.

5. Output: The result received by the output unit is finally presented in the required form, as for example on punched cards.

Software

The term software is defined as a system of computer which includes the programming, control instructions, training facilities, etc., providing to enable a computer to operate. In brief, it is a means by which the computer can be put to work.

Applications

Perhaps there is no field where the utility of computers are not felt. The following are some of the areas in which the computer are used:

1. Analysis: It is used to all work involving analysis.

2. Apportionments: Apportionment of common expenses to various departments or products.

3. **Budgetary control:** In preparing departmental and master budgets.

4. **Conversion:** To convert the amount into various currencies.

5. **Credit control:** It is helpful in classification and tabulation to customers.

6. **Financial accounts:** In preparing debtor's, creditor's and nominal ledgers.

7. **Interest:** In calculating simple and compound interest.

8. **Investment:** To analyse and maintain information about investments.

9. **Managerial information:** To produce information for managerial decision making about investments.

10. Mortgage and Investment accounts.

11. **Pay roll:** In preparation of tax, insurance, bonus, etc.

12. **Sales invoice:** In preparing invoice and sales budget.

13. **Shares and debentures:** It is used in the allotment of shares, payment of dividend and interest.

14. **Stock control:** In stock verification, reports.

15. **Time table:** In programming, staff working hours, production planning and control.

Advantages of computers

(*a*) Its speed of operation is very high.
(*b*) The volume of work which it can perform is large.
(*c*) It reduces the labour cost.
(*d*) The results shown by it are accurate and reliable.
(*e*) Furnishes upto date information for management.

Disadvantages of computers

(*a*) The initial investment on computers is very high.
(*b*) It may be subjected to obsolescence owing to increased technology of computers.
(*c*) It requires additional cost of maintenance such as air conditioning.
(*d*) It results in wastage of stationery in producing unnecessary records and increased labour cost in producing, handling and filing them.
(*e*) It is difficult to obtain experienced system analyst and programmers.
(*f*) Breakdown of machine leads to delay in producing results.

Reprographic service machines

Reprography is a term which implies any sort of process which enables a copy or a succession of copies to be reproduced from a master copy. The master copy is the original document which is written, typed or electronically prepared. Reprography in other words, connotes a process of duplicating original copy into multiple copies to meet the requirements of various people. With the increase in the size of business, there has developed a greater need for more number of copies of various documents, information bulletins and memos which are to be sent to various departments, branches, and other concerned persons. The reprographic service machines can be broadly classified into two categories, *viz.,* (1) Photocopying and (2) Duplicating machines.

I. Photocopying: Photocopying is a method of copying a document with photographic detail, and is generally used for obtaining one or at the most a few copies of such documents. The various methods of photocopying are as follows:

(a) Reflex photocopying: It resembles to ordinary photography.

Under this method, a negative is created by exposing the original to the light. With this negative any number of copics can be obtained. After developing in two baths of chemicals, high quality papers are produced.

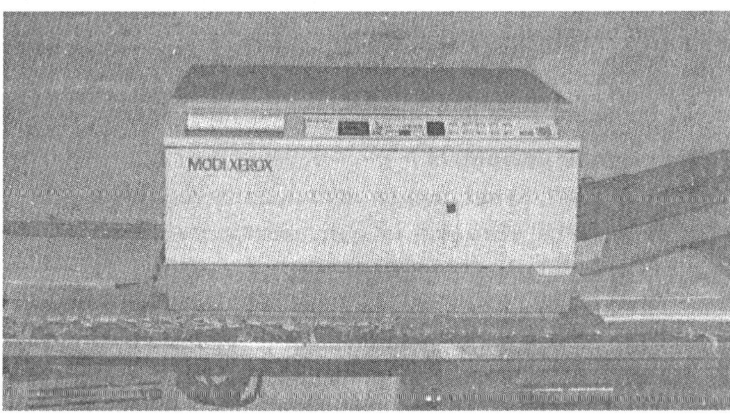

Photo Copying Machine

(b) Transfer diffusion: Under this method also, a negative copy is obtained but the multiple copies are obtained directly from the negative without the need for additional exposure and development. This involves the following steps:

(*i*) A negative is obtained as in the reflex printing.

(*ii*) The negative is associated with a positive paper and the two sheets are introduced together into the machine, where a diffusive action takes place to produce a positive image. The negative print is of no further use once it becomes dry.

(*c*) **Direct positive:** Under this method, it is possible to produce directly a positive copy without using a negative. A special type of translucent paper is used which yields a black image on white ground without the medium of a negative.

(*d*) **Heat transfer:** This equipment contains an infra-red lamp which emits heat. The original paper is passed through the machine along with a piece of special heat sensitive paper. When switched on, infra-red lamp emits heat which is reflected back by the light areas of the original but absorbed by dark areas. The heat sensitive coating of the copy (duplicate) paper darkens in those places where it comes into contact with the darkened areas of the original and thus produces the required copy.

(*e*) **Electrostatic:** This process is also known as Xerography. It can be explained to the original by means of a camera.

(*i*) A selenium-coated plate is charged with positive electricity and then exposed to the original by means of a camera.

(*ii*) A negatively charged powder is showered on the plate, adhering only to the positively charged areas, to provide a true copy of the original.

(*iii*) A sheet of paper is brought into contact with the selenium-coated plate from which it attracts a dusting of positively charged ink power to form an image of the original.

(*iv*) Lastly, the image is permanently fused into the paper fibres by exposing it to heat.

Applications of photocopying machines

The applications of photocopying machines are found in the following fields:

1. Correspondence: When the incoming letters are to be circulated to more than one department of a business, they may be duplicated and sent to every department.

2. Meeting: For preparing notices and agenda of meetings they may be duplicated and sent to all concerned persons.

3. Transmission of shares: Certain documents such as will of probates, letters of administration and power of attorney, death certificates can be duplicated prior to returning the originals to be members.

4. Statutory books: The contents of statutory books such as Register of members, Register of debenture holder, Register of directors, Register of mortgages and charges, etc., can be photocopied as a precaution against loss by fire.

5. Accounting records: Important ledgers, final accounts and other financial statements can be photocopied as a precautionary measure against loss of originals by fire.

6. Forms production: Important documents used for internal purposes such as Memorandum of association. Articles of association, prospectus and for external purposes such as purchase order, invoice can also be photocopied in case of need.

7. Drawing office: Plans, drawings, specifications, charts, graphs, contract deeds and other blue prints can also be photocopied to meet the requirements of more than one purpose.

Advantages of photocopying

(*a*) It produces the exact facsimile copies with all details of the original copy.

(*b*) It is cheapest form of duplicating when only a few copies are required.

(*c*) It obviates the need for checking with the originals.

(*d*) It is used when the number of copies required differs.

Disadvantages of photocopying

(*a*) When more number of copies are required, it is very expensive.

(*b*) Photocopies may fade over a period of time.

Duplicating machine

II. Duplicating machines: Duplicating is the name given to a process whereby a master copy is prepared from which a large number of other copies are automatically obtained. The important methods of duplicating are (*a*) stencil method, (*b*) spirit duplicating method and (*c*) offset lithography.

1. Stencil duplication: Under this method, the master copy happens to be stencil which is made up of a thin fibrous sheet covered with a plastic coating. The process of duplicating is described under the following points:

(*i*) The stencil is cut either through a typewriter or by manually writing on it and to check it whether everything has been properly typed or written.

(*ii*) It is inserted in the duplicator and fixed over the drum of the machine which is properly inked.

(*iii*) When the machine is operated, the ink is forced through the cuts in the stencil, which produces the exact replica of the original on the stencil papers.

(*iv*) When the large number of copies are required, an automatic counting device is set so as to get the required number of copies.

It is desirable first to make a trial and take a few samples of duplicated papers to ensure that exact replica is obtained. Otherwise it requires proper adjustments and proper inking of the machines. A good quality stencil can produce as many as 500 copies. The stencil can be preserved and reused when required.

Applications

(*i*) Duplicating of circulars for distribution to customers.

(*ii*) Duplicating office forms to save the time in the preparation of various documents and reports.

(*iii*) Documents used while holding meetings such as notices, agenda, proxy forms and minutes for the circulation among members.

(*iv*) Duplicating company documents such as final accounts, auditors' reports, board of directors' report for distribution among shareholders.

(*v*) Memoranda for the internal circulation of staff.

(*vi*) In duplicating the office manuals and news of the company for the distribution among employees of the organisation.

Advantages

(*i*) The quality of reproduced copy will be good provided the stencil is cut properly.

(*ii*) A large number of copies can be obtained under this method.

(*iii*) Stencils can be stored and reused whenever necessary.

(*iv*) Alteration on stencil can be easily made by use of special correcting fluid.

(*v*) The method is most economical compared to other method of duplicating.

(*vi*) It can be duplicated with different colours.

Disadvantages

(*i*) The duplicating papers used will not be suitable for making entries by pen.

(*ii*) Colours can be reproduced only by making separate run for each colours.

(*iii*) This method is expensive when only a few copies are required.

2. Spirit duplication: Under this method of duplication, a master copy is prepared on a piece of art paper one side of which has a glossy surface. It is either typed or written backing it with piece of special carbon paper. The master copy is then inserted in the duplicator and wrapped round the drum of the machine. When the machine is operated, the copy paper which is fed one by one is dampened with the spirit. The spirit on the copy paper dissolves a small proportion of the carbon coating of the carbon paper and leaves a positive image on the copy paper. About 100 to 200 copies can be obtained from each master copy before it is exhausted.

Advantages

(*i*) It is cheap mode of duplicating both the carbon and master copy.

(*ii*) It is the only method by which many colours can be duplicated simultaneously.

(*iii*) The process of duplicating is simple, compared to other methods.

(*iv*) The master copy can be reused for subsequent short runs.

(*v*) Copies obtained are neat and reasonably of good quality.

(*vi*) It may be reproduced on papers of varying weights and sizes or on cards to suit the requirements of management.

Disadvantages

(*i*) The image diminishes and becomes weaker as the duplicating work progresses.

(*ii*) The number of copies that can be duplicated is limited.

(*iii*) The quality of impression when compared to stencil duplicator is not so good.

(*iv*) Alteration of master copy is somewhat difficult.

3. Offset lithography: This machine resembles to the printing process and is used where printed copies are felt necessary as against stencil or print duplicated copies. The process of its functioning can be listed under the following steps:

(*i*) It involves preparation of a master copy by typing, writing, drawing, photographing or electrostatic process. The material used for the master copy may be metal or paper plates.

(*ii*) The master plate is fixed to the cylinder of the machine and it is first brought into contact with damping rollers which are inked.

(*iii*) The operation of the machine brings the inked plate into contact with rubber-covered roller (or blanket) which takes up the inked image in reverse. Because the positive image is transferred or offset to this rubber covered-roller, the machine is called offset lithography.

(*iv*) Finally, the paper is fed into the machine between the *blanket* and the roller receives the positive image, and thus the printed matter is ready for us.

Advantages

1. Economy: Large amount can be saved when compared to outside printing cost especially when it is used in the long run.

2. Quality: The quality of reproduced documents is the best when compared to two methods discussed earlier.

3. Consistency: The quality of printing is maintained throughout but not unlike spirit duplicating machine where the image diminishes as the work progresses.

4. Length of run: If metal plates are used as master copy, as many as 50,000 copies can be obtained. A paper plate is capable of producing 1,000 copies.

5. Speed of operation: This equipment can produce about 3,000 copies per hour.

6. Convenience: The delay, usually caused by outside printers can be overcome by owning this machine.

7. Quality of paper: Any quality of paper can be used for obtaining the printed copies.

Disadvantages

(*i*) Initial investment is very high.
(*ii*) It involves training of persons for operating the machines.
(*iii*) It requires more space for storing chemicals, paper, and master plates.
(*iv*) Separate runs are required for different colours.

QUESTIONS

Objective Type Questions

1. Define an accounting machine.
2. Mention four features of an accounting machine.
3. What do you mean by adding machine?
4. List out three varieties of adding machines.
5. State four features of adding machines.
6. Mention any four applications of adding machine.
7. List out the advantages of adding machines.
8. Distinguish between an adding machine and a calculator.
9. What do you mean by a printing calculator?
10. What do you mean by key-driven calculator?
11. What is a rotary calculator?
12. What is an electric automatic calculator?
13. What is an electric calculator?
14. What do you mean by a dictating machine?
15. State the features of a dictating machine.
16. List out any four equipment used in the mail room of an office.
17. What is a franking machine?
18. Mention any four types of typewriters.
19. What is a typing pool?
20. What do you mean by a punched card equipment?
21. What do you mean by a computer?
22. Distinguish between a Hardware and Software.
23. Mention any three types of time recording equipment.
24. What are reprographic service equipment?
25. Distinguish between photocopying and duplication.
26. What do you mean by offset lithography?

Analytical Type Questions

1. Outline the policies which guide mechanisation in an office.
2. State the preliminary arrangements that are to be made before installing machines in an office.
3. What factors determine the leasing of office machines. State the merits and demerits of acquiring office machines on a lease basis.
4. State the advantages and disadvantages of office machines.
5. Explain briefly the different types of adding machines.
6. Briefly explain different types of calculators used in an office.
7. State the applications, advantages and disadvantages of a dictating machine.
8. Briefly explain the various equipment used in a mailing section of an office.
9. Explain with merits and demerits the functioning of a franking machine.
10. State the features, merits and demerits of addressing machines.
11. State the principles involved in the functioning of a telephone. State advantages and disadvantages of a telephone.
12. Briefly explain different types of typewriters.
13. What is a typing pool? State its merits and demerits.
14. Explain briefly the various time recording equipment used in an office.
15. Explain the various types of photocopying machines.
16. What is a stencil duplicator? State its merits and demerits.
17. What do you mean by a spirit duplicator? State its merits and demerits.
18. What do you mean by an offset lithography? State its merits and demerits.

Essay Type Questions

1. Explain the various factors which influence mechanisation of an office.
2. Explain the objectives of office machines. Explain the preliminary arrangement that are to be made before implementing machines in an office.
3. Describe the functioning of an accounting machine. State the applications, merits and demerits of accounting machines.
4. Explain fully the features, applications, advantages and disadvantages of adding machines.

5. Explain clearly the types, applications, advantages and disadvantages of a calculator.
6. Explain the advantages and disadvantages of two important machines used in process of correspondence.
7. Describe the components of punched card machine. State its applications, advantages and disadvantages.
8. Explain the functions and system of computer. What are the advantages and disadvantages of a computer?
9. What do you mean by reprographic service machine? Mention the various photocopying machines with advantages and disadvantages.
10. Explain the advantages and disadvantages of various duplicating machine.

14

Communication

INTRODUCTION

The Word *communication* is derived from a Latin word meaning *Common*. Whenever there is an exchange of ideas or understanding between two persons on meeting each other on a common ground, it is known as communications.

One of the main purposes of maintaining an office is to get the work done through the people. The means to get the work done takes the form of communication. It is the process of meaningful interaction among persons in an organisation. It constitutes the life stream of all commercial and industrial enterprises. It is the main channel through which a business undertaking makes and keeps contacts with the outside world. The success of an enterprise to a large extent depends upon its ability to communicate effectively with its employees and customers. Every business, whether big or small, has to maintain contact with its suppliers, customers, creditors, government departments and the like. The function of communication in the business world consists of opening up and maintaining business relations as well as to initiate conduct and conclude business transactions. The reputation of a business depends to a large extent on the quality of its communication. It is, therefore, the duty of office manager to become familiar with the various means of communication and factors which determine a communication system.

Communication can take various forms such as oral and written. Even silence can be used to communicate. Similarly even gestial and facial expressions can be used to communicate. Communication can, therefore, be direct or indirect, conscious or unconscious. When one person communicates something to another person, the factors of perception and language come into operation. However, special mention must be made of language as a means of communication. Language involves signs, signals or symbols to which one responds. The most important symbols used are words and actions. Besides this, a manager in an office communicates not only by what he does but also by what he does not do.

For example, when the desk of an inefficient clerk is shifted from a private room to an open office without communicating him orally or in written form, the clerk has to interpret it in his own way. That is the missing symbol in this example which is supplied by the employee.

Definition and elements of communication

Communication may be viewed as the transfer of information from one entity to another no matter the entity being individual or body corporate.

Communication may be defined as "an exchange of facts, ideas, opinions or emotions and as a way that individuals or organisations share meaning and understanding with another".

L. Hall in his book *Business Administration* defines communication as "the act or any natural or artificial means of conveying information or giving instructions".

In the words of C.L. Littlefield and others "communication is the process of conveying messages. In order that communication may occur, messages must be composed, transmitted and understood".

There are four elements in a communication system. They are:

1. Transmitter: He is the first entity involved in the communication process. The transmitter must be well aware of (*i*) what to communicate, (*ii*) when to communicate, (*iii*) to whom to communicate and (*iv*) the media to communicate.

2. Message: This is the central theme of communication. This takes the form of information, ideas, instructions, facts and opinions which must be expressed clearly by the transmitter so that the receiver understands these in one sense only. According to Littlefield and others, the composition of message is to be based upon the following principles:

(*i*) Determine the purpose of the message. Usually there will be a central purpose of conveying certain information and other subsidiary information to be transmitted.

(*ii*) Plan the messages and arrange them in a logical sequence before communicating it.

(*iii*) Use natural conversational language. Aim for directness and simplicity.

(*iv*) Be complete and clear.

(*v*) Be brief.

(*vi*) Be courteous always. Being clear, complete and yet concise are long steps towards being courteous. Keep in mind the simple basic concept of the "your attitude", be considerate, friendly and helpful.

3. Media of communication: Choosing the right medium of communication is the third element of communication. It may be written, oral, visual or audio-visual. These are discussed in detail in the pages to follow.

4. Receiver: He is the other entity who receives the message communicatedby the transmitter. Since effective communication denotes reciprocal understanding, it matters how the receiver, (*i*) attends the message, (*ii*) understand the message, (*iii*) perceives the message and (*iv*) reciprocates the message.

Guidelines for effective communication

The following are some of the guidelines which must be followed for effective communication:

1. To be sure of what to communicate: It is necessary to know what one wants to communicate as for example, whether additional information is required or whether to initiate some action. It is only when the matter to be communicated is decided, it will have a chance to succeed.

2. To be clear in the use of language: The language to be used must be such that it is easily understood by the receiver. This will remove the barriers of faulty expressions and translations.

3. To watch as to how much to communicate: It is necessary to keep the quantum of communication only to the required extent. It should neither be too much as that might cause boredom nor too little as it may not be properly understood.

4. To use the suitable medium: It is desirable to select the right channel to communicate effectively. Illustrations, charts and diagrams can often help towards better understanding.

5. Listen attentively: It must be remembered that the receiver has to listen or read carefully or misunderstanding is likely to occur. The listener should try to place himself in the speaker's position so as to understand him fully (*i.e.*, projective listening). It is important that the listener should understand the speaker's viewpoint as clearly as possible. Therefore, the listener must also try to understand the speaker's feelings as well as his words.

6. To watch out for unintentional communication: It is not only the words which are important but also the tone in which one speaks out. For example, when an employee talks to his boss the boss unconsciously frowns and thereby communicates (may be even unintentionally) that he is not happy with what he is hearing. Therefore, bored looks, frons and fidgeting should be avoided.

7. Two-way communication: Communication is a two-way process and requires prompt reply for every message received.

8. To make sure that actions do not contradict the communication: The transmitter is judged not only by what he says but also by what he does. For example, if a superior advises his subordinates, the superior must practice first before he preaches.

Importance of communication

The importance of communication is reflected under the following points:

1. To improve better understanding between employer and employees: A good understanding between the employer and employee is the basis of sound management. Effective communication establishes and maintains an understanding between the employer and employees in all organisations.

2. To facilitate managerial function effectively: Communication is one of the important functions of management. It is through communication and instructions that orders are imparted from management to supervisor, from supervisor to subordinate and from instructor to trainee.

3. The shock of technological change is lessened: Through proper and timely communication of change in working conditions, wages and redundancy in the workers resulting from the introduction of automation, it is possible to reduce the shock and ensure that the change is more readily accepted by those affected.

4. Future capital is more readily obtained: Through the process of communication, it is possible to highlight the progress and prospects of the business. Shareholders and debenture holders are convinced about the prosperity of business through a net work of communication. Thus, a company can raise more capital when it requires more capital for further development.

5. Employees are given opportunity for communication with their employers: This facilitates the employees to share the complaints with the employer or may seek advice from the employer. The employer may often rely upon the information given by the employee to make a decision or improve methods.

6. It enhances prestige: Good communication between a company and its customers, suppliers and the general public will enhance its prestige. For example, neat, well written letters, invoices and other circulars will certainly improve the image of the business.

7. It improves public relations: A company uses communication in different ways to improve its image among the public by bringing out the quality of its products, the technology and its uses, the growth and development, the amount of profit earned by it and, the export of its goods, the award it has won and in so many other ways.

Objectives of communication and means of achieving it

The main purposes of communication are as follows:

1. To develop mutual trust between all employees: The aim of communication in modern management thought is to achieve a closer understanding between all employees including managers. This enables complete awareness of aims to know up to date information and job responsibility which enables every member to become a productive worker.

2. To solve number of problems: Communication theory is highly complex as it embraces not only the basic idea of communication but also to solve a number of problems. The scope of communication in this sense includes solving organisation problems, the correct treatment of employees, diagnosing individual problems, improving the climate within the concern, the development of employee and adopting a modern management philosophy.

3. To minimise misunderstanding: It was mentioned earlier that the communication skill lies in creating a favourable response in the individual as well as ensuring that he fully understands the message. The absence of a favourable response in an employee could lead to a communication blockage. He may attempt to withdraw from his operational role as a provider of information or he may not fully co-operate by withdrawing some information. From this point of view, the concept of communication relies heavily upon people getting on well together in situations which reduce antagonism to the minimum.

4. To encourage team work: There is an emphasis today to ensure that employees really become a part of a team in which everyone contributes and participates in the decisions that affect them. This philosophy goes a long way towards creating a higher degree of understanding, which is one of the main aims of communication. One example of lack of understanding is that about one-third of strikes are attributed to communication failure.

There are four approaches to achieve these communication objectives. These are as follows:

1. The mechanics approach: This approach concentrates on three areas. Firstly, it ensures that the message is as simple as possible and clear. Secondly, it chooses the correct channel taking into account factors such as economy, speed, efficiency, accuracy, time available, the importance of message and its acknowledgement. Lastly, it chooses the most appropriate way of passing the message such as face to face contact, a telephone call or a letter. The choice should take into account the reaction of the recipient, the response and the likely effect of the overall situation on the individual.

As regards the first area is concerned; this approach makes sure that the receiver of the message knows exactly what the sender intends to communicate. Further, every attempt must be made to remove any doubts which could be detrimental to the receiver. A two way technique can be adopted to assess the receiver's viewpoint and the possibility of some positive action being undertaken.

This approach also is concerned with ensuring clear understanding of the message by the receiver. The main causes for misunderstanding are poor educational level, inexperience, poor Intelligence Quotient (IQ), the use of abstract terms, technical jargon, inferiority feelings, confusing facts, false inference and value judgements. Therefore, it is necessary to check whether the receiver has understood. Sometimes, the sender of message may be responsible for misunderstanding the message. Several reasons can be cited in this connection such as, the sender may be under pressure at the time of conveying the message, he may not have sufficient time to 'Tune-in' to the receiver, he may misjudge the situation completely in his haste or he may employ the wrong approach with a certain individual. Other reasons for misunderstanding of message from the point of view of sender are; poor expression, incomplete message, poor listening to feed back and the use of the wrong channel. The following rules can be followed to reduce misunderstanding of message:

(*i*) Use simple, clear and concise words
(*ii*) Avoid elaborate explanations that may confuse
(*iii*) Develop precise, clear speech and writing
(*iv*) Do not rush if understanding is essential
(*v*) Be sensitive to the receiver's feeling
(*vi*) Weigh up the receivers ability to comprehend
(*vii*) Check carefully to make sure he understands

(*viii*) Try to reduce any suspicions of sender's intentions which may adversely affect the receiver,

Regarding the second area of this approach, the establishment of suitable channels for communication depends upon the desired communication network, the problems of communication that usually exists and the facilities that are offered. There are networks of communication known as one-way and two-way communication. Under one way communication, the message is passed downward and no opportunity is given for consultation. The assumption is that the receiver will understand and is ready to take action. The two-way communication is rather slow as more opportunity is given for consultation and participation between group members. In this process, everyone gets more satisfaction and becomes more adoptable to proposed changes. This also eliminates misunderstanding and enables each member to be aware of others performance and opinion and thus achieve co-ordination.

Regarding the third area of this approach, the actual means of communication available are speech, writing, actions, signs, gestures, silence and even facial expressions. Face-to-face oral communication is considered to be the best means. The signs as a means of communication will lose its impact very soon. As for example, no smoking sign is forgotten quickly or intentionally ignored. Silence, as a means of communication is used to express disgust, boredom, agreement, disagreement, displeasure, indifference and amusement.

2. The personal contact approach: The purpose of this approach is to establish better relationship between the office manager and members of staff under his control. The contact points are associated with the following topics:

(***i***) **Issuing-orders:** As far as possible it is better to avoid issuing orders to the staff as they will feel an antagonistic response if direct orders or commands are given to them. A better approach is to ensure that they know their job well and simply give them information about their job.

(***ii***) **Reprimanding:** Sometimes, the office manager will be forced into situations where reprimands have to be undertaken. However, it is always better to be impartial and everyone must be treated equally.

(***iii***) **Absenteeism:** Excessive absenteeism arises on account of sickness, domestic problems, lack of interest in the job, inherent problems involved in the job, managerial treatment and so on. It is advisable to meet out fair treatment with an appropriate degree of leniency based upon sensing the situation.

(*iv*) Late arrival: Some of the causes attributed to lateness are transport difficulties, domestic problems, lack of discipline and poor attitude. This can be avoided when the office manager allots the work on the previous day itself and by warning the employees coming late.

(*v*) Errors: Errors are committed owing to lack of concentration, poor selection, poor training and so forth. Most of the causes of errors are due to managerial ineffectiveness. The individual should be helped instead of blaming or reprimanding.

(*vi*) Slackening: Slackness or laziness may be on account of physical incapability, mental incapability, boredom, incorrect work load or an erratic supply of work. The office manager should take necessary steps to correct the situation.

(*vii*) Grievances: A grievance may be defined as any business situation or managerial act that appears to be unfair or unjust to an employee. When there are signs of grievances, the employee should be consulted with out delay. Dealing with grievances provides an excellent opportunity for the office manager to improve relationship because he can demonstrate understanding, fairness and willingness to consult and take the opportunity to establish a continual follow up contact with the members of staff.

(*viii*) Group discussion: The more informal type of meeting which is often held at short notice to discuss a particular topic is called a group discussion. This arrangement encourages the participation of all who are directly concerned with the topic and ensures that all information is disclosed and opinions are given before a decision is made by the group leader.

3. The Informative approach: Under this approach, the concentration is on improving personal performance. A sustained programme is essential to improve personal performance. This is possible by considering the following factors:

(*i*) Effective speaking: The ability to speak in public is essential in the modern business world. This is even more important for a manager who is judged by his ability to speak well. It requires learning many rules as well as practice to acquire the skill of effective speaking.

(*ii*) The art of listening: Effective communication depends on how well a person listens to the speaker. This requires concentration and to achieve this, the following points should be remembered:

(1) The mind must be tuned to the receiver.

(2) To use the spare time to assess the communication as thought is faster than speech.
(3) Display interest by indicating sole attention to the speaker.
(4) If it is difficult to remember, write down the salient points.
(5) Try to avoid criticising the delivery, but concentrate on the message.

***(iii)* Logical thought:** Logical thinking is necessary to solve problems, make decisions and to produce clear message. Logical thought is based on imagination, judgement and precise reasoning which determines the degree of success in a managerial job.

4. Psychological approach: The foundation of the psychological approach consists of a basic knowledge of human beings and their reactions in different situations. The main point to remember is if an individual is suspicious of another person's intention of sincerity in communication, the listener will dislike him. This approach concentrates on the following features:

(*i*) The psychological use of line managers, (*ii*) Careful analysis of job requirements so as to encourage personal development, (*iii*) A realistic personnel policy that provides more opportunity for staff to continue with their education and training, (*iv*) Complete openness in negotiations between staff and management, (*v*) Active participation by staff in all matters affecting them, (*vi*) Development of a climate, where friendliness, fair dealing and complete trust are of utmost importance.

Factors to be considered while choosing channel of communication

For an effective communication network, the following factors must be considered by an office manager:

1. Speed: Depending upon the urgency of message to be communicated, it is necessary to decide upon a speedier means of communication.

2. Accuracy: Important message must be communicated accurately so as to avoid misinterpretation. Written communication serves the purpose in this regard.

3. Safety: All important messages must ensure the factor of safety. When postal communication is restored to, it is better to send the message through registered post instead of ordinary post.

4. Secrecy: All messages communicated should be kept in strict confidence and should not be divulged to unauthorised persons.

5. Record: Certain communications need to be preserved for future reference. Written communication ensures this factor.

6. Impression: Certain means of communication alone can create better impact over the receiver. For example, oral communication is appreciated always when compared to written communication.

7. Cost: The cost of communication must be kept as low as possible.

8. Convenience: The channel of communication must always be convenient to the sender.

9. Staffing: The process of communication must involve less number of clerical staff.

10. Distance: The channel of communication to be selected depends upon the geographical area to be covered.

Types of communication

The communication system may be divided into the following types:

(1) Internal communication
(2) External communication
(3) Mechanical means of communication
(4) Staff locating system
(5) Visual means of communication

The above types of communication are shown clearly by the chart.

Internal communication

The process of communicating within the several departments of a business unit is known as internal communication. Internal communication enhances the efficiency of office work as office coordinates the efforts of people working in different departments. In a small office, internal communication is simple and easy. But in a large office, with a network of several sections, it will be difficult to establish quick contacts with various persons and it will be a time consuming process. Internal communication assumes importance on account of the following reasons:

(*i*) It improves the understanding between management (employer) and employee which is the basis of a sound management.

(*ii*) It enables the management in discharging its functions effectively. The two important functions of management, namely, directing and coordinating the efforts of workers are highly facilitated by the internal communication system.

TYPE OF COMMUNICATION

- Internal Communication → Oral, Written
- External Communication → Oral, Written
- Mechanical means of communication
- Staff locating system
- Visual means of communication

Oral	Written	Mechanical means of communication	Staff locating system	Visual means of communication
(*a*) Courses for	(*a*) Agenda forms	(*a*) Teleprinter	(*a*) Loud Speaker System	(*a*) Closed circuit Television
(*b*) Interviewing	(*b*) Annual Reports	(*b*) Telex	(*b*) Bells & Buzzers	(*b*) Films
(*c*) Joint consultation	(*c*) Bulletins	(*c*) Facsimile Telegraphy	(*c*) Light signals	(*c*) Notice Boards
(*d*) Meetings & conferences	(*d*) Journals	(*d*) Pneumatic Tube system	(*d*) Wire less call system	(*d*) Posters
(*e*) Speeches	(*e*) Memoranda	(*e*) Conveyors and gravity chutes		(*e*) Statistics graphs
(*f*) Telephone system	(*f*) Minutes			
(*g*) Television	(*g*) Office Manuals			
(*h*) Travellers	(*h*) Organisation Schedules			
(*i*) Trade unions	(*i*) Reports			
	(*j*) Correspondence			

(*iii*) It creates employees interest in the progress of the business through motivation.

(*iv*) Adequate and timely communication of changes in working conditions, wages, systems of production, management policies, etc., will have less shocking effect on the employees and such changes are readily accepted by those affected without any resistance.

(*v*) It enables to raise the finance more easily and quickly from the present shareholders and debenture holders by providing a steady flow of information about the business enterprise.

(*vi*) It provides an opportunity for the employees to communicate back to the management (employer). This serves as a feed back for formulating important policies.

Internal communication may take the form of oral or written communication.

Oral communication

The important channels of oral communication are as follows:

1. Course for trainees: This method is used to impart knowledge and to offer instructions by way of training the employees. This enables the new entrants to learn more about the nature of job and helps in discharging their duties efficiently.

2. Interviewing: This channel of communication is used to collect opinions from the employees with a view to provide better facilities to them. This method is also used for selection and promotion of employees.

3. Joint consultation: Joint consultation is a means of two-way communication, a forum at which the opportunity is given for discussing problems and securing mutual understanding. Under this method, the employer and employees discuss mutually the important issues of the business such as policy matters, proposed future development, new manufacturing methods, etc. The main purposes of joint consultation as a means of communication are as follows:

(*i*) It improves the relationship between employer and employees.

(*ii*) It creates interest in the employees in understanding and appreciating the policy and philosophy of the business.

(*iii*) It gives freedom, for the employees for self-expression in terms of decision making, production methods and so on.

(*iv*) It improves the attitude of the employees.

4. Meeting and conferences: Frequent meetings and conferences held at the company premises offers an opportunity for transmitting and provides an opportunity for discussion and debates which helps in decision making.

5. Speech: A speech given by the chairman of a company will help in communicating the progress, prosperity, problems, prospects and policies to employees and trade union leaders.

6. Telephone system: This is the most common form of oral communication used in business both for internal and external communication. Telephone communications can be divided into the following groups:

(*i*) **Direct exchange line:** This type is most suitable to a small sized office wherein a single connection line is obtained from the telephone exchange on becoming a subscriber to it. When the business grows into large size, additional connecting lines can be obtained, each line with a separate number.

(*ii*) **Private branch exchange or private telephone system:** This system is used to serve only internal communication. When a business organisation has several departments, it may not be possible for persons working in various departments to go to the place where the telephone is kept every time a call is received. At the same time, it may also not be possible to provide a separate line of telephone connected with the telephone exchange. Under such circumstances, a switchboard termed as 'Private Branch Exchange' (PBX), is used which is helpful in connecting the various extension lines. A person known as "Switch Board Operator" is specially recruited for this purpose whose main job is to connect the lines to various departments when a call relating to that department is received.

(*iii*) **Private manual branch exchange:** This system is used to make all connections between extensions as well as connecting outgoing and incoming calls. It involves the use of a switch board and is manually operated and hence the name 'Private Manual Branch Exchange' (PMBX). The difference between PBX and PMBX lies in the fact that the former is used to serve the purpose of internal communication only where as the latter is used to serve both the purposes of internal and external communication.

(*iv*) **Private automatic branch exchange:** It is a combination of PMBX system and the automatic dial operated system. Under this system, internal calls can be made automatically from one extension to another. Similarly, for outgoing calls connected with telephone exchange, it gives automatic connection. However, it requires manual operations for incoming calls.

7. Television: It is a combination of oral and visual means of communication. This is extensively used for advertisement as well as for offering instructions and educating the people as to the way of using the product.

8. Travelers: Sales representatives often constitute a vital link between the business and customers and serve as an important means of communication who help in bringing to the notice of customers and potential customers the availability of new product, its utility, the demonstration of product and the alternative uses for which the product can be put to and so on.

9. Trade unions: It serves as a vital channel of communication between employer and employees through which the changes in policy matters and other problems faced by the employees are settled mutually by the management and trade union leaders.

Written communication

The following are the important channels of written communication:

1. Agenda forms: An agenda is a programme of events which shall take place in a meeting. It is circulated before the meetings to all the members who are invited to attend the meeting. It serves as an advance intimation as to the matters which will be discussed in the meeting and as such constitutes a means of written communication.

2. Annual reports: The annual reports published by companies furnishes information to all its shareholders and debenture holders regarding the policy maters, progress and other developmental activities.

3. Bulletins: This channel of communication is used in some companies in order to keep abreast the employees with all important matters of the company.

4. Journals: Journals may vary from an ordinary leaflet to bound booklet. They are used to present the current information of the business such as existing vacancies, financial requirements and other highlights of the business.

5. Memoranda: In some big offices, as a part of day to day working, some instructions or information is circulated through the circulars. This especially happens when any cultural or national functions are celebrated or when any important persons visit the business enterprise.

6. Minutes: A minute is a written record of the proceedings of a meeting and the decisions, taken at the meeting. The minutes are circulated to all concerned members for their reference. Thus, it constitutes an important means of written communication.

7. Office manuals: Office manuals provide information relating to the rules and regulations, the expected standards and procedures to be followed by employees.

8. Organisation schedule or organisation chart: An organisation chart establishes the relationship between a superior and subordinates, their duties and responsibilities in the organisation. By knowing this relationship, the possible confusion is totally avoided.

9. Reports: A report contains the summary of findings and recommendations relating to a special problem investigated or studied. This helps management to take prompt action or in solving a particular problem based on the findings and the recommendations.

10. Correspondence: The day to day inflow and outflow of postal communication by far constitutes the largest means of communication. A big business receives and dispatches hundreds of letters every day to transmit and receive various kinds of messages.

External communication

The communication which takes place between the business unit and the outside world is known as external communication. External communication mostly takes place between the company and its customers, suppliers, creditors, prospective customers, government agencies and tax authorities. External communication is important for every business for the following reasons:

1. To increase the image and prestige of the business: A network of communication between a company and its customers, suppliers and general public will increase the prestige of the business. This can be brought about neatly by well written letters, prompt handling of correspondence and furnishing accurate and upto date documents such as statement of accounts, Debit Notes, Credit Notes, invoices and so on.

2. To improve public relations: Public relations can be improved by means of communicating effectively in respect of its working, improvements made, future prospects of the business, diversification of products, etc. Of course this requires attending immediately to the problems of shareholders, suppliers, creditors and thereby winning their confidence.

3. To improve the business: Improvement in the overall activities of the business can be effected with good communication. This can take place deliberately to achieve the result. As for example, through advertising and public relations or by a careful handling of day to day correspondence which eventually increases its prestige.

External communication can be oral or written.

Oral external communication

Among the various means of external oral communication, telephone occupies the most important channel. The main factors for this choice are its speed, the involvement of person directly in the process of communication and the fact that it can be used by any one. The most important recent development in external telephone services are as follows:

1. Wide area telephone service (WATS): Under this arrangement, a telephone subscriber in return for a fee which is monthly or quarterly can make any number of calls over long distance within certain specified large areas. The amount of the monthly or quarterly-charged depends upon the extent of the area covered.

2. Central exchange (Centrex): Under this system, the telephone section of an office has its own separate seven-digit number. Any call coming from outside the business can be made directly to any of the firm's CENTREX telephone section. Similarly, outgoing calls whether local or outstation, may also be made directly from the internal station to the external number. Under this system, the calls need not go through a switch board.

Written external communication

Two important means of written external communication are as follows:

1. Mail service: The importance of mail service can be best appreciated by the fact that in India everyday more than 10 lakh written communications are delivered by postal department. The comparative figure in U.S.A. is twenty five billion letters annually and this volume is steadily increasing. Owing to the increased cost involved under this channel of communication, the management of every organisation is serious about reducing the cost of the written external communication. Owing to the growing importance of this channel of communication, the mail rooms are now mechanised with new, faster and more efficient machinery such as addressing, folding, inserting, sorting, sealing, weighting and stamping machines.

2. Telegraphic services or wire communication: It is one of the means of handling messages quickly over relatively long distances. This channel is resorted to for delivering brief message which are more important and of urgent nature. Under this method, a form is filled with the name and address of the addressee, the message to be sent and duly signed by the addresser. It can also be typewritten with duplicate copies in which case the duplicate copy can be filed for future reference. The message to be sent through telegrams may be in English language or coded language known to the parties concerned. The use of coded language serves two purposes. Firstly, it maintains the secrecy of the message and secondly, coded words go to reduce the use of long phrases or even sentences. A code word according to postal regulations should not consist more than 5 letters.

Types of telegrams

1. Ordinary and express telegrams: Ordinary telegram is the cheapest form of telegram which takes more time to reach its destination when compared to express telegrams. Express telegrams receive priority over ordinary telegrams and its rates are also high.

2. Reply paid telegram: This type of telegram is used where a reply is expected from the receiver of the message. The sender pays the cost of reply at the post office where he sends the telegram. At the delivering post office, the telegraph clerk attaches a prepaid blank form along with the message of the telegram. This facilitates the recipient to complete the form if he desires to reply to the sender.

3. Multiple address telegram: This type of telegram is used to send identical messages to two or more addresses in the same free delivery area on payment of additional fee for every copy beyond the first.

4. Cypher telegram: This type of telegram is used to send message of confidential nature and is mostly used by defence and security departments.

5. Phonogram: This type of telegram can be availed of only by telephone subscribers. Instead of going to a post office for filling up a telegram form, the message can be communicated over telephone to the telegraph clerk with a request to transmit the message to the addressee. Similarly, any message received through telegram is also communicated to the telephone subscriber over phone by the telegraph clerk.

Mechanical means of communication

Mechanical means of communication has in fact revolutionised the business communication. The important channels of mechanical communication are as follows:

1. Teleprinter: A teleprinter resembles to a large typewriter in appearance. Infact, it is a combination of a typewriter and the telegraph system. A teleprinter consists of two parts, namely a key board and a receiver. Whenever any message is to be transmitted, the keys on the key board are depressed wherein, the transmitter automatically converts the key depression into electric signals and transmits them to the line. Then the receiver translates the coded signals and automatically prints the message on a tape or a sheet of paper. A teleprinter is usually hired from post and telegraph department. The rent payable depends upon the distance between the localities. It can also be purchased and installed for internal use of communication between head office and its branches. Teleprinters are used to transmit information quickly and accurately, particularly when oral communication is likely to lead to misunderstanding.

2. Telex: Telex is the name given by the post office to a teleprinter service supplied by them. Under this channel of communication, the message can be transmitted from one telex subscriber to any other telex subscriber, both between the home and foreign countries. The machine is connected to the post office. Whenever any message is to be sent ,a signalling button is pressed to call the telex clerk in the post office. Then the operator types the telex number required. When advised that the connection is made, the operator types the message. The operator at the receiving end acknowledges the message received on the same machine. The post office charges are paid on rental basis and also on the basis of number of messages sent.

3. Facsimile telegraph: This equipment is used to transmit quickly different drawings, formulae, or other information which cannot be ordinarily sent through a teleprinter. The equipment is connected to a post office. It has three control devices, *viz.*, Send, Stop and Receive. The message to be transmitted is reproduced on electro-sensitive paper which is wrapped round a cylinder. It is then inserted into the machine which is automatically transmitted at the receiver's end thereby reproducing a facsimile copy of the original.

4. Pneumatic tubes: This channel is more useful where messenger service is difficult to arrange and where space available is less for the free movement of messengers from one place to another. Under this system, papers are placed in small plastic cylinders and inserted into the tube. The cylindrical pipes are connected to various departments. The papers are carried from one place to another by pneumatic (air) pressure. It does not required specially skilled operators for transmitting the message.

5. Conveyors and gravity chutes: A slow-moving conveyor is installed in office where continuous flow of messages take place between different departments. Similarly, gravity chutes are provided particularly to carry parcels and other documents from an upper floor to a lower floor.

Staff locating system

In big factories, often it is felt that some of the departmental managers are to be consulted at short notice. Various means of locating staff through communication system are as follows:

1. Loud speaker system: Under this method, the telephone operator draws the attention of persons sought through a microphone. Similarly, any message that is to be communicated can also be broadcasted to all departments or sections.

2. Bells and buzzers: Under this method, a 'call list' is prepared and maintained which contains code numbers for each and every persons included in the call list. By sounding the bell, the attention of person is drawn to the office or wherever the services of the person are required.

3. Light signals: This is an improvement over the previous means of communication as it does not produce any sound which is disturbing. The code number corresponding to the person who is being called upon is indicated when the equipment is operated. Alternatively the number gets illuminated when the services of person are sought.

4. Wireless call system: This means of communication consists of a central transmitting station and a portable receiver which is provided for every executive to be called. When a call is transmitted for a certain person, only that person receives that call, and it continues until he answers the telephone and announces his availability.

Visual means of communication

The following are some of the important visual means of communication employed in big business organisations:

1. Close-circuit television: This is a combination of oral and visual communication. This means of communication is used for offering instructions in new methods, demonstration of a new machinery and for training of workers.

2. Films: Films are used by large sized business units for a variety of purposes such as education, recording test, research, training and work study.

3. Notice boards: It serves the purpose of communicating announcements, trade union matters, declaration of holidays and such other matters.

4. Posters: Posters are mainly used to convey messages through slogans and precautions. A poster appeals most and has a lasting impression when compared to notice boards.

5. Statistical graphs: Statistics as a means of communication is used to highlight the achievements and the progress made by the business. It is readily understood when compared to a textual matter. Common forms of presenting statistical data are diagrams, graphs and pictorial presentations. The most important information portrayed in the form of statistics are data relating to production, sales, profit earned, number of employees recruited, exports etc.

Report writing as a means of communication

Denyer in his book, *Office Administration* defines a report as "a means of communication in which the writer sets down some conclusion or recommendations from facts or circumstances which have been investigated."

L. Hall in his book Business Administration defines a report as "any written or oral communication in which according to the nature and purpose of the report, the reporter presents a collection of facts or a number of alternative propositions states his conclusions and submits his recommendations.

A report constitutes a means of upward communication in a business and which provides a means of feed back information for management for formulating the policies.

Types of reports

The reports prepared to communicate different types of information may be classified under the following types:

1. Routine reports: A report which is prepared to communicate the day to day functions relating to purchases, production, finance, sales etc., is termed as routine report. Such reports are prepared on a regular basis and they mostly contain facts rather than recommendations.

2. Special reports: A special report is prepared to offer recommendations on a non-routine matter.

3. Statutory reports: Statutory report is to be prepared by all public limited companies, a copy of which is to be submitted to the Registrar of Joint Stock Companies and to all the shareholders of the company.

4. Technical reports: This type of reports are prepared by technologists which contain more of statistics and figures rather than written textual matters.

Techniques of writing a report

The following factors must be considered while writing a report:

1. Simple language: The report must be written in simple language. The use of technical words and jargons must be completely avoided.

2. It must be clear: The report must be written in a clear and lucid style using straightforward language.

3. Write positively: It is desireable to write the report with the positive statement instead of negative one so as to avoid confusion.

4. Readability: The report must be written, keeping in mind the person to whom it is meant for. The writer of the report should read the report after writing it in order to satisfy himself that it is readable.

5. Layout: The general appearance of the report must be attractive. Otherwise it will create a bad impression. The layout of a report may take the form of (*a*) 'Tetter', in which case the opening salutation and the complimentary close is made use of, (*b*) a 'memorandum' form which dispenses with both opening salutation and complimentary close.

6. Arrangement of paragraphs: The report must be written in a number of paragraphs so as to bring out the matter clearly. Each paragraph must be numbered to facilitate reference. If the report is a longer one, each paragraph is to be written under a separate subheading.

7. Use of statistics: In order to create a good impression about the report, it is necessary to make use of diagrams, graphs and statistical tables which create lasting impression among the readers.

Barriers to communication

Although in recent times there is a considerable improvement in the process of communication owing to technological developments involving the use of electrical and electronic devices, still it has not brought complete understanding between the comminicator and communicatee. If the objectives of communication are to be achieved, the management must know the obstacles or barriers that hamper communication and try to solve such problems. Such barriers to communication are as follows:

1. Status barriers: One of the barriers to communication arises from status relationship in the organisation. In all organisations, the individuals acquire a status of their own. But this status depends upon the position of the individuals. An individual with a high status will keep himself aloof from others. Other individuals with lower status will communicate only those matters which the superior likes and withhold the unpleasant facts.

2. Language barriers: The use of language differs from person to person based on experience, knowledge of language orientation, etc. The sender may interpret certain concepts with his own frame of reference. But the same when communicated may be misinterpreted by the receiver according to his own understanding. This distorts the communication in the organisation.

3. Barrier of indifferent attention: Sometimes, when a manager is preoccupied with an urgent work, he may not listen to the communication sent by his subordinates. Very often it goes out of his attention because he overemphasizes his own job and underestimates his subordinates'. So, it becomes only a superficial message without paying full attention to what has been communicated.

4. Barrier due to premature evaluation: A good environment is to be provided in order to enable the communicator to communicate effectively and the listener to understand the message completely. Very often the executive will undertake to evaluate the communication without even understanding it. Such premature evaluation and response tend to stop the transfer of information.

5. Barrier due to non-fulfillment of expectations: Whenever a communicator communicates any message, the listener must take some action as a response. If no such response is evoked, a sender of communication may stop communicating in future.

Measures to overcome barriers to communication

(*a*) The *status* barrier to communication can be overcome by the superior by de-emphasising the notion of his status when communicating with subordinates.

(*b*) Language barrier can be overcome by using the language which means the same to all persons.

(*c*) The listener must cultivate the skill of emphatic listening so as to encourage the speaker to speak frankly and freely.

(*d*) The listener must also listen fully before a conclusion is arrived at.

(*e*) The listener must take necessary action as a response to the message communicated.

(*f*) The medium of communication must be properly selected.

(*g*) The message must be communicated at the right time. There should not be undue delay in the communication process.

(*h*) Information must be reliable, accurate, precise and clear.

(*i*) Two way communication is to be encouraged.

QUESTIONS

Objective Type Questions

1. Define communication.
2. Mention the four elements of communication.
3. Distinguish between internal and external communication.
4. Mention eight channels of oral communication.
5. What do you mean by joint consultation as a means of communication?
6. What do you mean by 'Direct exchange line' as a means of telephonic communication?

7. What is a private telephone system?
8. Distinguish between PMBE and PABE.
9. List out eight means of written communication.
10. What do you mean by Wide Area Telephone Service (WATS)?
11. What is CENTREX?
12. Distinguish between ordinary and express telegram.
13. Mention any four types of telegrams available in a post & telegraph department.
14. What do you mean by a teleprinter?
15. What is a telex?
16. What do you mean by facsimile telegraphy?
17. What do you mean by pneumatic tubes as a channel of communication?
18. What are conveyors and gravity chutes?
19. What do you mean by loud speaker system as a means of communication?
20. What is a wireless system of communication?
21. List out any eight channels of visual means of communication.
22. What is a report?
23. Distinguish between a routine and special report.

Analytical Type Questions

1. Explain the four elements of communication.
2. Outline the guidelines which are to be followed for an effective communication.
3. Explain the importance of good communication.
4. Explain the objectives of communication.
5. State the factors that are to be considered while choosing channels of communication.
6. What do you mean by internal communication? Explain its objectives.
7. Explain the various means of internal communication.
8. Explain the various telephone communication systems.
9. Explain the various channels of written communication.
10. What do you mean by external communication? Discuss its importance in a business.
11. Explain the recent trends of oral external communication.
12. Explain the various channels of written external communication.
13. Explain the various mechanical means of communication.

14. Explain the various means of staff to locating system.
15. Explain the different means of visual communication.
16. Explain the techniques of good report writing.

Essay Type Questions

1. Discuss the different approaches to achieving the objectives of communication.
2. Explain the different channels of communication.

15

Correspondence

INTRODUCTION

Correspondence is one of the most important functions of every office as it serves a connecting link between the business enterprises and outside world. The success of a good business to a large extent depends upon the prompt dealings between a business and those interested in a business. To deal with this function, in most of the large sized offices, a separate correspondence department is established. The function of correspondence is undertaken by correspondence clerks, typists and steno-typists. The correspondence is attended to by these people by getting advice from the executives concerned. In addition to the above persons, in modern days, a number of equipments are also used to facilitate quick communication and correspondence. Very often correspondence also takes place within the business unit which is known as internal correspondence or office correspondence or inter office correspondence. The correspondence which takes place between a business unit and outsiders is known as external correspondence. The importance of correspondence is recognised by all on account of two reasons, namely; (1) It builds or destroys the goodwill and reputation of the business. This is because, correspondence represents a contact between the business and its customers and the general public and (2) Correspondence may prove costlier if it is not properly undertaken.

Essential parts of a good business letter

Correspondence between the business and others take the form of letter writing. In order to create a good impression among the readers, it is necessary that letters must be written considering its essential parts. This not only facilitates quick understanding but also establishes goodwill of the business. While drawing business letters, the following parts of the letters must be duly given its place in the letter:

1. Letter head: Usually letter heads are printed by the business units which give the name, address, telephone number and other details of the business unit. Where a letter head is not used, a plain paper may be used.

2. Margin: A margin of 15 spaces on the left hand side and 10 spaces on the right hand side is to be provided for. In a letter head, it is determined by an alignment with the beginning of a letter head.

3. Reference: Often the letter heads will contain a place for the reference and where it is not provided, it should be typed at the left hand margin on the same line as the date. The reference number of both the company and the addressee is written under this heading.

4. Date: There are various ways of typing the date. The last letter or word of the date should coincide with the right hand margin. The correct way of typing a date is for example, June 15, 1999. The month should not be numbered and abbreviated.

5. Inside address: This contains the name and address of the person or the firm to whom the letter is to be sent. It is always typed in single spacing. There are two reasons for putting this on a letter. Firstly, to ensure that the original copy will be put in the correct envelope. Secondly, to enable the carbon copy to be correctly filed.

6. Attention line: Letters addressed to a firm are directed to an individual by the use of this line which comes three spaces below the address.

7. Salutation: It is the opening word of greeting in a letter. This is typed flush with the left hand margin three spaces below the address followed by a comma or a colon.

8. Subject line: This is typed two spaces below salutation in the centre.

9. Body of the letter: This is divided into a number of paras and typed in single spacing.

10. Complimentary close: This is typed two spaces below the last line of the letter. It should be typed three to four spaces away from the centre towards the right side. Only the first letter is typed in capital.

11. Signature: For the signature of the executive atleast five spaces are to be left out.

12. Name and designation: The name of the person signing the letter with designation is typed under this part of the letter.

13. Enclosures: This column is provided when any enclosures such as a receipt or a cheque are enclosed.

14. Identification: This consists of the initials of the person signing the letter in capitals immediately followed by the initials of the person typing in small letters.

15. Carbon copy: This means circulating copies. When it is necessary to send copies to persons other than the addressee. 'CC' shall be typed at the end of the letter followed by the name of the recipients.

16. Continuation sheet: When a letter occupies more than one page, the second and subsequent pages are described as continuation sheets. This is of the same size of the original letter head of the company.

Cost of letter writing and reducing cost of correspondence

Correspondence with others involves the following elements of cost:

1. Salary: This includes the salaries payable to the dictator, typist, filing clerk, messenger, etc.

2. Stationery: This includes expenses incurred towards procuring letter head, envelopes and carbons.

3. Capital cost: This involves expenses incurred on the investment and maintenance of typewriters, franking machines, dictating machines, etc.

4. Cost of stamping: This involves purchase of stamps and the labour of stamping or franking.

5. Wastage: This includes spoiled stationery, envelopes and lost stamps.

6. Cost of office space: This includes rent, lighting, insurance ect.

The increased cost of correspondence increases the office and administration costs of a business, which in turn increases the selling price to that extent. In order to reduce the cost of correspondence the following measures are suggested:

(*a*) The use of form or standardised letter which saves the dictator's time.

(*b*) The use of dictating machine which saves typist's time.

(*c*) The use of window envelopes which avoids typing of address on the envelope.

(*d*) The use of automatic typewriter to produce standardised letters.

(*e*) The use of franking machine which saves labour in stamping.

(*f*) The use of telephone instead of writing letters.

Methods of replying letters

The following are the methods of replying letters:

(*a*) By dictating letters either to a shorthand typist or a dictating machine.

(*b*) By dictating partly to the typist and partly by using a form letter, *i.e.*, a standard letter.

(*c*) By using a complete form letter.

(*d*) By drafting letters in the written form and sending them to the typist. This is especially used where correspondence relating to legal matters are involved.

(*e*) By jotting down the points, the private secretary may be asked to compose the letter in its full form.

(*f*) By handing over the incoming letters to the private secretary to deal on his own accord.

(*g*) By writing the reply on the bottom of each incoming letter and sending a duplicate (xerox) copy of it. But this is not a popular method of replying.

Techniques of letter writing

The following factors should be considered while dealing with correspondence:

1. Clarity: The message to be communicated must be simple to understand. Over 1,800 years ago Quintilian, a Roman said "one should not aim at being possible to understand, but at being impossible to misunderstand. Clarity can be achieved by writing to serve people rather them to impress them. Most obscurity comes not from incompetence but from a desire to impress and astonish".

2. Friendly: The letters must be written in a courteous manner so as to be appreciated by the reader. Under no circumstances, the reader should get offended by the contents of the letter.

3. Effectiveness: The effective use of language is called style. The best style is that which attracts the least attention to itself and is transparent so that the meaning is clear.

4. Brevity: It is said that brevity is to sole of wit. One of the requirements of good manners is we should not waste the time of others. In the words of Ruskin "say all you have to say in the fewest possible words". A useful practice is to use one or two words for many words.

5. Jargon: Jargon means language which is special to science, art, trade or profession. A Jargon which gains currency and which gets incorporated in the public or general language alone can be used in writing business letters.

6. Tact: The use of tactics should not upset the feelings of the recipient.

7. Positive approach: The business letter must be written with a positive approach so as to build confidence rather than use of negative approach which indicates helplessness.

Form letters

A form letter is a standardised letter used by business to answer all correspondence of a similar and recurring nature and to give the same information to all correspondents. Some examples of form letters are application for employment, acknowledgement of order, acknowledgement of complaints, debts collection letters and request for delivery of goods. Its chief advantages are:

(*a*) It ensures uniformity in writing letters.
(*b*) It saves the time of dictator and typist.
(*c*) It reduces the cost of postage as postal rates are less for printed matters.
(*d*) It speeds up replying the correspondence.

However, form letter suffers from the following disadvantages:

(*a*) The personal element is missing in form letters.
(*b*) The required style of letter cannot be adopted.
(*c*) Printed form letters do not receive that much attention when compared to typed letters.
(*d*) Form letter often needs to be changed depending upon changing conditions.

Follow-up of correspondence

Sometimes, the sender of the communication may not receive the reply from the communicatee. In order to expedite the process of communication, it is necessary to take follow-up action by the communicator. The following measures can be resorted to under such circumstances:

(*a*) To maintain a record of communication expecting the probable date of receiving the reply. Reminders can be sent when the replies are not received before the expected dates.
(*b*) The duplicate copy of the original may be sent which also serves the purpose of reminder.
(*c*) When reference copy is not available for future reference a fresh copy of the correspondence can be redrafted and it is sent to the communicatee.

Correspondence department

Correspondence department is one of the major and the most important departments in a modern commercial office. This is the department where external written communication is carried out which is very important for the success of all business enterprises. The size of correspondence department differs from office to office. The correspondence department consists of staff headed by the secretary. The correspondence clerks assist various executives in the process of drafting and standardisation of letters. The Stenographers will take down dictation of letters in shorthand and transcribe in the usual written form. Various equipment such as typewriter, dictaphone, duplicating machines are used in large size office to deal with correspondence. To handle incoming and outgoing mail, separate staff is recruited.

The correspondence department can be organised on the principle of centralisation or decentralisation. Under centralisation system, the entire process of correspondence is carried out at one common place under the supervision of a competent person. It offers the following advantages:

(*a*) The responsibility for handling the correspondence can be fixed on a single person. This system relieves all other departments of the burden of dealing with correspondence.

(*b*) It leads to reduction of mistakes and errors.

(*c*) Skilled and expert staff can be appointed for dealing with correspondence.

(*d*) Correspondence can be promptly undertaken, thereby saving time.

(*e*) It is possible to use mechanical equipment such as letter opening and sealing machines so as to increase the speed of handlıng correspondence.

(*f*) Proper use of postal articles are ensured. Pilferage and wastage of postal articles can be easily controlled.

(*g*) Special arrangements are possible with the post office.

(*h*) It leads to specialisation in terms of handling correspondence whıch ıncreases the efficıency of staff.

Under decentralised system of correspondence, the process of correspondence is looked after by each and every department of the business. This is best suited to a small sized business.

Arrangement with post office

Usually in a small business, for despatching the mail, a person is sent to post office. Similarly, for collecting the incoming mail, the postman's arrival is awaited or a person is sent to post office to collect the mail. In a big business, special arrangements are made with post office both for receiving and despatching the mail. Such arrangements take the following two forms:

1. Post box: A Post box facility is available in a large post office for the purpose of receiving the mail. It is rented out to all those organisations who would like to collect the mail in person at an earlier possible time directly from the post office. The post box will have two keys one of which is kept by the postal authorities and the second one is given to the hirer of the box. An agent of the hirer is usually authorised to collect the box in which is inserted all the unregistered mail. Any article which could not be inserted because of big size or for want of space in box it will be intimated through a slip by the post master.

The following rules are followed in case of delivery of mail through a post box:

(*i*) Before a post box is hired, the hirer has to pay the rent on a quarterly or yearly basis. In addition to payment of hire charges, the hirer must also deposit a certain amount with the post office.

(*ii*) The post office will give the original key of the post box together with a token number and a delivery ticket bearing that number.

(*iii*) The hirer or his agent has to surrender the ticket whenever he wants to open the box by the key.

(*iv*) The rent is to be made in advance and renewed before the expiry of the period.

The advantage of post box facility can be summed up as follows:

(*i*) The mail can be collected at the convenience of the hirer.

(*ii*) The token number can be used as a short postal address which serves the purpose of secrecy.

(*iii*) Mail is delivered more safely.

The chief disadvantages of post box facility are as under:

(*i*) It is not suited to deliver registered articles.

(*ii*) It is expensive.

(*iii*) It requires a reliable person.

2. Post bag: It is kind of special bag which is provided by the post office to the hirer in order to carry mail from or to the post office. The bag has the facility of locking. All the mails addressed to the hirer is placed inside the bag and it is locked. The hirer or his representative can carry the bag on production of delivery ticket. Then after emptying the bag in the correspondence department all the out going mail is placed inside the bag and locked and the bag is carried to the post office for posting.

Post office services

The following are some of the services offered by a post office to facilitate correspondence by business enterprises and to public at large:

1. Book post: This facility is available for despatching printed articles such as papers, leaflets or books through post at a concessional rate. The envelop or wrapper however, should be marked 'printed matter only'.

2. Certificate of posting: Usually no receipt is given by a post office when ordinary letters are posted. However, where it is desired that the sender requires an acknowledgement relating to the despatch of letter, he can obtain it by sending the letters under certificate of posting. This involves payment of additional expenses in the form of stamps. The receiving clerk will affix the date stamp on the receipt along with his signature. This certificate serves an evidence in time of disputes arising out of despatch of communication.

3. Recorded delivery: This is an alternate arrangement that could be utilised instead of sending documents through registered post. It is cheaper when compared to registered post and involve obtaining a proof from the post office for having sent the documents.

4. Business reply system: This facility is available for a businessman wherein unstamped reply cards or leaflets can be returned by the addressee to the sender of the communication without paying. The business man then makes an arrangement for meeting the postal expenses on all replies received. It is used more frequently to solicit business orders, guarantee cards, etc. The following procedure is involved under this system:

(*i*) To obtain a licence from the post master.

(*ii*) To deposit certain amount in advance to cover charges for a reasonable period.

(*iii*) The cards or envelopes must conform to a pattern laid down by GPO. All letters to be sent under this system must bear the name, the address of the business and the licence number. The words 'No postage required if posted in India' must be printed on the top right hand corner and the words 'postage will be paid by the addressor' on the top left hand corner in black vertical lines near the right hand edge.

(*iv*) The cards or leaflets returned by the recipients are then delivered to the addressor in the usual way and amount due towards postage is collected from the addressor.

5. Remittance of money through post office: The following are some of means of sending money to others through post office:

(*i*) *Money order:* This is more suitable for remitting small amount. It ensures safety and takes less time compared to remittance through banks.

(*ii*) *Telegraphic Money Order (TMO):* It is similar to money order with a difference that it is sent with greater speed.

6. Registered post: Valuable articles are sent through registered post which is considered to be safer when compared to ordinary post. The post office will issue a receipt to serve as a proof for having received the article to be sent under registered post. A modified form of registered post is to send the articles under 'Registered post with acknowledgement due', under this system, the receiver of the article will sign the acknowledgement receipt to indicate that he has infact received the article from post office. All important documents are mostly sent under this method.

7. Insurance parcel: Under this system, postal articles are sent by insuring the articles so as to cover all risks of loss or damage in transit. The post office acts as an insurer and indemenifies if the articles are lost or damaged.

8. V.P.P. (Value Payable by Post): Under this system, the sender of the article will realise the value of the article sent through the post office. The articles to be sent under this system must be registered. The postman before delivering the article will collect the value of the article from the addressee and then will remit it to the addressor. However, this is a costlier method of sending an article when compared to other methods.

9. Speed post: It is one of the fastest modes of delivering postal articles, both national and international in return for an additional charge. This system covers both mail and parcels. The tariff differs between place to place of delivery.

10. Railway letter: By a pre-arrangement with a post office, letters can be handed over at railway stations and will be sent by the next train to the station of destination.

11. Late posting: Under this system the articles can be posted at travelling post office, *i.e.*, sorting carriages, on mail trains upto five minutes before departure of the train.

12. Telegram services: It is one of the means of sending messages quickly over long distance. The rates of telegram depends upon the words used in the telegram form. The different types of telegrams used in the day to day dealings were discussed in the previous chapter.

Procedure of handline incoming mail

Inward mail assumes more importance as it affects the working of other departments and to safeguard the cash received through mail in various forms. Though no standard procedure is laid down for handling the inward mail, the following procedure is usually followed in a large sized organisation.

1. Receiving and opening the mail: In a small sized business, all incoming mail is handled by the secretary. But in a large sized business, a separate receiving department is incharge of receiving clerks who are supervised by a senior clerk. They should attend office atleast half an hour before it opens so that the mail can be distributed by the time the other staff arrives. Mail is received in any of the following ways: (*i*) Direct delivery by the postman. But this will take more time as one has to wait for the arrival of the postman, (*ii*) Mail collected from post box or post bag and (*iii*) Mail received through a peon from the post office.

When the mail received is less in number they are operated by hand and by a letter opening machine, if there are many. Letters opening machine cuts open the envelopes at a great speed, without damaging the contents. However confidential and personal letters are not opened but sent directly to the respective addressee. After opening the envelops, the contents are taken out for further processing. Sometime the empty envelopes are pinned or filed with the contents to serve as an evidence of the date received as indicated by the postal seal.

2. Scrutiny of contents: The second step involved in the handling of incoming mail is to scrutinise or verify the contents of the mail for the following reasons : (*i*) to know to which department the letters shall be sent and (*ii*) to verify whether all the enclosures are in accordance with the description given in the letter. The enclosures usually are in the form of cheques, bank drafts, orders, invoices, debit notes, credit notes, statement of accounts and so on. After verification of the contents or enclosures of the letter, the receiving clerk will sign the letter to conform that the contents received are in accordance with the description. The cheques and bank drafts are sent to cash department for taking necessary action. Wherever a large number of cheques and bank drafts are received through post, the receiving clerk will prepare a list of all such receipts and after totalling the amount, the list is sent to cash department. The procedure is followed to safeguard against theft of such instruments.

3. Date stamping: As soon as the contents of the mail are opened, a rubber stamp containing the details such as (*i*) serial number of the letter received, (*ii*) the date of receipt, (*iii*) the time of receipt and (*iv*) the initial of the clerk who opens the letter is affixed on every letter received. Alternatively, separate machines could be used for dating, numbering, and time recording. Such machines involve automatic change of figures with every stroke. In some office, the date stamping involves recording of additional particulars such as person who has received the letter, acknowledgement, replying, and filing references. This is shown below:

No........................	Received by......................................
Date......................	Acknowledged by............................
Time.....................	Replied by..
Initial...................	Filed by..

Sometimes, a modified procedure is followed in case of composite letters. A composite letter is one which is to be referred by more than one individual and hence circulated to all those concerned. In this case, a different type of rubber stamp is used to facilitate recording of information as is applicable to all the departments. Finally, it is sent to filing department for future reference. A specimen of the rubber stamp used is given below:

No.. Received.. Filed...	
Cashier... Sales Manager.. Cashier... Accountant..	Initials

4. Recording: In some of the offices, it is a practice to record the postal articles received everyday in a book known as Inward mail register or Letters received book. This process of recording serves as a source of evidence in case of doubt or dispute in respect in incoming letters. A specimen of this book is given below:

Inward Mail Register

Sl. No.	Date	Name and Address of sender	Nature of Mail	Subject	Department concerned	Remark	Initial receiving clerk

Sometimes instead of maintaining an inward mail register, a mail room list can be maintained. It is a list which contains particulars of all letters and articles sent to a particular department and the list is signed by the department-in-charge. A specimen of this is given below:

Mail Room List

Name of the Department..

Date....................................

Time.....................

Sl. No.	Name of sender	Address	Nature of the mail	Remarks

5. Sorting: After affixing the date stamp, the mail is sorted out in order to send it to the respective departments or individuals concerned. In small and medium sized business, trays are used to facilitate the sorting of letters. In large sized business, a cabinet with a number of pigeon-holes is made use of. Sorting of letters avoids wrong delivery and facilitates prompt delivery of letters. Where it becomes difficult to relate a letter to any of the particular department, it can be sent to secretary or office manager who in turn will decide as to which department it should belong to.

6. Distribution: At this stage, the letters are sent through peons along with a Mail room list for distribution to various departments or persons. Before the letters are handed over, the person who receives the letter will sign the mail room list. However, this practice is not followed in case of telephone and telegraphic messages.

7. Follow-up action: The handling of inward mail will be complete only when the letters received are actually acknowledged. All enquiry letters must be promptly replied and complaint letters carefully attended to. Similarly order letters should be executed and in case of delay in supplying materials and goods, it must be advised accordingly. If the letters received are of no importance, then they are not replied and can either be filed or destroyed. It is only after replying every letter that they are sent for filing.

Rules to be followed while handling incoming mail

The following rules are to be followed for ensuring an efficient handling of mail:

(*a*) All Registered mail must be recorded in a separate book and opened only by the senior incharge.

(*b*) A preliminary sorting is to be made on the basis of
  (*i*) Private and urgent mail
  (*ii*) Sealed envelopes and
  (*iii*) Unsealed envelopes

(*c*) All remittances and enclosures must be carefully checked and the contents ensured. A list of cheques and other modes of payment is to be made and it must be handed over to cashier along with cheques and bank drafts.

(*d*) All letters must be rubber stamped bearing the date and number of the documents.

(*e*) Letters are then classified on the basis of the references contained in them or on subject basis.

(*f*) Letters are then sorted out on the basis of the departments to which they related to.

(*g*) All empty envelopes should be checked to ensure that no cheque or other enclosures are left inside.

(*h*) Mail must be distributed to various departments and persons as soon as possible.

(*i*) When letters are to be routed through more than one department, a standard procedure is to be laid down.

(*j*) One or two massagers must be arranged to distribute all mail and other circulars to all the departments.

Procedure to be followed while handling outgoing mail

It is desirable to route all the outgoing mail through one person or department. This system fixes responsibility, controls the use of postage stamps and makes clerks to become experts in terms of postage rates. Outgoing mail is very important as it determines the reputation of business and its success. The outgoing mail consists of notices, circulars, replies to the enquires, price lists, orders and various other letters addressed to shareholders, creditors, suppliers, customers, prospective investors and government. Certain letters must be drafted strictly according to statutes and must be signed by a competent person such as secretary, while other documents are sent as a matter of routine. Such documents can be signed by some authorised person. The following procedure is involved in handling an outward mail:

1. Preparation of letters, circulars, notices, etc: Strictly speaking, preparation of the letters does not come under the procedure of handling outgoing mail. However, this is considered as one of the important aspects of correspondence which cannot be under estimated. The letters are dictated by departmental heads to the correspondence clerk. Letters relating to policy matters are dictated by chief executive. The letters so dictated are corrected and improved upon in all respects and they are typed or printed as the case may be. Finally, it is signed by the appropriate authority.

2. Collating: This step involves assembly of all documents which are to be sent along with letters. Some of the common enclosures are cheques, postal orders, invoices, orders, notices and agenda of meetings, reports, adjustments made through debit and credit notes, profit and loss account and balance sheet. All such documents are collated or assembled and attached to the main letter by stapling or by using pins, tags or clips. Care must be taken to see that no part of enclosure is missed. If the work of collating is more a collating machine is used.

3. Folding: Appropriate folding of all letters and other documents is one of the important steps in the handling of outgoing mail. Good and neat folding of papers is an art by itself. When the letters and other enclosures are more in number, folding machine is used which folds the letters uniformly and at a higher speed. After folding the letters and other enclosures they are inserted into envelopes.

4. Address writing: It is the duty of despatch clerk to write the address on all the outgoing mails in most of the offices. However, it is suggested that the typist himself should type the address on all the envelopes to ensure correct insertion of letters in the correct envelopes. Very often window envelopes are used to avoid writing of address on the envelopes. However, it requires proper folding of letters so as to make the address visible through window envelope. Sometimes, addressograph machine is used to write addresses when communication is made frequently with some fixed addressees to send notices, circulars price lists, etc.

5. Collection of mail: When the outgoing mail is handled by a central mail department, it has to receive the mail from various departments to despatch them promptly. To avoid congestion at the end of the day, the mail is collected by the central mail room from all the departments throughout the day. To ensure proper despatch of all mail, a time is to be fixed as deadline which depends upon the closing time of the office and also clearance time of post office.

6. Sorting of mail: The outgoing mail is then sorted out on the basis of weight so as to determine the amount of stamp to be affixed. Similarly, all registered letters are sorted out to facilitate quick despatch of such mail. This helps to avoid mistake involved in calculating postage expenditure.

7. Sealing and stamping: In a small organisation, the sealing of envelope is done with the help of a sponge and water bowl. However, if the number of envelopes are more sealing becomes a tedious job and, therefore, in large organisations sealing machines are used. Stamping of letters can be done again manually or mechanically. Under manual process, the postal stamps are affixed depending upon the weight of the articles. Where the letters to be despatched are more in number stamp emitting machines can be used in which rolls of stamps are inserted and the number used is recorded on a dial. However, it is necessary to have a separate machine for each denomination of stamp used. In big concerns, franking machines are used to seal the envelopes.

8. Recording: In every office, a despatch register is maintained to facilitate the recording of particulars of all the outgoing mail. It consists of columns for date of despatch, name and address of addressee, the amount of stamp affixed and column for the initials of the despatch clerk. The despatch clerk will fill in the particulars of every column of the register and he will put his initials on the record. A specimen of this record is given below:

Despatch Register

Sl. No.	Date	Name	Address of addressee	Amount of stamp used	Initials

The despatch register serves two purposes *viz.*, (*i*) it serves as a source of reference for having despatched the letter and (*ii*) to know the value of stamps on hand on the last day of stock taking of stamps.

9. Posting: This is the last step involved in the handling of outgoing mail. Posting is not necessary in case of local delivery by the messanger, in which case the messanger will resort to hand delivery against an acknowledgement signed in the book. In case of ordinary letters, they are inserted in the letter boxes fixed at convenient places by the postal authorities. Other letters to be sent under certificate of posting, registration, recorded delivery, speed post articles must be taken to post office and handed over to the clerks concerned. In all such cases, the receiving clerk of the post office will issue a receipt acknowledging receipt of postal articles for despatching. Alternatively, where the letters to be mailed are many, post box and post bags can be made use of.

Rules to be followed while handling outgoing mail

The following rules are to be followed for the efficient handling of outgoing mail:

(*a*) To decide whether the address on envelopes are to be typed i.e., at the time of typing or at the central despatching room by the despatch clerk.
(*b*) To avoid confusion, instructions must be clearly given on the top of every letter such as 'under certificate of posting', 'Registered post with acknowledgement due', 'Speed post', 'Recorded delivery', 'Air mail' and so on.
(*c*) Arrange for the collection of mail from all the departments throughout the day to avoid congestion, delay and confusion at the end of the day.
(*d*) Fix a deadline at the end of the day beyond which no letters are accepted for despatching on that day.
(*e*) Make sure that the letters are classified on the basis of inland and overseas mail and also on the basis of weight for affixing the correct amount of stamp.
(*f*) Use folding and sealing machines when large number of letters are to be posted.
(*g*) Use window envelopes to avoid letters being placed in the wrong envelops.
(*h*) Make necessary entries in the despatch register before mailing the letter.
(*i*) To check all the enclosures before the envelops are sealed and stamped.
(*j*) To take stock of stamps at frequent intervals to avoid its misuse.
(*k*) To paste all the receipts issued by the post office for having received articles in a special book.

Mechanisation of mail services

The recent trend in dealing with the correspondence in a large sized business is towards mechanisation of correspondence process. A large number and a wide variety of equipment and machines are used to quicken the speed and to maintain uniformity in communication process. The mechanism in the functioning and applications of such machines were already discussed in the chapter *Modern office appliances* earlier. Here, only a summary of the various machines used in modem business correspondence is made:

(*a*) A dictating machine to dictate the messages.
(*b*) A letter opening machine to open the letters carefully and not to damage the contents of the letter.
(*c*) Envelope sealing machine for reducing monotony and delay in sealing envelopes.

(*d*) Paper folding machines for neat and correct folding of letters and other enclosures.

(*e*) Stamp affixing machines and franking machines to enable quick stamping of letters.

(*f*) Addressing machines for quick writing of addresses.

(*g*) Collating machines, used to assemble related or consecutive documents or sheets.

QUESTIONS

Objective Type Questions

1. What do you mean by a form letter?
2. State the purpose served by a post box and a post bag.
3. What do you mean by recorded delivery?
4. Mention any four advantages of a form letter.

Analytical Type Questions

1. What are the essential parts of a good business letter?
2. What is the importance of and what are the constituent factors in the cost of letter writing in business?
3. What are the different methods of control over letter writing in a large office?
4. State the various methods of replying letters.
5. Explain the techniques of letter writing.
6. State the advantages and disadvantages of a form letter.
7. Explain the system of organising corresponding department. State the advantages of centralised organisation of correspondence department.
8. Distinguish between a post box and a post bag as facilities offered by a post office.
9. State the rules to be followed while handling inward mail.
10. State the rules to be hollowed while handling outward mail.

Essay Type Questions

1. Explain the procedure involved in handling the inward mail.
2. Explain the procedure involved in handling the outward mail.
3. Explain the various services offered by post office to a business unit.

16

Personnel Management

INTRODUCTION

In olden days, when business organisations were of small size, the number of employees were few in number. The problem of employees were also less and the employer used to attend to all the problems faced by the employees. Gradually the organisations grew larger in size and the employer could not attend to the problems of employees. There arose a gap between employer and employee and to bridge the gap, personnel management has been developed. The development of personnel management can be traced back to the period of Industrial Revolution. When the business organisations were expanded, they were managed by professional managers instead of owners. As a result of separation of owners and employees, the working and living conditions of the employees deteriorated. This led to the formation of trade unions with a view to redress their grievance. In England, a few pioneering Industrialists such as Robert Owen and Bolten paved the way for the development of modern personnel management. In U.S.A., the scientific Management movement led by F.W. Taylor gave opportunity for the development of personnel management. The Hawthorne Experiments conducted by Elton Mayo and his associates known as human relation movement gave further impetus to the growth and development of personnel management.

The development of personnel management in India dates back to 1929-31, during which period, the Report of the Royal Commission on labour in India recommended the appointment of Labour officers to check corruption while recruiting the employees. Until the period of Independence, to look after the welfare of employees, welfare officers were appointed. Subsequently with the enactment of Industrial Disputes Act in 1947 welfare officers soon became Industrial Relations Officers, who used to participate on collective bargaining, conciliation and adjudication with the rapid growth of Business organisations. The Indian industries demanded many skilled and semiskilled workers. This led the government to cover recruitment aspect of personnel management by law. The Apprentices Act of 1961 and the Employment Exchange (compulsory Notification of Vacancies) Act of 1959 has regulated recruitment in respect of workers. Today, all matters pertaining to personnel management are governed by statute in our country.

Definition and importance of personnel management

According to Littlefield and others, personnel management is "a programme of activities relating to obtaining and maintaining a competent and harmonious working group in which each individual is provided with opportunities for personnel development and is well utilised in the interest of the ogranisation".

According to British Institute of Personnel Management, London, "personnel management is that part of management which is concerned with the people at work and with their relationship within an enterprise."

According to Indian Institute of personnel management, "Personnel management is that part of the management function which is primarily concerned with the human relationships within an organisation. Its objectives in the maintenance of those relationships on a basis which, by considerations of the well-being of the individual enables all those engaged in the undertaking to make their maximum personnel contribution to the effective working of that undertaking".

According to William Spriegel, "personnel management is concerned with the attaining of maximum individual development under desirable working relationships between employers and employees and an effective moulding of human resources and contrasted with physical resources".

In order to study the importance of personnel management, it is worthwhile to consider the various aspects dealt with by personnel management. It includes three closely related aspects, *viz.*, (*i*) personnel aspects, (*ii*) welfare aspect and (*iii*) Industrial relations aspect. The personnel aspect includes recruitment, selection and placement of personnel, training and development, promotions and transfers, wages administration etc. The welfare aspect is concerned with the provisions of amenities to the workers such as better working and living conditions, health and safety, etc. The industrial relations aspect is concerned with organisations relations with employees, such as union management relations, collective bargaining process, disciplinary action, grievance handling and settlement, etc.

As regards the importance of personnel management, experts on management subject treat management as synonymous with personnel management. In the words of Rensis Likert "all the activities of any enterprise are initiated and determined by the persons who make up that institution. Of all the tasks of management, managing the human component is the central and most important task because all else depends on how well it is done". The importance of personnel management is felt on account of the following reasons:

1. **Specialisation:** Specialisation has become the rule of day and this is being created and maintained by the personnel department in an organisation.

2. **Growing size of business:** The increased size of business has resulted in the employment of more employees and this has led to more problems. It is the personnel manager who attends to all such problems and solve them.

3. **Handling of married women and part time staff:** The employment of married women and part time staff in large numbers create domestic and others problems and for handling these carefully, need for personnel management is felt.

4. **Ergonomics:** The development of this comparatively new science has emphasised that the environment in which people work determines the efficiency of their work.

5. **Education and training:** The need for training employees has assumed more importance and management has recognised this fact. To offer training and educational facilities, personnel management is considered more important.

6. **To meet the demands of trade union:** Trade unions demand the management to solve various problems faced by employees. The personnel manager acts under this situation as a kind of liaison officer.

7. **Shortage of staff:** Shortage of staff occur in some cases. In such cases, the personnel manager must tap all possible sources of recruitment.

Principles of personnel management

The following are some of the important principles of personnel management:

(*a*) Care and skill should be exercised in the selection of employees.
(*b*) Introduction to the job should be friendly, skilful, and adequate.
(*c*) Each employee should be made to feel that his efforts are really appreciated.
(*d*) Careful and thoughtful consideration should be given to the probable effect of each rule, notice and practice on employees.
(*e*) Employees should take part in planning those things which affect their working conditions.
(*f*) There should be a sense of security and reasonable freedom from worry.
(*g*) There should be a constant and intelligent effort on the part of management to be absolutely fair in every policy and practice.
(*h*) Each employee should have a feeling of pride in the worthfulness of his work.
(*i*) The organisational set up should be such that there is no confusion in anybody's mind as to his duties or responsibilities.
(*j*) Conditions should be such that working in the office should prove to be a satisfactory social experience as a means of making livelihood.

Personnel policies

To enable the personnel department to carry out its functions efficiently, it is necessary to formulate personnel policies in advance. According to Michael Jucious, "policies are basic rules established to govern functions so that they are performed in line with desired objectives." In the words of Edwin B. Flippe "a policy is man made rule or predetermined course of action that is established to guide the performance of work towards the organisation. It is a type of standing plan that serves to guide subordinates in the execution of their tasks." Personnel policies like any other managerial policy serves as a road-map for managers.

Importance of personnel policies

1. **It helps in achieving the objectives of organisation:** The formulation of policies makes the efforts of each workers as well as the management goal oriented.
2. **Uniformity in decisions:** Well drafted personnel policies bring continuity, uniformity and consistency in various decisions relating to the employees. They eliminate adhoc decisions, partiality towards some and subdual of others.
3. **Encouragement of decentralisation:** It is the distribution of work to different persons and departments. Personnel policies

accomplishes every type of work because of the existence of good relationship between the superior and the subordinate.

4. **Helps in controlling:** The personnel policies always enable to compare the actual performance with the predetermined performance and in case of any difference, it helps to take necessary steps to make actuals confirm with predetermined ones.
5. **It increases morale of workers:** The personnel policies which are nothing but the goals and the means to realise it enables the staff to know about the philosophy and objective of the organisation. They take policies as guide to accomplish the objectives. This increases the morale of workers.
6. **It guarantees security:** The personnel policies are common for both members and non-members of trade union. Therefore, workers need not necessarily fall a prey to the whims of the supervisors and managers.
7. **Guide to management:** Personnel policies guide the management as to who has to do the work, when and how. It also helps the management in solving personnel problems.

Objectives of personnel policies

As was mentioned earlier, policies serve as guidelines to the achievement of objectives of the organisation. The success or failure of a personnel policy is measured on the basis of the objectives, for which these were initially formulated. Personnel policies are formulated to achieve the following objectives:

1. Maximum use of human resources: The best use of manpower can be ensured only when employees are scientifically selected and placed on a suitable job. The process of matching the job with individuals is an important aspect in business organisation. Profits cannot be maximised as long as the business does not utilise the man power to the best of its capabilities. Personnel policies define the job and their responsibilities and then help in their proper handling.

2. Personnel development: Personnel policies must encourage healthy and constructive competition among the workers so that they may be motivated for their maximum development.

3. Sound industrial relations: The efficiency of a business to a large extent depends upon industrial peace. A harmonious relationship must prevail between employer and employees. Personnel policies aims at maintaining sound industrial relations.

4. Other objectives: These include (*a*) proper recognition of workforce and protection of their prestige and (*b*) safeguarding the interests of labour and management.

Contents of personnel policies

The important contents of personnel policies are as follows:

1. History of the growth of the business.
2. Employment practices and conditions of employment.
3. Grievance handling procedure.
4. Safety rules and regulations.
5. General practice such as procedure of getting pay leave policies, etc.
6. Relation between employer an employee.
7. Financial aid to employees.
8. Educational opportunities to employees.
9. Medical facilities to employees.
10. Leave pay, Holiday with pay.
11. Sickness benefits or allowances.
12. Freedom to discuss any matter of interest with management.
13. Social security and other compensations.
14. Collective bargaining.
15. Discipline.

Features of a sound personnel policy

P.W. Betts in his book "Office management" has outlined the main features of sound personnel policy as under:

1. Fair and just treatment of all staff.
2. A realistic salary, structure and compensation for high performance.
3. Genuine scientific selection of staff.
4. Ample opportunity for staff to continue with their education and training.
5. A reasonable working environment consistent with good health and safety, requirements.
6. The provision of modern welfare and social activities.
7. Sympathetic help for domestic and other difficulties.
8. Encouragement of a friendly atmosphere.

Factors affecting personnel policies

The following factors will influence in determining the personnel policies of an organisation:

1. Laws of the country: The various law and labour legislation govern the different aspects of personnel matters. Policies should be in conformity with the laws of the country.

2. Social values and customs: These are the codes of behaviour of any community which should be taken into account in framing the policies.

3. Management philosophy and values: Management does not work, together for any length of the time without clear broad philosophy and set of values which influence their actions on matters concerning the work force.

4. Stages of development: All changes such as size of operations, scale of technology, innovations, fluctuations in the composition of work force, decentralisation of authority and change in financial structure influence the adoption of personnel policies,

5. Financial position of the organisation: The personnel policies cost money which will be reflected in the price of the product. Because of this, prices set an absolute limit to organisation's personnel policies.

6. Union objectives and practices: How well the employees are organised? What is their bargaining capacity? What are their pressure techniques? All these factors are responsible for personnel policies.

7. Type of work force: The assessment characteristics of work force and what is acceptable to them is the responsibility of the effective personnel staff. A policy which is not appropriate is hardly worth implementation.

Duties and responsibilities of personnel manager

The duties and responsibilities of a personnel manager can be tabulated as follows:

Responsibilities	Duties
(1) Employment	*a.* Tapping the sources of labour supply. *b.* Selection of employees. *c.* Induction. *d.* Maintaining the records of all laid off.
(2) Transfers, promotions and separation	*a.* Establishment of policies regarding transfer.

	b. Establishment of policies regarding discharge and demotions. *c.* Dealing with separation initiated by the employee. *d.* Establishment & policies regarding promotions.
(3) Education and training	*a.* Training by organising courses for apprentices, supervisors, new entrants etc. *b.* Arranging film shows for trainees and supervisors. *c.* Organising suggestion school.
(4) Job evaluation, Job analysis and Merit rating	*a.* Analysing all jobs of office supervisory and managerial staff. *b.* Evaluation of each job according to some scheme that will show the relative works of each job. *c.* Conducting merit rating studies.
(5) Fixation of wages and incentives	*a.* Formulating of wage plan. *b.* Studies in cost of living and recommendations to management about the revision of wages and salaries. *c.* Supervising bonus or profit sharing scheme.
(6) Health and Sanitation	*a.* First aid facilities to be given. *b.* Providing health education. *c.* Conduct studies to eliminate fatigue, monotony and occupational disease.
(7) Safety	*a.* Impart safety education. *b.* To undertake studies relating to causes of accidents.

	c. Safety inspection and guidance of employees, safety committee. *d.* Formulation of safety practice code. *e.* Fire protection.
(8) Financial aid to employees	*a.* To look after employees' mutual benefits societies. *b.* Profit sharing plans. *c.* Mutual savings programmes. *d.* Workman's compensation Insurance.
(9) Employee service activities	*a.* To provide recreational activities. *b.* To provide housing facilities. *c.* Canteens. *d.* Transport facilities. *e.* Medical facilities.
(10) Research, Record keeping, reports and follow-up	*a.* Maintaining all files and records of employees. *b.* Periodic check of all records for promotion wage and salary increase, transfers, etc. *c.* Special reports to executives and supervisors. *d.* Personnel Audit.
(11) Joint consultation and labour relations	*a.* Setting up joint consultative committee and ensuring that the results of joint consultative bodies are disseminated. *b.* Encouraging and ensuring the upholding of harmonious labour relations.

Managerial functions of personnel management

The managerial functions of personnel management pertains to the activities concerned with planning, organising, directing and controlling.

1. Planning: It determines in advance a personnel programme. It involves ability to think, analyse and to take decision about personnel problems.

2. Organising: After the plan is formed, the people available have to be grouped and their relationship established in a way as to enable them to achieve organisational objectives. Organisation function involves grouping of the activities required to attain the planned objectives, defining responsibilities of the people in the organisation delegating appropriate authority to them to enable them to discharge their respective responsibilities and establishing structural relationship to generate coordination of the individual efforts towards accomplishment of the organisations objective.

3. Directing: This function is concerned with getting the work done through subordinates by the superior. It consists of issuing orders and instructions to the subordinates, to execute the functions of an office by implementing the plans. This function also resembles to leading, as it involves taking initiative and getting work done through the subordinates.

4. Controlling: This function is concerned with confirming the actual periodical performance appraisal, employee counselling, personnel research, etc, with the plans. This function leads to innovations and new idea relating to planning, motivation, etc.

Advantages of having a personnel manager

1. Reduction in the burden of top executives: Top management is relieved of the personnel function by delegating the function of personnel management to the personnel manager. Thus, top management can devote their time in discharging other most important functions of the management.

2. More attention can be paid to personnel problem: More time can be devoted to personnel problems by the personnel managers to attend to the problems and needs of employees. This results in the improvement in personnel relationships throughout the organisation.

3. He serves as a line between employees and management: The personnel manager bridges the gap between management and employees by representing the problems of employees to the management and by communicating the solutions offered by the employer to the employees.

4. Serve as a means of communication: The personnel manager in a way helps in improving the communication process as it is he who conveys the problems of employees and who in turn communicates the decision taken by the management.

5. Improvement in health, welfare and safety: There will be an overall improvement in health, welfare and safety as the personnel manager, directly or indirectly, can play in important part in providing them with a suitable environment to work.

6. Increases profitability: The losses arising out of sickness, accident, excess labour turnover can be minimised. Consequently, production increases and this results in more profit.

7. Better public relations: By developing a good employer- employee relationship, the company's public relationship also improves. Consequently, a company having bad industrial relations is likely to find its public image somewhat tarnished.

Recent trends in personnel management

The following are some of the recent trends in the area of personnel management:

1. The selection and utilisation of minority groups: From the stand point of recruitment and selection of new employees, emphasis in modern days is to select neglected and weaker sections of the society. The policy formulated by the government and the excess government regulation has added more importance to this changing trend.

2. Better methods of training and placing disadvantaged individuals: Recognising the social responsibility of business, industries in modern days are hiring, educating and training those employees who are physically handicapped, ex-service men, etc. Who would not other wise be eligible for such employment.

3. Automation of personnel records: With the introduction of data processing equipments most of the enterprises are making use of automatic machines for maintaining personnel records. Instead of making use of paper files, magnetic tapes are made use of for storing applicants' data, performance rating, for job history, test results, promotions, payroll data and the like.

4. Merit rating: It is conducted by recognising the management potential through experimentation with samples of the individuals behaviour rather than total reliance on tests and interviews.

5. Determining employee opinions and attitudes: The management is heavily relying upon the opinions of employees instead of depending upon outside consultants. Management of organisation has now fully understood that incorporation of employees' feelings and opinions in formulating plans will motivate the employees and thus increase their efficiency.

6. Employee morale: The importance of employees morale is recognised in most of the organisations today. Research is undertaken to study the effect of good working conditions on employees, better employer and employee relationship, better motivation so that morale of employee is improved and better performance achieved.

7. Basic and applied research by personnel management: Increased emphasis is made on research covering a wide range of topics in the area of personnel management. Some of the topics relates to technical and managerial obsolesces; organisational and environmental aspects and so on.

QUESTIONS

Simple Questions

1. Defines personnel management.
2. Defines personnel policy.
3. State any four features of good personnel policy.

Short Answer Questions

1. Outline the principles of personnel management.
2. Discuss the importance of personnel policy.
3. Defines personnel policy. State its contents.
4. What are the advantages of having a separate personnel manager?
5. Explain the recent trends of personnel management.

Essay Type Question

1. Explain the responsibilities and duties of the personnel manager in a modern business.

17

Recruitment and Selection of Office Staff

MAN POWER PLANNING

It is considered as the most valuable and important assets of an office. Leon C. Megginson in his book "Personnel and Human Resource Administration" views manpower as the total knowledge, skill, creative abilities, talents, and aptitudes of an organisation's work-force as well as the values, attitudes and benefits of an individual involved. In the words of Bruce P. Coleman, manpower planning is the process of determing manpower requirements and the means for meeting those requirements in order to carry out the integrated plan of the organisation. Many factors have contributed to the greater interest of manpower planning in modern days. These factors are (*a*) Job requirements are changing fast with the change in technology, (*b*) Increased need for skilled workers, (*c*) National concern about labour and employment, (*d*) Increased mobility of human resources, (*e*) Changing patterns of modern management process, (*f*) Mechanisation and automation introduced in the office and (*g*) Expansion in the size of offices.

Objectives of man power planning

The important objectives of manpower planning are:

1. Making correct estimate of manpower requirements: This is the first and foremost objective of manpower planning. The forecast of manpower helps in recruiting the right type of men, for the right job. The additional staff in an office are created by discharge, retirement, transfers, promotions. Employees under such an organisation are not available all of a sudden. Manpower planning helps in this regard.

2. Managing manpower according to the need of the office: Manpower planning avoids over staffing and under staffing in office. To a large extent, the staff available within the office can be utilised without relying on external sources. It gives encouragement to the existing employees and in turn creates favourable psychological climate for motivation.

3. Help in recruitment and selection: Sound manpower planning helps in recruitment and selection also. It helps in pursuing sound procedures of recruitment so that best staff may be available at the time of requirement. It also reduces the cost of recruitment.

4. Maintaining production level: Man power planning undertakes to estimate the separation of staff on various grounds in advance. By proper planning, it makes alternatives arrangement for substituting the staff who might leave the job. This is possible by two types of analysis known as work load analysis and work force analysis.

5. Other objectives: The other objectives of manpower planning include making employee's development programmes effective, establishing industrial peace, reduction in labour cost, and effective utilisation of labour force.

Types of man power planning

Man power planning can be of two types, *viz.,* (1) Short term planning and (2) Long term planning.

1. Short term man power planning: It involves matching the present employee with their present jobs so that they may perform their function efficiently. However, it may not always be possible to have a perfect match between jobs and individuals. So, necessary adjustments have to be made in the jobs so as to make employees fit for the job. The problems under such circumstances can be studied under he following :

(*a*) *When the employee is less qualified than the requirements*: Under this circumstance, the following steps can be taken; (*i*) providing training, (*ii*) change in the job and (*iii*) transfer.

(*b*) *When the employee is more qualified than the requirements*: Under this circumstance, the abilities and skills of the employee is not to be exploited to the maximum extent and hence the following adjustments can be made (*i*) Job enlargement, (*ii*) Additional charge and (*iii*) Promotion to higher jobs.

2. Long term man power planning: In the long term planning, the management plans the manpower requirements for a longer period, usually between 10 to 15 years. Long term planning considers such factors as organisations structure, technology, methods of production, possible expansion of business and so on.

Man power planning can also be classified under the following types :

1. **Replacement planning:** It is connected with recruitment or promotion to fill expected loss of manpower. It considers age, health problems and identified sources of replacement.
2. **Adaptive planning:** Under this planning the future events are known in advance and alternatives are considered and best course of action is taken.
3. **Contingent planning:** Under this planning, potential hazards are identified and advance strategies are developed.

Steps in manpower planning

The steps involved in manpower planning have been beautifully summarised by Geisher in his article "Man Power Planning": An emerging staff function." According to Geisher, Manpower planning is the process including forecasting, developing and controlling by which a firm ensures that it has the right number of people, and the right kind of people, at the right place, at the right time, doing work for which they are economically most useful. Manpower planning consists of the following steps:

(*a*) Forecasting future manpower requirements.

(*b*) Making an inventory of the present manpower resources and assessing the extent to which these resources are employed optimally.

(*c*) Anticipating manpower problems by projecting present resources into the future and compare these with the forecast requirements to determine their adequacy, both quantitatively and qualitatively.

(*d*) Plan the necessary programmes relating to selection, training, development, transfer, motivation and compensation to ensure that future manpower requirements are properly met.

Procedure of appointing office staff

The procedure involved in appointing a person to an office can be explained under the following headings:

(1) Receiving of labour placement requisitions.

(2) Recruitment of employees.

(3) Inviting application forms.

(4) Checking reference.

(5) Screening out unqualified applicants.
(6) Conducting employment tests.
(7) Conducting oral tests.
(8) Conducting medical examination.
(9) Final approval.
(10) Placement and induction.

The above steps are explained here under:

1. Receiving of labour placement requisitions: The function of appointing the required number of employees to an office starts with receiving the labour placement requisitions. A labour placement requisition is a request made in written form from various departments. It contains particulars such as (*a*) Job specifications, (*b*) Educational qualifications, (*c*) Experience, (*d*) Skill, (*e*) Age requirements and (*f*) The number of persons required for such department. The actual number of persons required for such department arises owing to the increased volume of work and on account of labour turn over. The office manager determines the skills of employees to be selected. The labour placement requisitions which are received from time to time by the office manager or personnel manager is consolidated so that all the required members of the staff and clerks for all the departments may be appointed at the same time. This also reduces the cost involved in procuring the labour force.

2. Recruitment of employment: The term 'recruitment' applies to the process of attracting potential employees to the office. It is a systematic means of finding and inducing available candidates to apply for the job in the office. Since it is the process of searching for prospective employees, it is concerned with determing the possible sources of supply of labour and the recruitment practices and techniques. As the ultimate success or failure of the office depends upon the right type of employee appointed, it is essential that the office manager taps the right source of supply for the labour force. There are two sources of recruiting the employees, *viz.*, (*i*) Internal source and (*ii*) External source. This is presented in the following chart.

SOURCE OF RECRUITMENT

INTERNAL SOURCE	EXTERNAL SOURCE
1. Promotion.	1. Friends, relatives and present employees.
2. Transfer.	2. Institutes and colleges.
3. Recalling retired employees.	3. Advertising.
4. Trainees.	4. Employment exchanges.

5. Deputation.

5. Waiting lists.
6. Recruitment through Trade Unions.
7. Use of special consultants for recruitment.
8. Professional organisation.

(*i*) *Internal source*: The internal sources of supply of manpower refers to recruitment from within the organisation so as to avoid the complications and expensive procedure of recruiting persons from external source. Internal source of recruitment offers the following advantages:

(*a*) It enhances the general morale of the employees in the organisation.
(*b*) It builds loyalty among the employees by creating a sense of security.
(*c*) It reduces labour turn over in the organisations.
(*d*) It creates a sense of sincerity among the staff.

However, internal recruitment suffers form the following disadvantages:

(*a*) It severely narrows down the areas of selections.
(*b*) It leads to stagnation and conservation in the service.
(*c*) Fresh candidates with talents are denied a chance of entry into the organisation.
(*d*) It does not compel the existing employees to keep abreast of new development in the area of office administration.

The following are the important sources of internal recruitment:

1. Promotion: Under this source, vacancies are filled up through promotions from the lower cadres. This gives encouragement to the employees in general besides creating vacancies at the lower levels which gives employment opportunities to the unemployed.

2. Transfers: Very often existing employees who are found competent to take up a newly created vacancy may be transferred to the department where he is more suited. Thus, transfer involves the change of place of work by an employee without any change either in status or recruitment.

3. Recalling retired employees: When no qualified and competent staff or managers are immediately available to fill up the vacancy caused by the retired employees, their position can be filled in recalling the retired staff or manager. But care must be taken to see that he has necessary ability and interest to continue in the office.

4. Trainees: The concept of "Management Trainees" has become very popular in modern days, wherein the prospective employees are offered training even before they are appointed as full time employees. On successful training, if the candidates are found suitable, they are absorbed without resorting to external source.

5. Deputation: This source of recruitment is available only to big organisation which open branches in different localities. Instead of recruiting a stranger who may not have adequate experience it may be desirable to depute some of the experienced staff and other managers, until the new branch is firmly established. Subsequently, it can be left to the choice of the deputed staff either to continue with the branch or comeback and resume the work in the main office.

(*ii*) *External Sources*: It refers to recruiting the employees from outside the organisation. External source of recruitment offers the following advantages:

(*a*) A wider field of selection is available.

(*b*) Fresh candidates with variety of skill and a broad outlook may be attracted.

(*c*) Experienced and trained employees may be procured.

External source of recruitment suffers from the following disadvantages:

(*a*) Prolonged training has to be given to the new recruits which involves huge expenses in training.

(*b*) It reduces incentive to work hard among the existing workers because they feel that, however excellently they may work, they have no chance of getting promotions in their organisations.

The following are the important sources of external recruitment :

1. Friends and relatives of the present employees: The office manager may consider the recommendations of friends and relatives of the existing employees. It is presumed that the present employees who are loyal to the organisation will be in a position to introduce good, honest and efficient workers.

2. Management institutes and colleges: Under this source, the office manager keeps contact with management institutions and educational institutions to recommend suitable candidates for appointment. However, candidates who complete the course alone are considered for recruitment. This source of recruitment is useful for recruiting supervisors and managers at middle and higher levels of management. In India, recruitment through management institutes and universities is not common. This is due to absence of close contact between educational institutes and the business establishments.

3. Advertising: Under this source, the employer gives advertisement with the necessary details in newspapers, trade journals, radio and television. Press advertising gives full particulars about the job requirements, educational qualifications, experience, salary offered or expected and other service conditions. Suitable candidates are appointed through tests and interviews.

4. Employment exchange: In India, the government has set up employment exchanges in all important towns. These exchanges are useful for providing jobs to unemployed persons. Those interested in getting jobs have to register their names in employment exchange. The employer informs the employment exchange about the vacancies available from time to time and the exchange sends a list of suitable candidates for consideration and selection.

5. Waiting lists: Some of the applicants who had applied previously but not selected may be given an opportunity to come and take up the vacant job.

6. Recruitment through Trade Unions: Trade union leaders often recommend the required number of persons to the office manager. But there is a danger in this source of recruitment, in the sense that the person recruited through the recommendations of union leader would always support the union and may work contrary to the ideas and ideologies of the organisation.

7. Use of Special Consultants: Consultancy service of recruitment and selection are popular in foreign countries. These agencies are mostly business firms whose incomes are derived from fees charged from clients. Many such agencies are well staffed with competitive specialists and maintain high standards of ethical practice. In India, we have Tata Consultancy Service, ABC consultants, Ferguison and company etc.

8. Professional organisation: Where professional persons such as a cost accountant or chartered accountant or a secretary are to the recruited, professional bodies could be consulted. Such organisations, keep the names and addresses of the members who qualify professional educational qualifications. In India, we have the Institute of cost and works accounts of India, the Institute of Chartered Accountants of India, the Institute of Companies Secretaries of India besides number of other organisations such as the Institute of materials management, the Institute of Personnel Management, the Institute of Chartered Finance analyst and so on.

3. Inviting application forms: After resorting to any of the above discussed source of recruitment, the next step in the selective process is receiving of filled in application forms from the prospective employees. The office may some times issue a standard blank applications forms. Usually the candidates themselves are asked to write applications on their own to know their abilities and handwriting. The application forms must bear three important categories of information. They are (*a*) Biographic data such as name, age, sex and status, (*b*) Education and past experience and (*c*) Reference. Application forms should be as simple as possible and must incorporate questions relating to the fitness of the applicant to the job. Different colours of applications forms are to made use of, for different categories of employees.

4. Checking testimonials and references: A testimonial is usually associated with a document in which one person, usually, the employer, gives his opinion concerning the character, ability and qualifications of another person, usually an employees or ex-employee. It is addressed as "To whom so ever it may be concerned". A reference is more commonly descriptive of the document in which the "reference" expresses his opinion about the referee to the person requiring it. However, it is also possible to give a reference in the form of an oral statement to the inquirer. There is no legal obligation on the part of an employer to provide a testimonial or reference of an employee or ex-employee and no action can be taken against him for refusing to do so. If, however an employer is prepared to give a testimonial or reference, he must take a note of the following when preparing it:

(*a*) To avoid making any statements that may be defamatory of the employees.

(*b*) Not to write or speak in praise of an employee whom he knows has been inefficient in his work or dishonest.

(*c*) To state only what he bonafede believes to be true.

When sending a testimonial or reference, the employer would be well advised to address the documents to the person requesting it, and to ensure that the envelop is addressed to that person and clearly marked "Confidential".

5. Screening out unqualified and incompetent applicant: In these days of unemployment it is common, to observe that thousands of applicants apply for the job though all of them may not be really competent for the job. With increased application forms, it becomes difficult even to select the right candidate. So unless incompetent applications are screened out, it involves too much of time and more confusion in selecting the right candidate. For screening out the undesirable applicants, a criterion may be fixed. First of all, incomplete application forms may be out rightly rejected. Then on the basis of experience, merit, age, skill and such other criterion, the incompetent candidates may be screened out. Now, it becomes easy to deal with a limited number of applicants and this facilitates the selection of right candidate.

6. Conducting Tests: Lee J. Cronhach in his book Essentials of educational testing defines a test as "systematic procedure for comparing the behaviour of two or more persons. In the words of Milton L. Blun, "a test is a sample of an individual's behaviour, performance or attitude. Employment tests can be classified under the following categories:

(*a*) *Performance test*: It is designed to measure what the applicants know about a particular job or their degree of proficiency in performing job. For example, an applicant's shorthand skill can be tested by dictations. Similarly a typists speed can be judged by asking him to type a letter, a file clerk might be asked to code and file a series of documents.

(*b*) *Aptitude test*: This test measure an individual's potential to learn.

(*c*) *Intelligence test*: Under this test, the candidate's mental ability, debating power and reasoning abilities are known while performing a job.

(*d*) *Interest test*: This type of test is designed to measure the applicant's preferences for certain activities compared to other activities.

(*e*) *Personality test*: This type of test is not very much popular as it lacks validity. Personality test is devised for the purpose of measuring such characteristics as emotional adjustments, self-confidence, originality and other traits.

All the above mentioned tests must be properly administered as they serve the purpose of (*i*) scientific selection, (*ii*) training, (*iii*) vocational guidance, (*iv*) forecasting the success of employees and (*v*) placing the employees on the right job.

The test administered must possess the following features: (1) Reliability, the test must reveal the same result even if different persons conduct the test. (2) Validity, it tests the areas for which it is designed. (3) Objectivity, there must be one and only one answer to each and every question. (4) Comprehensiveness, all possible type of questions relating to the area is to be included. (5) Utility, it should be simple, easy to conduct, and it must involve less expenses.

7. Conducting oral interviews: Spriegel defines interview as the purposeful exchange of ideas, the answering of questions and communicating between two or more persons. An interview is an art of conversation through which competence of a person for the job is measured. While conducting interviews, the interviewer looks for symptoms that indicates the fitness or unfitness of a person for a job. The purposes for which an interview is conducted are as follows:

(*a*) To find the right applicant who will fulfill the duties most satisfactorily.

(*b*) To assess each candidate so as to get an accurate picture about his character and capabilities.

(*c*) To know more information which is not provided in the application form.

(*d*) To reassess any doubtful information supplied on the application form.

(*e*) To provide a full description of the vacancy and answer any relevant queries.

(*f*) To reach complete agreement with the successful applicant.

For the sake of conducting interviews, a selecting committee is constituted which is headed by the office manager. The selection committee should not be unduly large. Interviews can be effectively conducted through a well-developed procedure which is generally as follows:

(*a*) *The setting for the interview*: Environmental factors play an important role while setting the stage ready for conducting interviews. A comfortable waiting room must be provided for the candidates. The interview room should be kept apart from the busy premises of office. The furniture in the interview room must be arranged so as to give a friendly informal and homely atmosphere.

(*b*) *Conducting interview*: The process of conducting the interview should be simple and straight forward. The interview committee can ask questions to test the ability of the applicant and to reveal his character an personality. They can also provide more details of the job that applicant is expected to perform.

(*c*) *Assessment of the performance*: The interview committee develops a rating scale of assessment of the different qualities and abilities of the candidates. The assessment process infact begins from the time of candidate's entry into the interview room and continues throughout the interview period.

(*d*) *Communication of result*: The interview committee will decide the best candidates to be selected based on the merit of performance in the interview. The selected candidate is then communicated about his selection and a time is given to him to come and report to the duty on the specified date.

8. Conducting medical examination: The medical examination as a step in selection is used to examine the physical fitness of employees to a job. A proper matching of job requirement with physical ability results in greater utilisation of manpower. It is also necessary to check the spread of disease from persons to person, as otherwise it involves payment of more compensation. Medical examination includes:

(*a*) Family medical history, (*b*) Personal history of previous illness, (c) Height, chest and weight measurement, (*d*) Physical examination of skin, (*e*) Examination of eyes, nose, ears, and teeth, (*f*) Checking up of heart and blood pressure and (*g*) Blood test.

9. Final approval: This selection of an employee in small organisation will be made by the office manager himself. But in large sized business enterprises the final selection lies with top level management. The office manager, therefore, acts with the authority delegated to fulfil his responsibility to assist the top management in the acquisitions of personnel. Thus, it is the top level management which has the authority to finally select a candidate but not the office manager.

10. Induction: The selection process is not complete until the selected employee is put on the job and introduced to his co-workers and the supervisors. In many cases this step is totally forgotten and there is a gap between the selection of employees and their success. This process of bringing the gap is known as induction. It involves the orientation of new employees to the work situation. He must be introduced to the policy and philosophy of management including the history of the business, the products manufactured, the organisation's structure, rules and regulations and specific duties and responsibilities involved in the job. Introduction of job serves as an excellent starting point for the business to sell themselves and infuse confidence in new employees.

11. Service agreement: A service agreement is usually entered into between the employer and employee, particularly when the post is highly responsible one. It consists of the following:

(*a*) Name and address of the employer and employee.

(*b*) Duties and responsibilities attached to the post.

(*c*) The various reasons for discharging the employee.

(*d*) Duration of contract and the length of probationary period if any.

(*e*) Deposit of money to be made by the employee as in the case of cashier.

(*f*) The number of holidays per annum to which the employee is entitled.

(*g*) Hours of work.
(*h*) Period of notice regarding termination of service.
(*i*) The remuneration payable.
(*j*) Any covenant restraining the employee (management trainee) not to leave the job for two or three years after completing training period.
(*k*) Provision for the payment of salary in case of sickness or disability.
(*l*) Benefits relating to pension, provident fund, insurance schemes ect.
(*m*) Previlege and amenities to be given such as housing, medical and transport facilities.

The service agreement is signed both by the employer and employee. A copy of it is retained by the employer and another copy is given to the employee, for his reference.

QUESTIONS

Simple Questions

1. What do you mean by manpower planning?
2. State any four objectives of manpower planning.
3. Distinguish between short term and long term manpower planning.
4. Distinguish between recruitment and selection.
5. State the merit of internal source of recruitment.
6. What do you mean by performance test?
7. What do you mean by aptitude test?
8. What do you mean by intelligence test?
9. What do you mean by interest test?
10. What do you mean by personality test?

Short Answer Question

1. What do you mean by service agreement? State its contents.

Essay Type Question

1. Explain the procedure involved in selecting an employee to an office.

18

Time Keeping System

MEANING AND OBJECTS OF TIME KEEPING

Time Keeping refers to the method of recording the arrival and departure time of workers in an organisation. The recording of time is usually done twice during the day. However, when the employees leave the office premises during lunch interval the time recording is done four times. Thus, the time recording is done four times a day for which a separate department is established which is known as time keeping department. The timekeeper is incharge of this department. His office will be near the entrance gate of the business establishments. His duty is to maintain proper recording of time spent by the employees in the organisation.

The objectives of time recording can be enumerated under the following:

(*a*) To maintain attendance records to meet statutory requirements.
(*b*) To serve as a disciplinary check on workers.
(*c*) To calculate the number of hours worked in order to calculate wages.
(*d*) To maintain punctuality of attendance among the employees.
(*e*) To check late arrival of employees into the organisation.
(*f*) To apportion overhead expenses on the basis of hours worked in the organisation.
(*g*) To calculate the labour cost of product or service.
(*h*) To prepare and analyse the statistics of labour, records for determining productivity and control of labour cost.

Methods of time keeping

Time keeping methods can be broadly classified into two, categories: (1) Manual method and (2) Mechanical methods

1. Manual method: Under this method, the recording of time is done by employees. The following are the two manual methods employed to record attendance time of employees.

***(A)* Attendance register method:** The attendance register which is used to record incoming and outgoing time of employees in an organisation is known as daily muster roll. Under this method, attendance time can be recorded in any one of the following two ways:

(*a*) The attendance time can be recorded by the time keeper himself. He will enter the arrival and departure time of worker in the business establishment.

(*b*) The attendance register may be kept inside the time keeping office and the employees are required to sign both at the time of entering and leaving the organisation noting down "time in" and "time out".

This method is very simple to operate and is best suited to a small sized business organisation. However, this method suffers from the following disadvantages:

(*i*) Employees are held-up near the gate at the time of arrival and departure.

(*ii*) It involves extra clerical costs for maintaining individual attendance record.

(*iii*) It cannot act as a check on the dishonest practice of noting down wrong time by the employees.

(*iv*) Sometimes gatekeeper behaves partially towards some workers which vitiates the accuracy of the wage records.

***(B)* Disc method:** Under this method, every employee is allotted a disc or a metal token which bears his identification number. All the discs are hung in a spike and kept at the entrance of the gate, a few minutes before the commencement time. As an when a worker enters into the gate, he removes his disc from the spike file and puts into a box or hung it on another spike file which is kept for this purpose. To record the time of employees coming late, the box is replaced at regular interval each indicating the extent of late attendance. Alternatively, employees coming late may be required to report the timekeeper so that the exact time of arrival may be noted. With the help of discs in the box, the attendance time is recorded in a book. The missing discs indicate the absence of an employee. This method suffers from the following disadvantages:

(*i*) A worker may insert two discs inside the box one of himself and the other of his friend.

(*ii*) It involves a large amount of clerical work. There is every possibility of committing mistakes while writing attendance with the help of discs and discs cannot offer any proof in case of disputes, doubts, etc.

2. Mechanical methods: Mechanical methods are used in modern days to save time and ensure greater accuracy. The machines record the exact arrival and departure time of all employees. Thus, it avoids possible disputes and difference in opinion. Mechanical devices are used in medium and large sized organisations because of heavy investment involved on it. The following equipments are used under this method:

(A) Dial Time Recorder: The features and functioning of this equipment can be summarised as under:

(*i*) It consists of a large dial on which there are about 150 holes corresponding to the number of workers.

(*ii*) A clock is fitted with the circle of the dial together with a dial arm which operates from the centre of the circle.

(*iii*) The worker entering into the gate turns the dial arm. He then presses it into the hole corresponding to his clock number. The time of his arrival is recorded on a sheet of paper kept inside the machine.

(*iv*) The same procedure is followed before the employee leaves the factory gate.

Advantages

(*i*) Time is recorded strictly according to pay roll order.

(*ii*) Provision can also be made out not only to record time, but also to calculate wages.

Disadvantages

(*i*) A worker can record the time of an absentee.

(*ii*) Time of arrival and departure are separated out on two different sheets of paper which require additional clerical work.

(*iii*) A worker cannot see the time he has booked and disputes may arise afterwards.

(B) Card time recorder: This is a machine which is fitted with a clock on each side of which there is an "in" and "out" rack which contains the cards of the employees. The worker who enters into the gate takes his card from the "in rack", inserts it into the machine on pressing a lever, the time of arrival is recorded on this card.

Then the card is placed in the "out' rack. At the time of departure from the office, the employee removes his card, inserts it in the machine to record the time of departure and finally places it in the "in" rack.

Advantages

(*i*) For each and every employee, time is recorded individually.

(*ii*) The absence of an employee can be checked by a mere look at the "Out" rack.

(*iii*) This can be taken as a basis for wage calculation.

Disadvantages

(*i*) An employee can record the time of an absentee.

(*ii*) Controlling and checking card become difficult.

(C) Autograph or signature type time recorder: This type of machine is most commonly used in small sized business organisations where supervision for time recording does not arise. Its features can be listed out as follows:

(*i*) It is a machine which is fitted with a clock and is connected to a printing mechanism on a roll of paper.

(*ii*) To operate the machine, the incoming or outgoing employee opens the shutter by pressing a lever which is at the side of the machine. This enables to uncover a small signature window.

(*iii*) The employee signs in this signature window and as he signs, the day and time is automatically recorded.

(*iv*) When the lever is released, the paper roll inside the machine (which now bears the employee's signature, day and time) is advanced, the shutter slides back over the signature window and the machine is ready for the signature of the next employee.

Advantages

(*i*) Recording of time is automatic and accurate.

(*ii*) Employees cannot alter the recorded time.

Disadvantages

(*i*) The workers name appear in different order, but not according to payroll order.

(*ii*) Signature may not be legible.

Overtime

Usually overtime work in an office is not encouraged. But, whenever it arises it is adjusted towards leave or absence. However, in foreign countries there is a shift towards the policy of overtime work and it is recognised as valued from the point of view of both trade union and labour laws. It is now a commonly accepted fact that the overtime salary is paid in the same way as in the case of overtime wages payable to direct workers in factories. Overtime work is felt necessary only during the end of the month or a quarter. Where detailed reports are to be prepared or excess work is involved as in the case of preparation of dividend list, the office manager must evolve a clear policy in terms of over time involved, its payment, length of notice required to be given to employee, maximum overtime and so on.

QUESTIONS

Simple Questions

1. State any four objectives of time keeping.
2. Mention any two manual and two mechanical methods of time recording.
3. What is a muster roll.
4. What is a disc? What purpose does it serve?
5. State two advantages and two disadvantages of dial time recorder.
6. State two advantages and two disadvantages of card time recorder.
7. What do you mean by autograph time recorder?

Short Answer Questions

1. State with advantages and disadvantages, the manual methods of time recording.
2. State with advantages and disadvantages the mechanical method of time recording.

Essay Type Question

1. Explain the various methods of time recording.

19

Wages and Salary Administration

INTRODUCTION

On of the major problems that confront the management of every organisation is the determination of a satisfactory wage and salary structure. This problem has been further complicated because many indirect methods of remuneration have been devised which have social and psychological implications with an employee's salary. From the point of view of employer, the selection of a particular system of salary payment determines the future earning capacity of the organisation. From the point of view of the employee, choosing the appropriate plan plays a prominent role in determining employee's satisfaction, productivity, morale, and turnover. Therefore, management of every organisation must determine the amount of salaries to be paid to the employees. The determination of salaries payable to employees is based upon thorough analysis of all factors affecting such remuneration.

Wages *Vs.* Salaries

According to Alford and Beatty "wages are the aggregate earnings of an employee for a given period of time such as a day or week and are equal to the product of an hourly rate times the number of hours or the product of a piece rate times the number of pieces, plus any premium bonus earned.

Salary is compensation paid to an employee for personal services rendered on a weekly, monthly or annual basis.

When construed in a broad sense, wages cover all forms of compensation paid to the employees of an organisation. Accordingly, wages include basic wages, bonus or any other form of monetary payment. By its popular usage, the term wage is used to denote the remuneration given to those employees who are employed on production process. On the other hand, the term salary is used to denote payment of remuneration to those employees who manage, supervise and control the activities of employees. Such category of employees belong to the group of Managers, Supervisors, Accountants, Inspectors, Foremen and the like.

Wage and salary policies

It is very difficult to prepare a comprehensive wage and salary policies in an organisation. Usually the following matters are included while compiling a wage and salary policies:

(*a*) Basis of remuneration, *i.e.*, number of hours worked, or number of units produced should be fixed for various groups of employees.

(*b*) Establishment of wages and salary level that will enable the organisation to maintain production costs that are competitive, thus assure stability.

(*c*) Determination and use of fair wage differential between jobs based upon the skill, experience, responsibility and working conditions required.

(*d*) Measurement and recognition of individual merit through merit rating or through incentive system of wage payment.

(*e*) Establishment of fair standards of performance which can be reasonably and consistently attained.

(*f*) Establishment of a plan of promotion from within the organisation that will assure every employee an opportunity for advancement consistent with his ability and performance.

(*g*) Establishment of a normal work week schedule indicating the hours of the day and days of the week in which the work is to be performed.

(*h*) Determination of extra remuneration for overtime work. Special work schedule should be anticipated and arranged whenever possible, to allow the worker to adjust himself, to the new situation.

(*i*) Determination of wage and salary payments to be made during vacations, holidays and sick leave to various groups of employees.

(*j*) Provisions for giving prompt attention to complaints on wage and salary matters in order that adjustments that may be made before grievances develop.

Characteristics of a sound salary plan

The following are the essential characteristics of a sound system of wage payment:

(*a*) The system must be agreed upon both by the employer and the employees.

(*b*) The salary system must be such that it must minimise labour turnover.
(*c*) It should reduce absenteeism and late attendance.
(*d*) Wage system should include incentives for efficient and exceptional type of workers.
(*e*) The cost of operating the system must be less.
(*f*) The system of salary payment must take into account the working conditions of the employees.
(*g*) It should guarantee a minimum amount of wages and salaries.
(*h*) Salary system must be flexible and capable of being adjusted in case of need.
(*i*) Salary system must be commensurate with the earnings of the business enterprise.
(*j*) It should be consistent with government policy.

Methods of remunerating office employees

The remuneration paid to office employees is known as salaries. The salary scale is fixed to different categories of employees in advance and these scales shall be applicable to different grades of employees.

Fixation of salary scale has the following advantages:

(*a*) The employees will know at what rate they are remunerated.
(*b*) It helps to know about their future scales.
(*c*) It helps them to know the increments they are going to get from time to time.
(*d*) It helps them to know the maximum salary they will get and thus enable them to plan the spending accordingly.
(*e*) It eliminates the secrecy with regard to salaries which prevent jealousy and hatred among the employees.

Salary scales are fixed by taking the following factors into consideration:

(*a*) Different scales are to be fixed for different categories of work.
(*b*) Salaries to be fixed must be such that, it attracts new employers.
(*c*) A lower rate must be fixed for beginners and higher rate for experienced employees.
(*d*) There must be flexibility in the fixation of salary scales.
(*e*) The salary scale must include deferred increment when employees have been on maximum scale for years.
(*f*) The salary scale must be easy to understand and simple to operate.

Types of salary scales or method of salary payment

The following are different methods of remunerating office employees:

1. Grade scale: When the job is classified according to the nature of work involved, then different grade scales are applicable to different employees. For example the clerical work is classified into first division clerk, second division clerk and so on. Accordingly, different salary scales are implemented for different grades of clerks. Similarly other jobs can be graded on the basis of experience, educational qualifications, responsibility involved, judgement, initiative, efficiency and so on.

2. Merit scales: Under this method, the scales are fixed on the basis of merit of employees. The merit of employees are judged by the following factors:

(*a*) Loyalty to work.
(*b*) Output in terms of quantity.
(*c*) Quality on the basis of accuracy, neatness, etc.
(*d*) Ability to do work under different situations.
(*e*) Ability and willingness to assist others.
(*f*) Ability to do variety of work.
(*g*) Regularity and punctuality in attendance.

The merit of the employees are to be assessed at frequent intervals preferably twice in a year. Records must be maintained to access the merit of employees. A five point rating scale can be used as mentioned below for the sake of judging the merit of employees.

Much Below Average	Below Average	Average	Above Average	Much Above Average

Or

Indifferent	Fair	Good	Very Good	Excellent

Clerks may be rated accordingly to above characteristics and scales are fixed according to merit rating of employees.

3. Age scales: This is not a very popular method of fixing the salary scale. But, this method can be combined with a grade scale so that each clerk will be paid atleast the minimum for his age or the minimum for his grade which ever is greater.

4. On the basis of salaries paid in other offices: Under this method the salaries payable in other establishments are taken as the basis for payment of salaries. This method, therefore, involves a survey to be conducted in various organisations with a view to analyse the salary structure payable in those organisations.

5. Long service premiums: Under this method, a certain incentive is paid to those employees who are in long service in addition to the usual salary scale. The premium payable is in recognition of service of employees and varies according to the period of service rendered.

6. Bonus: Bonus is paid to employees based on output and the profit earned by the organisation.

7. Fixed salary: Employees in an office can also be paid a fixed amount of salary. This is applicable in case of apprentices, management trainees and retired employees who are absorbed into the organisation.

8. Incentive system: The term "incentive" has been defined as "the stimulation of effort and effectiveness by offering monetary inducement on enhanced facilities". It is clear from this definition that an incentive could be a monetary or non-monetary incentive like fringe benefits. Incentives can also be paid to individual worker or collectively to a group of employees. In the former case, the employee directly gets his share of premium for his increased efficiency, while in the latter case, the incentive is shared by all the employees in an agreed proportion for their collective effort. The incentive systems have the following characteristics:

(*a*) In all incentive systems of wage payment minimum salary is guaranteed.

(*b*) For every job, a standard time is fixed by conducting time and motion study.

(*c*) If a worker completes the job within the time allowed; he will be paid incentive bonus on the time saved.

Essentials of good incentive system

David W. Belcher, in his book "wage and salary administration" enumerates the following essential requirements of a good incentive system of wage payment:

(*a*) All incentive salary plan should be explained and discussed with all employees and supervisor before it is installed. Employees' acceptance and cooperation is much more necessary to avoid confusion and disputes in respect of salary payment.

(*b*) The plan should allow for earnings to be in direct proportion to an employee's work which is above the standard.

(*c*) An incentive plan should be easy to understand and calculate by the employees.

(*d*) The incentive should be paid in the same month during which the efforts are put. It should not be postponed to the future month.

(*e*) The difference between the guaranteed and the incentive pay rate should be large enough to encourage extra effort on the part on the employees.

(*f*) The standard once set should not be chanced unless; (*i*) there is an error or (*ii*) a change in work condition has been effected.

(*g*) The standards should be scientifically set and it must be within the reach of employees to attain it.

(*h*) The entire work process should be standardised such as standard work methods, standard work places, standard materials, and standard control process.

(*i*) Equitable adjustments should be provided for an employee who fails to meet the standard for reasons beyond his control.

(*j*) Standard of work must be based on establishment and recognised quality requirements.

(*k*) A good working condition is to be created to enable the workers to attain the standard.

(*l*) No upper limit should be fixed for employee's earnings.

Types of monetary incentives

1. Halsey system: This system was introduced by F.A. Halsey, an American Engineer in 1891. The features of this incentive system are (*a*) A standard time is allowed for each risk. An employee who takes standard time or more than standard time receives his time rate. (*b*) If the work is completed in less than standard time, the employee is paid an incentive of 50 per cent of the time saved. The remaining 50 per cent of the incentive is shared by the employer.

Advantages

(*a*) Time wages are guaranteed and thus, it offers security to the employees.

(*b*) As the incentive is also shared by the employer he is interested in improving the working conditions in office.

(*c*) This method of wage payment is comparatively easy to operate and understand

Disadvantages

(*a*) Workers are dissatisfied because employers share half of the incentive earned by the employees.

(*b*) It is difficult to fix a standard time in actual practice.

2. Rowan system: This incentive system of wage payment was introduced by James Rowan of Scotland. Under this system also the incentive is paid on the time saved as in the case of Halsey System, but the basis of calculating the incentive differs. Under this method, the bonus hours are calculated as the proportion of the time taken which the time saved bears to the time allowed and are paid on the basis of time rate system.

Advantages

(*a*) This system is more suitable for beginners and slow workers.

(*b*) The employer benefits more from this system ($66^2/_3$ per cent of incentive) and so he provides good working conditions in the office.

Disadvantages

(*a*) This system of wage payment is not easily understood by employees.

(*b*) This system is not beneficial to employees at high level efficiency.

3. Taylor's system: This system was devised by F.W. Taylor in 1880. The features of this system of wage payment may be summarised as; (*a*) Wages or salary is not guaranteed, (*b*) A standard is established for each and every task by means of time and motion studies and (*c*) Two different piece rates are applicable for payment of salaries and wages. The first rate is called as a low piece rate. Low piece rate is used to remunerate those employees whose efficiency is below standard and high piece efficiency is below standard and high piece rate for those who are above standard.

The main purposes of Taylor's differential system are: (*a*) to discourage less than average workers by denying guaranteed wages and fixing a low piece rate for lower level of work performance and (*b*) for rewarding the efficient workers by offering a high piece rate for higher level of performance.

Advantages

(*a*) This system attracts only the efficient workers.

(*b*) With the efficient labour force, the output will increase considerably.

(*c*) The incident of overhead will be less with the increase in production.

Disadvantages

(*a*) This leads to discontentment among employees particularly learners and substandard employees by setting a low piece rate.

(*b*) This method is also not suitable for those employees whose efficiency is just below the border line, *i.e.*, efficiency level is by small margin.

(*c*) It does not guarantee even the minimum day wages, which frustrates the employees.

(*d*) Employees develop hatred and jealousy with each other because of differential wage rates.

Indirect monetary incentives

Indirect monetary incentives are allowed on the understanding that employees contribute to the profit earning capacity of the organisation. This can take two forms; *viz.*, (1) Profit Sharing and (2) Co-partnership.

1. Profit sharing scheme: Under this scheme the employer agrees to pay a certain predetermined amount of profit in addition to usual salary payable to the employee. Profit sharing scheme differs from organisation to organisation in terms of coverage and method of distributing profit. In some organisations, it is restricted only to executives, while in other organisations it is extended to all employees. Again in some organisations, it is paid for the year during which profit is earned, while in others the payment of profit is deferred. This is to enable the employees to get sizeable fund at the time of retirement, disablement etc. The method of distributing profit also differs from organisation to organisation. In some cases, length of service is taken as the basis for determining percentage of profit. In other, a fixed percentage of total salary constitutes the basis.

Advantages

(*a*) It reduces the excess labour turnover.

(*b*) It increases the all round efficiency on account of increased efforts of employees with a view to earn profit.

(*c*) It eliminates conflicts between employer and employees.

(*d*) It leads to better cooperation, team spirit and increases efficiency of employees.

Disadvantages

(*a*) Usually the employee has no control over profit and it is not directly related to his effort.

(*b*) Unless merit rating is conducted, both efficient and inefficient workers get profit at the same rate.

(*c*) Payment of profit is at long intervals, usually once in a year and the share received by employees are negligible.

(*d*) Employees share only profit, but not losses.

(*e*) When workers are habituated to the payment of profit on regular basis, non-payment of profit in a particular year leads to discontentment.

2. Co-partnership scheme: Co-partnership confers upon employees the opportunity to share in the capital of the business in order to receive the part of the profits that accrue to their share of ownership.

Co-partnership differs from profit sharing in two respects; (*i*) In co-partnership, employees invest capital into the business, whereas in profit sharing scheme the employees do not contribute capital and (*ii*) In co-partnership, the employees share profit and losses, if there is any, whereas in profit sharing scheme, the employees receive only profit but they are not called upon to bear losses.

Fringe benefits

Fringe benefits refers to supplementary compensation paid in addition to direct remuneration to the employees. Fringe benefits are assuming more importance in recent years. A survey on payment of Fringe benefits in USA revealed that the average amount of Fringe benefits paid by organisations were 32.7 per cent of the total salary bill. The offering of fringe benefits to employees have the following advantages:

(*a*) It reduces excess labour turnover.
(*b*) It increases morale of employees.
(*c*) It improves the loyalty of employees towards employers.
(*d*) It increases productivity of employees.
(*e*) It increases job satisfaction of employees.
(*f*) It offers job security to employees.

Types of fringe benefits

1. Paid holidays: Employees are paid on National Holidays and festivals that fall on a working day for example, Independence day, Labour day (May Day), Republic day, etc., are treated as holiday with pay.

2. Leave with pay: In most organisations, staff are allowed to avail leave of about 15 days in a year. In some cases, the leave allowed is more and different types of leave is permitted. Such leave days are paid as in the case of holidays.

3. Sick leave: In most organisations, certain number of days of sick leave is provided. These sick leave when not availed can be carried forward to the following year. In some cases, sick leave can be encashed. In other cases, it can be adjusted at the time of retirement in which case the retirement period gets advanced to the extent of sick leave not a availed.

4. Educational facilities: In some organisations, the employees are sponsored to take up higher education while they are in service. All the educational expenses incurred by the employees are reimbursed by the organisation. Similarly, they can also be deputed for undergoing training and all expenses are met by the organisation.

5. Insurance: This is one of the common fringe benefit extended to employees by the employers. This is done as per the requirements of statute.

6. Pension and provident fund: This is a fringe benefit which benefits the employees after they retire from the organisation. Under pension programme, no amount is deducted from the employees' salary. Whereas in case of provident fund, the employees also contributed a certain percentage from their salary.

Non-Monetary incentives

Non-Monetary incentives are offered with a view to attract better employees, encourage loyalty, reduce excess labour turnover, promoting better health and reduced absenteeism with a view to build up a happy and contended staff. Non-monetary incentives are sometimes provided at a free of cost, while in some other cases it may be subsidised. This usually takes the following forms:

(*a*) Canteen facility
(*b*) Medical facility
(*c*) Transport facility
(*d*) Housing facility
(*e*) Recreational facility
(*f*) Co-operative store

QUESTIONS

Simple Questions

1. Distinguish between wages and salaries.
2. Define salary.
3. State the features of Halsey incentive system.
4. State the features of Rowan incentive system.
5. State the features of Taylor's incentive system.
6. Distinguish between co-partnership and profit sharing.

Short Answer Questions

1. State the matters to be included while preparing a statement of salary policy.
2. Explain the characteristics of sound salary plan.
3. Explain the three incentive system of salary payment.

20

Work Measurement

INTRODUCTION

Work measurement is one of the means of controlling office operations. The basis for controlling such operations is termed as work standard. By comparing the actual operations with the standard it is possible to assess the efficiency in the performance of office operations. There are number of methods used for measuring the performance of office activities. Some methods are as simple as counting the number of units produced by office staff, while others are more sophisticated ones.

Definition, objectives and advantages of work measurements

Zane Quible in his book "Introduction to Administrative office management" defines work measurement as "a system designed to determine what comprise a fair day's work from the standpoint of both the employer and the employee. This system helps to assess employee productivity in terms of the amount of time consumed to produce a unit of output".

The objectives of work measurement can be outlined as under:

(*a*) To determine the level of productivity so as to compare the expected and actual output of an employee.

(*b*) To facilitate planning and scheduling of office activities. This system also enables to know how much time is required to complete a work and the number of workers required to complete a job.

(*c*) To determine the alternative method and process of performing a work if the efficiency of an employee falls much less than the standard production.

(*d*) To determine the cost of operations in an office. The unit cost of operation can be compared with unit cost of operation of other companies or with budgeted cost to know the efficiency or otherwise of the office.

(*e*) To distribute the work load equally among all the office staff.

The advantages of work measurement can be listed as under:

(*a*) It facilitates in exercising better control over the office activities.

(*b*) It enables to know whether a department of the office is overstaffed or understaffed.

(*c*) It helps in locating and eliminating bottlenecks if there are any.

(*d*) The result of work measurement can be used in work simplification process.

Work measurement programme

The work measurement programme involves the following steps:

1. Preliminary organisation of the programme: This step consists of determination of the objectives of the programme, the selection of the technique, and fixing the time limits for installing the programme.

2. Staffing: This step consists of fixing the duties and responsibilities of the staff incharge of work measurement programme. This step also includes obtaining the consent of such staff to conduct the work measurement programme.

3. Collection of important data: This step involves collecting data from different work units. To collect data, it is necessary to train the staff appropriately.

4. Analyze the data and develop the standards: This step involves in analysing the data and in fixing up the standards.

5. Instructing employees: This step involves instructing employees the expected level of production from them.

6. Follow-up: To make work measurement programme more successful, it must involve follow-up action. The actual performance is compared with standard performance to know efficiency. Subsequently remedial measures are taken to improve upon the efficiency or the programme itself may have to be modified.

Work measurement techniques

The following techniques are used in the work measurement programme:

1. Production records: Under this method, the production records serve as the basis for determining the standard. In this case, the time taken by an employee to perform a job is considered as a source of measurement.

Each employee will maintain a separate record to note down the details of work produced and the time taken to do the job. This record is to be maintained on long term basis to even out any fluctuations. By dividing the total work units by the total time taken, a standard is determined.

2. Work sampling: Under this method, a random sample of observation relating to an activity being performed by the employees is recorded. Such observations are made to determine the percent of the total process that each activity consumes. This technique is illustrated below:

Activity	Number of Observations	Percent	Time	Units Produced	Standard
A	B	C	D	E	D÷E
1.	20	20%	100 Min.	250	0.40
2.	40	40%	50 Min.	100	0.50
3.	10	10%	200 Min.	200	1.00
4.	20	20%	100 Min.	50	2.00
5.	10	10%	50 Min.	125	0.40
	100	100%	500 Min.	725	

In the above illustration, it is assumed that 100 random observations were made. The number of times the observations were made is given under column B. The total time involved in performing all the 5 activities is given under column D, *i.e.*, 500 minutes. Activity number 1, constitutes 20 per cent of total process in terms of the number of observations. Activity number 1 also constitutes 20 per cent or 100 minutes of the total time consumed by the total work process. The number of units manufactured is indicated in column 'E' The particulars of column 'D' when divided by column 'E' gives the standard for each activity. This method can be simplified by making use of random Table numbers.

3. Time study: Time study is a technique undertaken to know the actual time involved in the performance of a job. Every standard employee is supposed to complete a job within the scheduled time. Time study is undertaken with the help of a stop watch. A time study technique involves three steps, *viz.*, (*a*) Identify the job and sub divide the various elements of job. (*b*) Record the time taken by every element of the job on a continuous basis, (*c*) Fix the standard on the basis of the time taken by each element of the job.

4. Micromotion study: A motion study is a technique used to know the movements of various organs of an employee while performing a job. A micro motion study is undertaken to study the motions of the organs of an employee when he works on a machine. The purpose of this study is to avoid all unnecessary movements while performing a job and thereby to reduce the fatigue of employees. Micromotion study provides necessary data for setting standards by means of analysing motion picture to find out the time involved for every element of job. To record the motion pictures a micro-chronometer is used. It is a machine which has a special timing device attached to the camera which enables the unit of time to be photographed on each frame of the motion picture. Then the time taken by each element is obtained by deducting the time that appears on the first frame of every element from the time that appears on the last frame of the same element.

5. The predetermined standard time data: This technique is based on the assumption that if same work is performed in similar conditions then time taken will be same irrespective of the situation. So, for office operations of repetitive nature, predetermined standard time can be used to exercise control.

6. Performance levelling: It is a technique used to adjust the standards to accommodate average employees. As work measurement studies is undertaken on a continuous basis, it may fail to consider the differences among employees arising out of rest pauses, coffee breaks, etc. To make standards more reasonable, they must be adjusted in the light of the above conditions, performance levelling is essential in order to make work measurement a success. But determination of standards at a very high level may not be achieved by employees. Hence, such standards are not taken very seriously by the employees. So to make standards more acceptable, it must be determined by expert persons who are trained specially for this purpose.

7. Work standard: The work standard constitutes the basis of work measurement. To make work measurement technique more effective, the determination of work standard more accurately is very essential. Otherwise the reliability of the technique cannot be apprehended. The standards set should be acceptable by the employee. Work standards offer the following advantages :

(*a*) It increases the efficiency of employees.

(*b*) It helps in communicating with employees, the level of output expected of them.

(*c*) It helps management in deciding as to what course of action is to be taken for employees whose efficiency is far below the standards.

(*d*) It reduces the supervision as employees are aware of the targets which they have to achieve.

(*e*) It helps in introducing incentive system of wage payment.

(*f*) It improves the morale of employees by enabling them to achieve the standard.

Types of standard

The following are the important types of sta ndards established in office:

1. Quantity standard: It is a standard which is expressed in a quantitive term as for example, the number of units produced per hour. Quantity standard can be a subjective or an engineered standard, while the former is more arbitrary, the latter is more reliable and accurate.

2. Quality standard: This standard is not capable of expressing in numerical terms, but used to measure the accuracy and acceptability of work. The examples of work where quality standards are used relate to typing, filing, keypunching, arithmetical calculation in preparing invoices and so on.

3. Descriptive standard: This standard like quality standard is not capable of quantitative expression, but identify acceptable descriptive characteristics of areas within an office. The examples of areas where this type of standard is used are office layout, purchase of office stationery and other expenses such as office lighting.

QUESTIONS

Simple Questions

1. Define work measurement.
2. List out any four objectives of work measurement.
3. List out four advantages of work measurement.
4. Define time study.
5. Define micromotion study.
6. What do you mean by performance levelling?
7. List out the advantages of work standard.

Short Answer Questions

1. Explain the steps involved in a work measurement programme.
2. Explain the different techniques of work measurement.

21

Office Control

DEFINITION, OBJECTIVES AND ADVANTAGES OF CONTROL

Control is one of the important functions of management. The managerial function of control consists in a comparison of the actual performance with the planned performance with the object of discovering if all is proceeding according to plans and if not, the reason for the same. According to Hoontz and O'Donnell, control implies measurement of accomplishment against the standard and the correction of deviations to assure attainment of objectives according to plans. In words of Mary Cussing Niles "Control is an aspect and projection of planning. Whereas planning sets the course control observes deviations from the course and initiates action to return to the chosen course or to an appropriately changed one." Henry Fayol defines control as "in an undertaking control consists in verifying whether everything occurs in conformity with the plan adopted, the instructions issued and princiles established. It has for object to point out weakness and errors in order to rectify them and prevent recurrence. It operates on everything—things, people and actions." Control is essential for the success of office operations. Without control, the efficiency of office operations will fall, quantity and quality of work will suffer and employees may even question the authority of management.

The objectives and advantages of control as has been enumerated by Zona Quible is outlined below:

Objectives of control

(*a*) To increase the operative efficiency of the organisation.

(*b*) To assess the degree to which anticipated result and actual results conform.

(*c*) To coordinate the various elements of a process or a task.
(*d*) To increase the likelihood that the objective of the organisation will be achieved.
(*e*) To assist the office employees in performing jobs more efficiently.
(*f*) To maximise the profits of the organisation decreasing the amount of work that has to be redone and by reducing the misuse of materials.

Advantages

(*a*) Control helps to maximise the profits of the organisation.
(*b*) Employees' efficiency improves because they are cognizant of quantity and quality of output requirement.
(*c*) The organisation has a yard stick by which to measure its operating efficiency.
(*d*) Because control identifies the areas in which actual and anticipated results do not coincide the various work processes can be modified so as to result in greater operating efficiency.
(*e*) Scheduling deadliness can be met more frequently.

Steps of control

1. Establishment of standard: Control cannot exist unless three are some kinds of plan or standard. Plans and standard set the level for achievement and accomplishment. Plan or standard may be quantitative, qualitative or monetary.

2. Keeping a record of actual performance: Accurate and authentic records of performance must be maintained in order to institute control procedures.

3. Appraisal and evaluation of actual or expected performance against set plans or standard: Evaluation involves two activities: (*i*) Measure of performance in concrete or numerical term and (*ii*) comparision, with set plan or standard. Measurement or performance is the most difficult of these two. Qualitative standards like efficiency and morale are hard to measure. When actual performance meets planned performance, the situation is said to be "in control". When performance fails to meet the plan, the situation is considered "out of control."

4. Finding out strategic control points: Finding out strategic control points means finding out the exact places or spots where the performance should be evaluated in order to obtain the best results at the least cost.

5. Provision for taking corrective steps against deviations of performance from plan or standards: The first four steps are concerned with fact finding. They provide data, facts or statistics which point to the need for action and also indicate the direction in which correction measures should be taken. Effective control cannot tolerate needless delays, excuses, endless compromises or excessive exceptions.

Features of control

(*a*) Control is not the beginning of the process of management but an end function. It is a following of the other functions of management. It works on the basis of a plan and judges how the different factors men, materials, machinery and money are organised and co-ordinated for the best performance.

(*b*) It is mainly forward looking. A manager can not control the past. But he reviews the past events and applies the benefits of previous experience to make improvements in future.

(*c*) Control is a dynamic process. As plans and objectives may change according to the needs of the situation, control must also adjust itself to them. The control system should be flexible.

(*d*) Like planning, control is a continuous activity. According to Koontz and O'Donnel "Just as a navigator continuously takes readings to ascertain where he is relative to a planned course, so should the office manager continuously take readings to assure that his department is on course".

(*e*) Control is exercised at all levels of management though its nature and degree differ accordingly to the level.

(*f*) If Control is identified with individuals. Control may be directly related to materials, process or even finance, but ultimately there is some human being whoever he may be, that is responsible for the defect in material, shortcomings of the process or financial lapse.

(*g*) Control does not necessarily mean curtailment of the rights of the subordinates. It is not the same thing as interference as was pointed out by M.P. Follet long ago.

Essential of good control procedure

1. Simplicity: Control system should be as simple as possible. The fewer the forms or records that are maintained, easier the system to operate and, therefore, lesser the chances to err. A simple system of control is also easily understood by people.

2. Low cost: The control system should not be a very expensive system.

3. Adequate and timely information: Enough information should be gathered for making decision. Economic balance should be maintained in the cost of information and its value. Information should be obtained at the appropriate time.

4. Flexibility: The control system should be flexible in its operations.

5. Permit management by exception: Only such situations that required corrective actions are brought to the immediate attention of the management or supervisory personnel, ordinary situations may be handled by the person in charge.

6. Force planning and corrective action: A control system should be designed so as to force managers to look ahead. Good control should foster better planning for future operations.

Control over organisation

Every enterprise needs sound and clear cut plan of organisation for its smooth running. Control over organisation structure is necessary in order that it may be worked according to the plan and purpose. Control is exercised through the following means:

(*a*) An organisation chart is the first step in such control. A good chart is indispensable to clarify organisational relationship.

(*b*) Some organisations circulate organisation manual. These contain not only the structural charts of the whole enterprise and its part but also a summary statements of the ascertain duties and delegated authority of every executive.

(*c*) One effective way to ascertain how well to plan of organisation in functioning is to analyse the demands upon executive time and attention in the form of interviews, telephone calls, reports and correspondence.

(*d*) Another approach is through review of inter-departmental disputes and differences.

(*e*) In a large enterprises, organisation control is left in the hands of an individual executive but entrusted to a staff department like O & M department composed of specialised personnel.

Forms of control

1. Operational control: This control is exercised at the clerical level as for example to verify the degree of accuracy of work performed by the clerk.

2. Supervisory control: Under this control, the supervisor checks the performance of work of every employee. The supervisor will compare the work with the standard work and advises if the actual work deviates from the standard work.

3. Managerial control: This type of control is also termed as overall control. This involves the establishment of standards for various procedures of performing work in every department, obtaining feedback from every department, solving problems concerned with major problem, making decision and revising plan if need be. Thus, an office manager is concerned with overall control of various jobs performed in office.

4. Senior management control: This type of control is exercised by top level management and the matters considered for exercising control are master budget, mechanisation and automation policy, use of new technology and so on.

Limitations of control process

(*a*) Control is exercised on factors which are internal to the organisation. But sometimes poor performance is caused by external situations like government action, market developments, violent changes in demand, discovery of a new technology and so on. Controlling these external factors is practically beyond the power of management.

(*b*) Control requires the determination of standard. Many things like production process and quality can be standardised in qualitative terms. But there are other areas which do not permit a measurement *e.g.*, of loyalty, leadership, morale, and discipline. The difficulty in measurement, of such qualitative factors limits the application of control procedures.

(*c*) Control proceeds on the assumptions that persons responsibility can be fixed and the person responsible will take corrective action. It is difficult to pin point responsibility on individuals and even if responsibility can be located, it does not necessarily follow that corrective action will be taken.

(*d*) Some of the obstacles in the process of control are finding out the causes of variations. Pin pointing the exact spot where variations occur is not easy. A defect in the quality of a product may be due to bad raw materials, inefficient labour or unsound organisation practices. Time is also an important factor. Ascertaining and correcting deviations may involve the stoppage of work which may cost more than the deviation.

Planning and scheduling of office work

Planning is concerned with what is to be done, how it is to be done, who is to do it, and where? The result of unplanned work is haphazard when compared to properly planned work. This results in waste of money, time, and materials. Proper planning enables effective supervision and enables to know in advance the obstacles which hinder the programme of work. The planning process require the following facts:

(*a*) The work to be done, *i.e.*, the nature of work, the quantity of work and the time available for doing.

(*b*) The resource and the capacity of the force available for doing the work.

(*c*) The order of doing the work *i.e.*, the preference to be given for various works planning process involves the following steps:

(i) Analysis of the work to be done: The office work is analysed according to the person, the time and the methods of doing the work.

(ii) Knowing the present position of the work: This involves knowing the quantity of work-in-progress, the quantity of work to be don and capacity of the working force and responsibility of assigning the work.

(iii) Anticipate fluctuations in the volume of work: Based on seasonal or other fluctuations in the work it is desirable to know the volume of work expected.

(iv) Improve systems, routine and standards: This is concerned with developing improvements on routines, systems and standards which serves as basis for performance of work and its control.

(v) Organisation of training work: It is concerned with supervision of all the trained workers so that the planning department may carry out its responsibilities maintaining standards.

The following forms are used in organised planning of office work:

1. The routine sheet: The routine sheet used in planning office work is some what different when compared to production work. The greatest use of the route sheet is on routine work where it is identical or repetitive such as preparation of orders, invoices and so on. The work to be completed will pass through from one department to other departments as per the routines laid down in the route sheets. This avoid confusion and avoids taking excess time than the usual time.

2. Records: A record is maintained in the planning room to be used to write the time each route sheet leaves room and the time it is returned. This is to facilitate the planning department to know the extent that is performed in the office and availability that could be used by assigning further work.

Scheduling of office work

The term scheduling refers to the fixation of time for completing a work. Scheduling office work has not assumed that much importance when compared to scheduling of production work, yet it is estimated that 75 per cent of all work in an average office can be saved. In preparing office schedule, the following factors are to be considered (*a*) The actual time required for the work, (*b*) The actual time required for the work travelled between two points, (*c*) An allowance for probable delays which can be foreseen. The important devices used while scheduling office work are: (*a*) schedule logs, (*b*) work chart, (*c*) work schedule calender and (*d*) GANTT chart. However, rebuilding is always to be followed up to make it more effective.

Quality control

Quality control is one of the techniques of control which is used to increase the operating capacity of office staff. In the absence of quality control, errors go unnoticed. The image of the company diminishes, spending more time to do the spoilt work which reduces the profit in the long run. Quality control technique is based on standards. Once the standard of the quality is determined, the actual work can be compared with the expected standard. If there is differences between the two, corrective, measure are taken to set right the differences. The following techniques of quality control are commonly used:

1. Total inspection: Total inspection refers to complete checkup of every unit of work done by every employee to determine whether the work meets the required standards of quality. Otherwise it involves taking corrective measures. The examples of work where this technique could be used are typing, calculation, complication of statistical data and so on.

2. Statistical quality control: This technique is used to overcome the time involved in "total inspection" technique discussed above. This technique makes use of statistical elements such as sample distribution curves and control limits. The sample element simplifies the control technique as it is based on the study of a sample selected against total output. Normal distribution as an element of statistics helps in knowing the number of errors committed in relation to a specified number of errors committed in relation to a specified number of work units. For example, average number of mistakes that may be committed for every hundred words may be restricted to two. Any typist who commits more mistakes exceeding two maybe warned or penalised. Control limit as one of the elements of statistics help in fixing the limits beyond which no mistakes should lie.

Budgetary control

Budgetary control is the control of a firms monetary resources with a view to achieve the goals of the firm. Budgetary control of a company is achieved through the use of budgets. A budget is an estimate of future financial needs of the company arranged in a definite manner for a specified period of time. According to George R. Terry, budget is as estimate of future needs arranged according to an orderly basis, covering some or all the activities of an enterprise for a definite period of time. Budgetary control may be described as a process of finding what is being done and comparing actual result with the corresponding budget data in order to approve accomplishments or to remedy differences either adjusting the budget estimate or correct the causes of the differences. Van Sickle defines budgetary control system as "a carefully worked out financial plan including the procedure involved in its operations for conducting the various divisions of a business for the ultimate purpose of earning project."

Purpose of budget

Broadly speaking there are three main purpose of a budget:

1. Planning: A budget is a plan of an organisation expressed in financial terms.

2. Coordination: A budget is a constructive aid to all departments within an organisation in achieving their common goals.

3. Control: A budget is intended to serve as a means of control, a yardstick for measuring performance against predetermined targets and standards. A budget is a means towards an end and is not an end itself.

Preparation of the budget

Usually a person is designated as chief budget officer and is responsible for the preparation of the complete budget. Most frequently, the controller of finance acts as a chief budget officer because of his knowledge of the activities of the company and of the financial figures associated with those activities. The chief budget officer serves as a coordinator between divisions or departments in budget preparation. Usually the heads of these divisions together with selected staff representative will serve as budget committee of the company. The committee receives and approves all forecasts and subsequently prepares periodic results showing comparison of actual performance with the planned budget.

The budget of office function contains only expenses but no revenues as office functions do not directly generate any income. However, before making allocation of expenses it is necessary to make an estimate of cost of each type of work, that is performed in the office. The allocation of cost on office function relates to (*a*) salaries and wages, (*b*) fringe benefits, (*c*) depreciation, (*d*) furniture, (*e*) telephone charges, (*f*) printing and stationery, (*g*) posts and telegrams, (*h*) taxes and insurance, (*i*) maintenance cost and (*j*) training cost.

Operating the budget

Any budget regardless of how carefully it may have been prepared, must be followed in operation if it is to achieve its full purpose. Too frequently, the budget is prepared and then forgotten until it is too late to remedy or remove the factors that block the planned progress. Changes and variations should be brought to the attention of the budget committee as soon as possible in order that their effect may be anticipated and adjustments made to counteract them.

Each department is made responsible for the preparation as well as control of the budget. Various departments are then co-ordinated through the controller and a budget committee is established for the whole enterprise. For operating the budget, attention must be paid to:

1. Recording of operations: Good budgetary control requires a sound accounting procedure to be established that will provide a picture of actual operations in terms of sales, production, income, expenditure and so on. This enables the budget controller to keep a constant check on operations.

2. Operating reports: There are regular reports to be submitted to the budget controller showing comparision of actual and budgeted figures and the reasons for variations. On the basis of these reports the budget committee may recommend revisions in the budget.

Advantages of budgetary control

(*a*) It helps in the process of planning by reducing it to concrete numerical goals. Through the budgets, the executives know what they are to produce or sell, how much they can spend, how much income to expect and so on.

(*b*) It provides an effective means by which top management can delegate authority and responsibility without sacrificing its overall control limits for each department or division are laid down in the budget.

(*c*) It keeps expenditure under check and constantly reminds employees and management of the targets and goals to be achieved. It helps in the continuous utilisation of resources and promotion of efficiency.

(*d*) As a control device, it supplies the means of checking results and comparing performance, of revealing weaknesses and making corrections.

(*e*) The budget is not merely an instrument of planning, but also a tool of co-oraindation. It brings together the activities of various sections, departments and divisions in an overall perspective.

(*f*) It helps in determining the polices of the organisations.

(*g*) It gives complete information in advance regarding the amount of capital needed for the budget period.

(*h*) It gives the idea of where executive action is required.

(*i*) It aids in measuring performance of each department of the organisation.

(*j*) It promotes co-operation among the different executives for determining future plans.

Cost control

The term cost control when applied to office organisation denotes the ways of keeping costs as low as possible. The objectives of cost control have been summarised by Zane Quiable as listed out below:

(*a*) To develop standard cost for various office operations.

(*b*) To develop within the employees a desire to be conscious.

(*c*) To assist in the development of efficient operating procedures.

(*d*) To allocate the costs of operations to the appropriate functions.

(*e*) To identify operations that are inefficient.

There are three important techniques used to control office costs. They are: (*a*) cost analysis, (*b*) use of standard cost and (*c*) cost comparision. Under cost analysis technique, the total cost is broken down into various elements and each element is expressed in terms of percentage of the office cost under standard cost technique, standard cost is developed for each element of office cost is compared with the actual cost to know whether it has exceeded the standard. Remedial measures are then taken to reduce the cost where it is incurred in excess of the standard.

Under cost comparision technique, actual cost incurred in office is compared with past year's cost to know whether current year's cost exceeds the previous year's cost. If it has increased, the reasons for the same is ascertained and appropriate measures are taken to keep costs under check.

QUESTIONS

Simple Questions

1. Define control.
2. State any four objectives of control.

3. State any four advantages of control.
4. State any four features of control.
5. Mention any four forms of control.
6. What is a route sheet.
7. What do you mean by scheduling office work?
8. What do you mean by quality control?
9. Mention three techniques of quality control.
10. State the purposes of budget.
11. What do you mean by cost control?

Short Answer Questions

1. State the advantages and limitations of office control.
2. Explain the steps in control process.
3. Write a note on planning and scheduling of office work.
4. Explain the techniques of quality control.
5. State the advantages of budgetary control.
6. State the objectives and techniques of cost control as applicable to office.

Bibliography

E.C. Eyre, *Office Administration*, Rupa & Co.

S.K. Sahni & G.S. Sundaresh, *Office & Management*, Oxford & IBH.

J.C. Denyer, *Office Management*, The English Language Book Society & McDonald & Evans Ltd.

G. Mills & O. Standing Ford, *Office Organisation & Methods*, A.H. Wheeler & Co. (Pvt.) Ltd.

S.P. Arora, *Office Organisation and Management*, Vikas Publishing House.

P.K. Ghosh, *Office Management*, Sultan Chand & Sons.

John J.W. Menner & B. Lewis Keeling, *Modern Office Management*, Taraporevala Sons & Co. (Pvt.) Ltd.

C.L. Littlefied, F.M. Rachel & D.L. Carult, *Office & Administrative Management*, Printice Hall of India (Pvt.) Ltd.

William H. Lejjingwell and Edwin M. Robinson, *Office Management*, Tata McGraw Hill Publishing Co. Ltd.

Zane & Quible, *Introduction to Administrative Office Management*, Winthrop Publishers.

Ricks & Gow, *Information Resource Management*, Ronald Publishers.

Claude S. George Jr. *Management for Business and Industry*, Printice Hall of India Pvt. Ltd.

L. Hall, *Business Administration*, English Language Book Society.

Arun Monappa & Mirza Saiyadain, *Personnel Management*, Tata McGraw Hill Publishing Co. Ltd.

Harold T. Amrine and others, *Manufacturing Organisation and Management*, Printice Hall of India Pvt. Ltd.